LAXMI MURTHY is consulting editor with *Himal Southasian*, the region's only political review magazine, published from Kathmandu. She also heads the Hri Institute for Southasian Research and Exchange, a research unit under the Himal banner. She is currently based in Bangalore and has been active in the autonomous women's movement in India for more than twenty-five years.

MITU VARMA is project director at Panos South Asia and has been leading the project on which this book is based. She is also director for Film Southasia, a biennial festival of documentaries for the region, and editorial advisor for *Himal Southasian*. She is based in New Delhi and is a founder member of the Community Radio Forum—India.

GARRISONED MINDS

WOMEN and ARMED CONFLICT
in South Asia

Edited by
LAXMI MURTHY and MITU VARMA

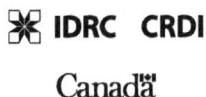

PANOS
SOUTH ASIA

SPEAKING
TIGER

IDRC CRDI
Canada

SPEAKING TIGER PUBLISHING PVT. LTD
4381/4 Ansari Road, Daryaganj,
New Delhi–110002, India

First published by Speaking Tiger 2016

ISBN: 978-93-86050-51-9
eISBN: 978-93-86050-49-6

10 9 8 7 6 5 4 3 2 1

The moral right of the authors has been asserted.

Typeset in Minion Pro by SÜRYA, New Delhi
Printed at Sanat Printers

This work was carried out with the aid of a grant from the
International Development Research Centre (IDRC),
Ottawa, Canada.

The views expressed in this book do not necessarily represent
those of IDRC or its Board of Governors.

Contents

Preface

Heeding Women's Voices from
Militarised Zones in South Asia

Putting together this book has been a voyage of discovery as well as an acknowledgement of the strength, courage and resilience of women who live their daily lives under the shadow of the gun in South Asia. It started with the idea of combining journalism and research to track the lives of women in three different conflict scenarios across the subcontinent—post-conflict Nepal; the long drawn-out struggles in the Northeast of India and Kashmir; and at the frontlines of battle in Khyber Pakhtunkhwa, Balochistan and the Federally Administered Tribal Areas of Pakistan.

Panos South Asia, a media support organisation for the region, backed by Canada's International Development Research Centre (IDRC), selected and trained twelve young and mid-career journalists to work under the guidance of research institutes and mentors to bring out the voices of women in these militarised zones through both mainstream media and in the form of this book.

The participating research institutes were the Hri Institute for Southasian Research and Exchange, the Uks Research, Resource and Publication Centre on Women and Media, Pakistan, the Alliance for Social Dialogue (ASD) and the Social Science Baha (SSB), Nepal and the Tata Institute of Social Sciences (TISS), Guwahati. Laxmi Murthy from Hri, Tasneem Ahmar and Shaista Yasmeen from Uks, Deepak Thapa from SSB, Hari Sharma from ASD and Sanjay Barbora from TISS guided the journalists through their research. Senior journalist and founder editor of The Wire, Siddharth Varadarajan, also mentored them in his individual capacity. Navsharan Singh, Senior Programme Specialist at IDRC, provided valuable inputs and direction as well.

Farzana Ali, Shazia Irram Gul, Syed Ali Shah and Muhammad Zafar from Pakistan; Thingnam Anjulika Samom and Yirmiyan Arthur Yhome from the Northeast of India; Shazia Yousuf and Zahid Rafiq from Jammu and Kashmir; Darshan Karki, Deepak Adhikari, Sewa Bhattarai and Trishna Rana from Nepal were the selected journalists. The twelve journalists faced the challenge of gathering material and interviewing people under very difficult circumstances. They had to take particular care to protect their sources as well as themselves from the myriad state and non-state actors operating in their area of research, especially as it also happens to be where they live. Together, they produced fifty-five media reports in a variety of forms, ranging from feature articles in print and multimedia to documentaries for television and radio.

Their work immediately yielded results: the reports led to intense public debate and discussions about the issues raised. Baburam Bhattarai, the former Prime Minister of Nepal, as well as senior policy makers, civil rights activists and senior journalists across the region took note of the hitherto missing voices of women from the discourse around militarisation. We seek to retain the buzz created by this process and keep the debates alive through this book, with the hope of ultimately prompting ameliorative action for the women who continue to live in unimaginably grim circumstances with quiet courage and firm resolve.

Mitu Varma
Project Director,
Panos South Asia

Introduction

Garrisoned Minds:
Women and Militarisation in South Asia

LAXMI MURTHY

We can call her Nasreen, Jwala, Dilshada or Zareefa. Or even Ruqaiya, Luingamla or Kushal Rakshya. Perhaps Rose, Shabana and Sharmila are more familiar faces of resistance. She has many names and many visages. She has loves and desires. She dares to dream of a future for herself and her people, despite living under the shadow of the gun, the acrid odour of devastation clogging her nostrils. For the most part she is stoic, for the garrison is also her home, her workplace, her field and her playground. Sometimes, she cries out in anguish, but the sound is muted, for there are few who want to hear. Her suffering and courage would be the stuff of legend, if only legend consisted of ordinary women carrying out extraordinary acts, going about the daily business of survival, displaying super-human strength in countering a mighty military juggernaut.

Militarisation and violence as a response to conflict has come to represent a global social order rather than a political exception. As anthropologist Kamala Visweswaran writes, military occupation 'increasingly informs the politics of both democracies and dictatorships, capitalist and formerly socialist regimes, raising questions about its relationship to sovereignty and the nation-state form' (Visweswaran 2013). South Asia is particularly afflicted by the ideology of militarism.[1]

While military spending across the globe has been in decline for the third year running according to a 2015 report[2] by the Stockholm International Peace Research Institute (SIPRI), it is on the rise in Asia. US spending on defence fell by 6.5 per cent, while China and Saudi Arabia have substantially increased their military expenditure, with Saudi Arabia's increase of 17 per cent making it the largest increase among the top fifteen spenders worldwide. It must be noted however that despite the budget cuts, the US, with an expenditure of 577 billion US dollars, still leads the world in military spending, followed by China at 145 billion US dollars. India is the ninth-highest spender on its military, with 38 billion US dollars. Pakistan ranks twenty-seventh with an expenditure of 7 billion US dollars.

The priority accorded to the military becomes clearer when the outlay on it is seen as a percentage of the GDP.[3] For one, Saudi Arabia is spending more on its armed forces than ever before; military expenditure now amounts to at least 10.4 per cent of the kingdom's GDP, according to an estimate by SIPRI. In contrast, the US's enormous military spending amounts to only 3.5 per cent of its GDP. For China, the proportion falls to 2.1 per cent, which is less than India's 2.4 per cent. These figures represent official government spending, and do not even attempt to estimate the outlay on arms by non-state actors in the fray.

Violent nation-building

It is clear that the world over, increased militarisation is a response to the anxieties of nation-building and an aggressive patriotism.

Feminist scholars have demonstrated how militarism closely

---

[1]'Militarisation', or the process by which a society organizes itself for military conflict and violence, and 'militarism', an ideology that reflects the level of militarisation of a state, are used interchangeably in this anthology.

[2]http://www.sipri.org/media/pressreleases/2015/milex-april-2015

[3]http://www.forbes.com/sites/niallmccarthy/2015/06/25/the-biggest-military-budgets-as-a-per centage-of-gdp-infographic-2/#2715e4857a0b5803d5584064

intersects with patriarchy and nationalism (Chenoy 2002). Notions such as 'national honour' and 'national pride' form the basis of militarised nationalism, which can be both defensive in trying to retain territory as well as manifested in offensive incursions to annex territory and gain control over resources.

Rubina Saigol (2008), using the Pakistani example, articulates the notion of the nation being essentially feminine in construction, narrated on the body of women who become emotionally-laden symbols of the nation, self, the inner, spiritual world and home. A connection is made between the homeland and mother: both are perceived as being in need of protection; both are loved and admired; both are respected; there is a willingness to die for the honour of each. The desire for this land/woman is constructed as a hyper-masculine desire; the desire to possess it, take pride in it, love it, protect it and even die fighting for it against invaders. A logical corollary of this construction is that women's bodies are treated as territories to be conquered, claimed or marked by the assailant. When the feminine self comes to signify the nation, communal, regional, national and international conflicts are then played out on women's bodies, which become arenas of violent struggle. Women are humiliated, tortured, raped and murdered as part of the process by which the sense of being a nation is created and reinforced. Women's reproductive power is also appropriated to prevent the 'undesirable' proliferation of the enemy's progeny.

Bina D'Costa (2011) argues that the foundation of present-day nation-states in South Asia rests on the silencing of women's experiences of violence during these epochal moments. She suggests that sexual crimes against women, for example, during the Liberation War in Bangladesh in 1971—rape, unwanted pregnancy, abortion and the taking away of infants born out of rape—were not an unfortunate by-product of war but inherent to the very foundation of the nation-building project. She suggests that acknowledging the ubiquity of sexual violence against women of all identities would have complicated the post-Independence narrative as well: 'In this new patriotic space, which required nation-building to make peace with the two conflicting identities (the religious and the ethnic), it was crucial to silence women's experiences of the Liberation War.'

Gender-based violence against women then becomes an essential component of the assertion of nationalism. Women are violated in a sexually-specific manner, their bodies are marked in particular ways that are meant to be reminders of their being not just women, but the honour of the community/nation, while men of the 'other' community/nation are emasculated and humiliated in a show of dominance. Needless to say, women's own identities are transformed and subsumed in this process of state-formation and nation-building.

The Partition of India in 1947, and subsequently, the birth of Bangladesh in 1971 were accompanied by unparalleled bloodshed and sexual violence. The subcontinent has yet to come to terms with the trauma. It has defined generations of South Asians and formed a backdrop for the contentious relationship between India and Pakistan today. The steadily growing militarisation in the region must be viewed in the light of the nuclear build-up by the two countries, their dangerous political brinkmanship and sabre-rattling. Each nation also has its own share of conflicts within and without.

Seema Kazi (2014) notes that while there has been considerable research on the economic effects of militarisation, highlighting the link between defence spending and underdevelopment, there has been less focus on the overlap between militarisation for external defence and the use of the military for domestic repression. She highlights how, over decades, rising military expenditures within three major South Asian countries—India, Pakistan and Bangladesh—have reflected the increased use of the military within state borders, on their own citizens.

Fractious frontiers

The military in Pakistan has been deployed in the Northwest, along the porous border with Afghanistan. This volatile region, far from being a lawless frontier land of violent medieval tribes as it is commonly depicted, must be understood against the backdrop of the colonial strategy of using borderlands as buffer zones in the imperialist project. The violent nation-building exercises of postcolonial governments in the Indian subcontinent represent the same continuum of authoritarianism, utilitarianism and plunder of resources.

A host of special legal regimes and arrangements continue to characterise the troubled relationship between these rugged frontier lands and the centre. The Murderous Outrages Act of 1877, designed to subjugate the fierce Pashtuns, was the precursor to the undemocratic Frontier Crimes Regulation enacted in 1901 that governs the semi-autonomous Federally Administered Tribal Areas (FATA) to date. Pashtun opposition and anger over having arbitrarily been divided by the Durand Line drawn up by the British has thus been dealt with as a law and order problem, through draconian laws and 'political agents' vested with immense power.

Defence analysts (Rana et al 2010) have described how, during the Afghan War, more than 15,000 Arabs, Uzbeks and Chechens were settled in FATA to fight a 'holy war' against the Soviets across the border in Afghanistan. These outsiders were given shelter in the tribal areas under the traditional cultural norms of asylum, the 'Pakhtunwali'. Almost a thousand madrasas were established, preaching jihad against 'infidels'. Backed by Saudi Arabia and the West, and having waged a successful battle against the Soviets, this new combat force, the mujahidin, transmogrified into the Taliban, which unleashed an autocratic regime deploying utilitarian interpretations of religion to maintain an ideological hold enforced by the gun. After 9/11 and the subsequent declaration of the 'war on terror', this impoverished region emerged as one of the main theatres of war on the global stage, since the government of Pakistan, under pressure from the US, was forced to make, at least publicly, a U-turn on its policy of support to the extremists.

However, scholars have warned against pinning the process of Talibanisation and militarisation on external factors alone. Farzana Bari (2010) highlights poverty, poor governance and the structural weaknesses of the state, which have all contributed to the rise of religious extremism. Men were forcibly recruited, displaced and had their homes and businesses snatched away. They were forced to grow beards and shun western dress. For women, however, besides imposing the 'shuttlecock' burqas and curtailing their mobility and public interaction, the impact of Talibanisation became a life and death issue. Denied access to health care, even during childbirth, kept away from education through violent means, and prohibited from moving around without male escort, women were made completely dependent on men. On the one hand, women's bodies became a site of scripting a more fundamentalist form of Islam, while on the other, the official discourse of victimhood and violation of women's rights (such as public flogging, stoning and other atrocities on women) was used as justification for military operations.

As veteran journalist Zahid Hussain points out in his introduction to the essays from Pakistan in this volume, the displacement of millions of people as the result of the conflict was a devastating outcome. In one of the largest displacements in the history of the country, more than five million people have been uprooted since 2004. Ejected from FATA and parts of Khyber Pakhtunkhwa due to militancy and military operations, they have been pouring into safer places for succour. For how long is anybody's guess, since rebuilding their devastated region could take decades, says Hussain.

Shazia Irram, in her moving essay 'No Woman's Land' about the devastation that is FATA today, bears witness to women's suffering as well as their resilience despite acute privation. Between a rock and a hard place, women make the best of the difficult 'choices' they are forced to make. In this ravaged frontier land, where 'mortar', 'drone', jangi jeyyaz (war aircraft) and karrpeo (curfew) are part of everyday conversation, there is an ominous normalisation of violence.

The families in camps have yet to draw the benefits of the purported 'end of hostilities', and most of the thousands of camp inmates cannot hope to leave any time soon. More remarkable is the stoic way in which women bear witness to the inexorable transformation of an idyllic mountain paradise to a ravaged land hazy with grenade and mortar dust. Physical displacement mirrors the emotional and economic dislocation that places immense burdens on women whose shoulders are already drooping with the weight of the death, disappearance and torture of their male family members. Prolonged camp life has also been taking a heavy toll on future generations compounding their suffering due to malnutrition and ill-health. Besides, their disrupted education means an uncertain future. The marked absence of the broader discourse around women's development, and health in particular, is reflected in the focus on women as reproductive beings alone. Inadequate access to health care during pregnancy and delivery has been well documented, but the lack of an integrated approach by policy makers to women's overall health has not been as strongly critiqued. Likewise, with a gender perspective missing from the official response to the conflict, women who have lost male members of their families, or female-headed households, lack access to compensation packages offered by the government. Sadly, the daily misery of a displaced people does not make it to the front pages of a media saturated with sensational stories of horror.

The ghastly murder of the dancer Shabana by the Taliban drew international attention to a scenic and hitherto unknown corner of the world: Swat. Farzana Ali's essay dwells on a little-discussed topic in conflict writing: the performing arts and their role in community life. Does entertainment matter? How crucial is music and dance to the lives of people, when survival needs are not met? The clampdown by the Taliban on all things construed to be 'against Islam' has gone virtually unchallenged by the state, allowing an extremist fringe to destroy a syncretic culture that had been nurtured in this valley of incredible beauty. Ali also explores the delicate interstices between tradition, culture and religion, to identify cleavages that can be exploited by both extremists and the state, and in the process further erode women's rights.

The flip side of this repression, according to Dr. Farzana Bari, is that '...various forms of patriarchal control of the Taliban over women's lives created tension between public and private patriarchy.' Her research found that men, who were forced to take over women's work outside the house, suddenly found themselves realising the extent of women's labour in agricultural and other subsistence operations: 'The gender consciousness that men and local communities gained due to terrorism/Talibanisation can now be leveraged in shaping the reconstruction policies and programs to change gender relations in post-conflict communities of FATA and Swat.' Such engagement would be in keeping with the Pakistani women's movement's long history of struggle for democratic and secular values as well, and its vociferous resistance to various military dictatorships and the Islamisation project of Zia ul-Haq. However, the time for this has yet to come in the tribal areas. As Shazia Irram reminds us, there is not even one woman delegate in teams undertaking peace talks with the Taliban and other militant groups.

In Balochistan, Pakistan's largest but most under-developed province, complex geopolitics, sectarian strife and a war over the control of rich natural resources at both the domestic and international levels have resulted in shrinking spaces for women. Syed Ali Shah and Shaista Yasmeen show how militarisation is exacerbating an already bad situation. Acute poverty, unemployment, malnutrition and illiteracy in this neglected province have fuelled numerous separatist armed movements. Counter-insurgency operations have created a situation where the abnormal is the normal, and beleaguered women struggle even to undertake everyday tasks. Shah and Yasmeen highlight the near absence of women's voices in the decision-making arena—in both traditional spaces as well as modern peace-building mechanisms. Yet these are stories, unfortunately, that few dare to tell in all their bare reality. Perhaps because no one dares to hear these truths. The media in Balochistan is vulnerable to attack merely for reporting from the ground about death and disappearance, disease and delivery.

If there is a sliding scale of vulnerability, then the Hazara minority of Balochistan would surely occupy the lower end, with the women among them hanging on to the very edge. Daily routines taken for granted in more privileged parts of the world—attending school and college, going to the hospital or the market, doing one's job—are activities laden with risk. And yet, they sally forth, the Hazara girls and women, determined to gain an education despite bomb blasts and suicide attacks. Quetta-based journalist Muhammad Zafar's essay is a searing account of the agonizing trepidation with which members of this Shia minority step out of their homes every single day. Other scholars too have pointed out that for Hazara women, who seem to be targeted more for their ethnic identity than their gender, the palpable sense of fear has taken an emotional and psychological toll on the entire community (Brohi & Gul Khattak 2014). Zafar highlights the lack of support from state agencies as well as secular civil society, which has resulted in the Hazaras stepping up to help the more destitute amongst them.

Ghettoisation has been another inevitable outcome of the lack of security for this minority community which has been forced to turn to itself. It is also no surprise that seeking asylum in safer havens is a route many Hazara families take. With only a few exceptions, it is the male members who leave, and the women who valiantly hold the fort, attempting to wrest control over their lives in small but significant ways, even if it is to take up karate.

Women in arms

The events of the past three decades the world over have demonstrated that women are not inherently 'peaceful' or non-violent. Women's roles in armed militancy in insurgencies in different parts of the world from northern Sri Lanka and Nepal to Palestine and Peru have been well documented. However, apart from the more dramatic female suicide bombers of the Liberation Tigers of Tamil Eelam (LTTE), women have largely played enabling roles to aid the war. This support follows traditional gendered roles, such as cooking, sewing uniforms, first-aid, fundraising, recruitment, sacrificing their husbands and sons (rarely daughters) to the cause. They have also increasingly moved into surveillance, aiding financial transactions and other crucial activities. Fewer are involved in active combat and policy-making roles.

Margaret Gonzalez-Perez's extensive global study of female

militants provides insights into domestic and international terrorist movements in the Americas, Asia, Africa, the Middle East and Europe, in which women played an active and supportive role. Interestingly, Gonzalez-Perez (2008) suggests that women are more active in domestic militant groups that fight against their own rulers, rather than external forces, because these movements offer more opportunities for transforming their own secondary status in their societies. This might be one way in which to analyse the role of women in Nepal's Maoist insurgency, launched in 1996.

Political scientist Deepak Thapa, in his incisive introduction to the Nepal essays in this volume, paints the backdrop of the insurgency, which mirrors the situation in Balochistan, FATA or indeed, conflict areas around the region: poverty, illiteracy, inequality, exploitation and alienation from the government. He traces how, instead of dialogue, the strategy of increasing state control, the suspension of civil liberties and the imposition of draconian anti-terror laws led to a spike in human rights violations during the 'People's War'. A political ideology that promised equality and freedom from oppressive social structures thus was an attractive proposition to thousands of women, who joined the Maoists as combatants, as well as political workers, fundraisers and supporters. Although the figure of 40 per cent women combatants, put forth by Maoist leaders, has been challenged, women undoubtedly made up a significant part of the 'People's Liberation Army' (PLA). Several women rose high in the ranks of the PLA, fearlessly leading men into battle, challenging the mainstream vision of compliant and soft Nepali women.

Kushal Rakshya, a platoon commander profiled by Deepak Adhikari talks about how battle fatigues and the gun gave women power hitherto unknown to them in their civilian life. Modelling themselves on male soldiers, adhering to masculine notions of strength, courage and sacrifice, women combatants refused to ask for privileges, even to deal with female physiological conditions like menstruation, pregnancy and childbirth. Adhikari's gripping narrative tells the story of this courageous woman proving her fighting skills on par with men, since it was important to show that women too were as capable of combat and therefore deserving of rank, privilege and honour. Even though the party espoused an ideology of equality, gender equity was a daily battle, and one that was often lost. Indeed, the bitterness and disappointment was acute when the aftermath of the war brought not peace but renewed battles, many of them the same old ones. Some, like Kushal Rakshya, with all the zeal of battle-ready soldiers, have plunged themselves passionately into new ventures and social causes. But for others, the sense of betrayal engendered by the peace agreement overshadows whatever gains the end of the war managed to achieve.

In her essay 'The Battle Within', Sewa Bhattarai joins feminist scholars who have documented conflict through women's eyes, convinced that women have a different story to tell, a story that complements but sometimes contradicts the grand male narrative of war. Bhattarai's sensitive telling of the travails and triumphs of dynamic women like Anoopam, Comrade Namuna and Dharamsheela Chapagain is an attempt to give voice to the marginalised. Whether combatants or political workers, they brim with energy, conviction and hope. Their passion for the cause and determination to surmount all hurdles is often belied by their leaders' cynical political manipulation.

The emphasis on their performance in war and the valorising of aggressive masculinity was reflected in how women looked and acted, even in their personal lives. Bhattarai tells of how women emerged from the war with conflicted views on motherhood. Some were disillusioned by the party that had promised to make careers easier for mothers, while others look ahead, visualising social institutions that share the family's responsibility for childcare. If such radical approaches to women's productive and reproductive labour were operationalised, even to a small degree, this would indeed be a positive outcome of women's active engagement with the war.

The opportunity for reform and rebuilding social institutions is ripe in Nepal, with a freshly minted Constitution attempting to take on board multiple and sometimes contradictory claims to representation and equity. Darshan Karki reminds us that the revolution is still an unfinished business for the Madhesis, who inhabit the Tarai. Marginalised and dispossessed and hitherto kept out of mainstream politics, the Madhesis are now staking their claim to the Nepali state. However, women's voices in these struggles are as yet muted, due to the strong feudal culture binding Madhesi women, who were relatively untouched by the upheavals of the Maoist insurgency. As one of Karki's interviewees baldly states, men are reluctant to share even a small piece of the roti. With the turbulent Nepali state attempting to balance contesting claims, appeasement of Madhesi demands has not been to the satisfaction of the ongoing movements in the Tarai, which have also turned violent.

As in many parts of the world, when underlying causes of conflict have not been addressed, there is no 'post' war harmony. Simmering discontent and bitterness in an uneasy 'peace' is most-often sought to be suppressed by aggressive troop deployment and repressive colonial laws to crush the aspirations of the people—whether for independence, self-determination or varying degrees of autonomy—vis à vis strong centralised regimes. This everyday nature of occupation defines the rhythm of life in these margins.

On the boil

As Sanjay Barbora in his introduction to the essays in this volume from Northeast India reminds us, '...in amplifying the experiences of women in conflict, the shortcomings of modern state-making and nation-building in the geographical margins of the country come into sharp focus'. The Northeast periphery of India, strategically located on the Eastern corridor and sharing a contested border with China and a porous frontier with Burma, is a cauldron of seething discontent. Armed insurgencies have erupted in almost every corner of these territories, declaring separate nationhood, demanding more political autonomy and control over their resources. Each uprising has been met, not with talk, but with brute force combined with a plethora of national security laws that make a mockery of civilian authority. Despite evidence that dialogue and conciliation is the most effective—and ethical—way forward, the increasing militarisation of the polity, far from tackling issues, has made them more intractable vis à vis the rule of New Delhi. Additionally, as Barbora points out, 'It is no coincidence that despite the increasing presence of more armed personnel on the ground, the number of incidents of violence between different ethnic communities has only increased over the past three decades. In almost all cases, it has been the economically weak and marginalised sections that have been killed or displaced.'

As a result, while the military in Pakistan is fighting a prolonged battle against invaders, in large swathes of India, many of which are periodically declared as 'Disturbed Areas', the state is fighting its own citizens. Women's bodies are prominent sites for this assertion of power. The desire to assert collective identity, whether of the nation or of the community, is transformed into what Veena Das calls 'the desire to humiliate the men of other nations and communities through the violent appropriation of "their" women' (Das 2007).

The use of sexual violence to humiliate and subjugate a people has been evident in the Northeast over the decades. Journalist Thingnam Anjulika Samom, bringing to bear her formidable story-telling skills, traces the blood-spattered history of defiance to central rule, a struggle that was accompanied by death, torture and sexual violence inscribed in the hills and valleys of Manipur. Breaking free of the deafening silence around sexual violence, some women did not remain victims at the hands of the Indian security forces, but were transformed, through collective memorialisation and iconography, to galvanise resistance. From the Naga teenager, Rose Machui Ningshen, in 1974; Luingamla in 1986; Elangbam Ahanjaobi in 1996; Thangjam Manorama in 2004, as well as countless women who were forced to remain silent, the security forces have treated the Northeast as a colony, committing crimes against humanity with impunity. Special laws like the Armed Forces (Special Powers) Act, 1958 (AFSPA) which allow the armed forces to act against the country's own citizens in areas deemed to be 'disturbed' and commit grave human rights violations with impunity, reflect the agenda of the just-departed colonial masters: suppress with brute force.[4] Samom reminds us that given the deep stigma around sexual violence in Manipuri society —as in most of the rest of the world—as well as structural impunity for perpetrators, few cases have been successfully prosecuted, and fewer victims have received justice. She draws attention to another significant but less discussed aspect of prolonged conflict and militarisation: the tensions and cleavages between communities; mutual suspicion and hostility; the blurring of lines between the benevolent and despotic and the utter fragility of individual and collective bonds.

It is this tenuous social fabric that filmmaker and journalist Yirmiyan Arthur Yhome explores through her evocative journey, 'This Road I Know'. 'How does one relate to age-old neighbours, waking up one day to see them at war?' she asks. To explore ethnic divides in a land ravaged by conflict, she transports us to her childhood. We drive with her down the highway, straddle the Naga hills and snake down the beautiful valleys awash with ethnic tension. As the main protagonist on the road, Arthur tells a compelling tale, of her slow realisation that the Indian Army was not the source of syrupy sweet jalebis alone, the growing trepidation that the presence of jackboots brings, the attempt to make sense of the dailyness of military occupation. With generations growing up under the shadow of the gun, with every family having its own horror stories to narrate and pass down in community memory, with every town and field having borne witness to atrocities and suffering, it is little wonder that the flame of resistance is kept aloft and burning. Secessionist movements, armed militancy and even human rights and civil society movements are fuelled by collective memory, where the individual plays out the aspirations of the community, desperate to achieve that ephemeral homeland. Arthur's stories are touching, the poignancy stemming from the sheer ordinariness of the misery of living under the rule of an oppressor. Like Samom, Arthur draws

---

[4]The AFSPA is modelled on the colonial-era Armed Forces Special Powers Ordinance enacted in 1942 to suppress the Quit India movement.

our attention to the women intervening when '...structure and civility collapses'. They wave the white flag; walk through jungles to negotiate with hostile armed militia; strip naked to expose the brutality of the Indian Army; weave shawls to commemorate a young woman whose life was snuffed out in the grandiose project of 'national security'; demand to know where the state has forcibly disappeared their husbands and sons; and go on a fast for the repeal of a draconian security law. In so doing, they also stand up and insist on being counted in any nation set to emerge from the debris of decades of conflict.

Collaborators and collateral damage

Contextualising the essays from Kashmir in his introduction entitled 'A History and its Witnesses', Siddiq Wahid draws attention to the fact that the Kashmir issue is not only a bilateral dispute between Islamabad and Delhi, with both laying claim to the territory. He foregrounds the third and most significant player: Kashmiris themselves. He traces the genesis of the problem to when the British, in an attempt to control one of the border regions, encouraged the creation of Jammu and Kashmir State in 1846 under Maharaja Gulab Singh. Alienation and assertion of a separate identity have run through successive resistance movements. The post-Independence period has in fact witnessed the increasing mobilisation of military power to quell rebellion, instead of dialogue and discussion to deal with democratic dissent. Armed might, along with a plethora of draconian national security laws legitimising what Wahid terms the 'assertion of raw power' by the state, has characterised the decades that followed.

If sacrificing one's life for a just cause has been valorised to make sense of horrific deaths in the ranks of militants and civilian supporters, the life of collaborators is possibly a fate worse than death. Srinagar-based journalist Shazia Yousuf's elegant prose offers a glimpse into the lives of the families left behind by the Ikhwanis, the armed militia of 'surrendered militants' set up by the Indian Army in Kashmir. The anguished stories effectively engender compassion for the women whose helplessness and shame is movingly described. Convenient labels of 'victim' and 'perpetrator' do not accurately fit those left behind to live out what Yousuf terms a 'widowhood of shame'. This counter-insurgency strategy left in its wake death, destruction, and families that could not hold up their heads in a land where pride and dignity are the foundation of the struggle for azadi, freedom. The women, who had little say in their husbands joining the Ikhwan, are torn between love for their men and for their land. Their isolation is complete. Their suffering is not on the agenda of even human rights groups. Negotiating the murky ground between traitorousness and family loyalty, Yousuf's interviewees conduct themselves with utmost dignity, urging the reader to see the real perpetrators of injustice: a state that prohibits self-determination and an army that uses brute force as well as devious means to suppress aspirations for freedom.

If calls for azadi are the life-blood of the self-determination movement in Kashmir, less audible are the cries of pain of the survivors of collateral damage. Zahid Rafiq's skilfully crafted essay, 'Shadows of a Dark Night', is a stark reminder of how sexual violence can have lifelong reverberations on the lives of many. His main protagonists' extreme fear of retaliation by the Indian Army for disclosing rape by its men eighteen years ago is testimony to the vice-like grip of the security forces in what is said to be the most militarised place in the world. Far from seeking justice for the rape of two sisters, one of them a minor, even speaking about it is laden with terror. The perpetrator, an Indian army officer, who has a name and a face, is still at large. Breaking the silence has severe consequences, and without a cushion of support, few women dare take the risk.

Rafiq also takes us back twenty-five years, to the twin villages of Kunan and Poshpora, where one night of terror left more than thirty women raped and tortured by security personnel. The women are speaking out now, with fifty young women, some of whom were not even born when the incident took place, petitioning the legal system in order to press for accountability. The process has been difficult, demanding great staying power in order to navigate the complex interplay between the politics of memory and assertion of state identity. For questioning the hegemonic state and its armed wings takes extraordinary courage. Bina D'Costa, writing in the context of war crimes during Bangladesh's Liberation War, points out that when victims of injustice are acknowledged, whether through law courts or war crimes tribunals, '...they are inevitably accompanied by social and political disputes over their importance and meaning' (D'Costa 2013). A manifestation of these contestations is the tensions between 'hard fact' in accordance with evidentiary requirements of law, and the more subjective public and individual memory. More challenging is the fact that bearing witness is but one of the first steps on the long road to justice.

Mobilising for peace

What we are witnessing in South Asia today is a growing culture of occupation, and what scholar Cynthia Enloe describes as '...an increasing diffusion of military ideas into popular culture and into social workings'. Inspired by Hannah Arendt, she interrogates the relationship between cultures of authoritarianism and authoritarian states (Enloe 2012).

It is worth reiterating that militarism is not, as is popularly imagined, merely the build-up of arms, arsenal or standing defence forces, or even the enactment of legislation that gives inordinate power to the armed forces. It is more insidious. It is a belief system that endorses military values in civilian life and believes in the construction of a strong masculinity that is also a necessary component of state power. It legitimises the use of violence as a solution to dissent and conflict—whether internal or external.

More difficult to resist than the wresting of control and undermining of civilian authority by violating the boundary between civil and military power, is the blurring of the distinction between military and civil administration, where the military is used as an arm of civil governance in territorially remote regions, and also as a corporate entity, with its tentacles in civil financial institutions (Siddiqa 2007).

When the military mindset is pervasive and has seeped into every social institution and defines the world order itself, anti-militarism then calls for the active questioning of power and authority in every sphere. While one of the steps is certainly sharing and representation in decision-making, it demands a re-think of centralised forms of decision-making, prioritising more grounded, accountable forms of power-sharing and resource allocation. Indeed, it demands revisiting the very notions of nationhood, citizenship and belonging.

The essays in this anthology represent an important contribution to this discussion by highlighting the impact of militarisation on women in South Asia. In-depth research and analysis, coupled with superb storytelling about the women routinely subsumed by the security discourse, provides humane and solidly grounded evidence of what it means to confront militarisation. Only when women's lives matter and when every individual's story is heard, can the military mindset be challenged.

Bibliography

Bari, Farzana. 2010. *Gendered Perceptions and Impact of Terrorism / Talibanization in Pakistan.* Islamabad: Heinrich Böl Stiftung.

Brohi, Nazish and Saba Gul Khattak with Beena Sarwar (Ed). 2014. *Women's Voices. Women in Conflict Zones: The Pakistan Study. Community Conversations in Balochistan and Swat.* Women's Regional Network, Afghanistan, Pakistan and India. Islamabad: Women's Regional Network.

Chenoy, Anuradha M. 2002. *Militarism and Women in South Asia.* New Delhi: Kali for Women.

Das, Veena. 2007. *Life and Words: Violence and the Descent into the Ordinary.* Berkeley: University of California Press.

D'Costa, Bina. 2011. *Nationbuilding, Gender and War Crimes in South Asia.* London, New York: Routledge.

——. 2013. 'War Crimes, Justice and the Politics of Memory' in *Economic and Political Weekly.* March 23 Vol XLVIII No 12, Mumbai.

Enloe, Cynthia. 2012. *Militarization, Feminism, and the International Politics of Banana Boats.* Theory Talk #48. May 22.

Gonzales-Perez, Margaret. 2008. *Women and Terrorism: Female Activity in Domestic and International Terror Groups.* London: Routledge.

Kazi, Seema. 2014. 'States of Denial' in *Himal Southasian,* October.

Rana, Muhammad Amir, Safdar Sial and Abdul Basit. 2010. *Dynamics of Taliban Insurgency in FATA.* Islamabad: Pakistan Institute for Peace Studies.

Saigol, Rubina. 2008. 'Militarization, Nation and Gender: Women's Bodies as Arenas of Violent Conflict' in Ilkkaracan, P. (ed.), *Deconstructing Sexuality in the Middle East: Challenges and Discourses.* Aldershot: Ashgate.

Siddiqa, Ayesha, 2007. *Military Inc.: Inside Pakistan's Military Economy.* London: Pluto Press.

Visweswaran, Kamala. 2013. *Everyday Occupations: Experiencing Militarism in South Asia and the Middle East.* Philadelphia: University of Pennsylvania Press.

PAKISTAN

Introduction: Multiple Cleavages

ZAHID HUSSAIN

The thirteen-year-long war in Afghanistan has had devastating effects on Pakistan, turning the country into a new battleground for militants. Thousands of Pakistani civilians and military personnel have been killed in the recent wave of terrorist attacks and fighting in the country's northwest. The economic and political cost of the war has also been huge, threatening to completely destabilise the country with catastrophic consequences for regional security.

The war came to Pakistan after the US invasion and toppling of the Taliban regime in Afghanistan. Thousands of Al Qaeda and Taliban fighters fleeing bombardment from US troops crossed over unguarded mountain trails and disappeared into the lawless tribal areas of Pakistan. The inhospitable mountainous region, which had been used by the American CIA and the Pakistani ISI in the 1980s as a base for their covert operations against the Soviet occupation forces in Afghanistan, was turned by militants into a hub for the battle against their erstwhile patrons.

The region, officially known as the Federally Administered Tribal Areas (FATA), has a long history of fierce independence. Home to more than six million people, this is undoubtedly the least developed place in the country. Occupying less than 5 per cent of Pakistan's total area, it is divided into seven semi-autonomous administrative units or 'agencies': Bajaur, Mohmand, Khyber, Orakzai, Kurram and North and South Waziristan. The thick forests and numerous caves that dot the harsh mountainous landscape make the region a natural redoubt for insurgents. Six of the agencies border Afghanistan; two are at the heart of the current tribal unrest: North and South Waziristan. The separation is mostly a matter of administrative convenience and it is generally more useful to think in terms of one Waziristan.

This 5,000-square-kilometre swathe is the largest of seven tribal agencies on Pakistan's western border with Afghanistan. Most of Waziristan's population of one million is composed of Wazirs and Mehsuds, two of the most fiercely independent Pashtun tribes, whose homeland extends into Afghanistan. Waziristan is a land of high, difficult mountains and deep, rugged ravines. With its long porous border with Afghanistan's Paktia and Khost provinces, Waziristan had become a major trouble spot for US and Afghan forces, particularly as Taliban insurgents regularly escape to the Pakistani side after attacking coalition posts.

In 2002, Pakistani troops entered the tribal areas for the first time in fifty-five years, albeit under an agreement that confined the army to development work. The main objective was to secure the border and prevent Al Qaeda operatives fleeing US and other NATO forces in Afghanistan from entering tribal areas. But the treacherous mountain passes made it impossible to fulfil the mission.

Foreign fighters moved freely through the region, using it as a base for cross-border attacks on NATO forces in Afghanistan. Pakistani military leaders were reluctant to launch military operations to drive the foreigners out, a policy of appeasement that later cost Pakistan hugely when the militants turned against Islamabad.

Early in 2004, under pressure from the US, Pakistan launched an offensive against Al Qaeda in South Waziristan, but it soon turned into an undeclared war between the Pakistani military and rebel tribesmen, spreading into other tribal areas. Despite the deployment of a huge number of troops, the military's efforts have yielded only questionable gains.

In the first several years after the US-led attack on Afghanistan, the militants based in Pakistan conducted attacks almost exclusively in Afghanistan, seeking to drive the US-dominated coalition forces from the country and overthrow the US-supported government.

Since 2007, they have also turned their guns on the Pakistani military and security agencies, launching attacks of increasing sophistication and intensity, as well as perpetrating an escalating and more violent wave of suicide bombings against civilians in major urban centres across Pakistan. A distinctive Pakistani Taliban movement has evolved, with the agenda of establishing its retrogressive rule not only in the tribal areas, but also in the adjoining Khyber Pakhtunkhwa province.

The emergence of the local Taliban movement occurred simultaneously with Pakistan's battle to flush out Al Qaeda fighters from the borderlands. This did not happen overnight; it was a consequence of war in Afghanistan and the military operations carried out by Pakistan. It also contributed to severely undermining the age-old administrative structures of the tribal areas. The members of the tribal council (or maliks) through whom the federal government established its authority were either killed or driven out by the militants. A new crop of Pakistani militants or Taliban emerged to fill the vacuum created by the collapse of the administrative system in FATA, over which the Pakistani government had at best tenuous control.

Clampdown on culture

The situation worsened in 2006 as the Taliban closed down shops selling video films and audio music, as well as Internet cafes, declaring them 'un-Islamic'. The Taliban also ordered barbers not to shave men's beards. People were prohibited from playing music, even at weddings and traditional fairs, which had earlier provided some form of entertainment to the public.

In December 2007, some forty militant leaders from the tribal region and elsewhere gathered in South Waziristan to unite under the banner of a new organisation called Tehrik-e-Taliban Pakistan (TTP). With thousands of fighters, the group seeks to enforce draconian Islamic rule in the tribal areas and neighbouring Khyber Pakhtunkhwa. This emergent Taliban grouping mostly came from the ranks of the mainstream Islamic political parties, which had ruled northwestern Pakistan from 2002 to 2007.

Most of the leaders had long experience in fighting US forces in Afghanistan while attempting to overthrow the government of President Hamid Karzai. But now they turned their wrath against Pakistan's security agencies and the military. Within a year, the TTP had swept through almost all the tribal territory as well as part of Khyber Pakhtunkhwa. By the middle of 2009, Taliban fighters had advanced to the districts of Swat and Buner, only 112 kilometres from Islamabad.

A massive army operation in 2009 pushed back the advancing Taliban, but the insurgents maintained their hold on some of the tribal territory. That August, US drone aircraft killed TTP leader Baitullah Mehsud (who had been blamed for the 2007 assassination of former Prime Minister Benazir Bhutto); the attack was one of the highest-profile successes of the CIA's aerial campaign in the tribal areas. But the insurgency was not dampened by the death of a prominent leader; he was replaced by an even fiercer commander, Hakimullah Mehsud, who unleashed a fresh wave of deadly terrorist attacks across the country to avenge his comrade's death. Thousands of Pakistani civilians and military personnel were killed in terrorist attacks and suicide bombings in crowded markets and other civilian targets, as well as at security installations.

The militant attacks are no longer confined to the distant mountains. The port city of Karachi, a metropolis of 18 million people that is also Pakistan's economic capital, has become a significant militant hub and source of funding. The economic and political costs of the spreading militant violence have been huge, threatening to destabilise the country.

The rise of the Taliban and the increasing military operations to tackle militancy dismantled the earlier colonial administrative structure in tribal areas. After the creation of Pakistan in 1947, the tribes pledged their loyalty to the new government, and in return, the authorities withdrew regular army troops from the region, replacing them with locally recruited paramilitary forces. But ironically, Pakistan retained the British colonial administrative and legal structure more or less intact, so that the tribes were deprived of basic civil and political rights and other protections under Pakistani law. Only in 1997 did residents gain the right to vote. All power in each agency rests with a centrally appointed political agent who operates through the maliks; some of these agents are chosen by the tribes, others by the government.

Bearing the brunt

The perpetuation of the old colonial administrative arrangement is largely to blame for the continuing lawlessness, neglect, and the lack of social and economic development in the region.

Less than 30 per cent of tribal children attend school, and of this group, 90 per cent drop out before completing their education. Smuggling, gunrunning and drug trafficking are rife. Abject poverty has also been a factor for tribesmen joining militant groups. However, the main victims of the conflict are local people caught in the crossfire. Among the most vulnerable are women.

Rising militancy and violent extremism has had the greatest devastating effect on Pakistani women. Whether it is the death of close family members or their displacement from homes, women bear the major brunt of the conflict. Additionally, in many instances, women are specifically targeted in the name of religion or culture.

The rise of the Taliban and imposition of a regressive version of sharia took a huge toll on women. Women constituted 60 per cent of the workforce in the agricultural sector in FATA, working at a subsistence level. But with the rise of the Taliban, women were prohibited from working in the fields and confined to their homes. Female students were forced to quit schools due to Taliban's' threats. Despite the difficulties, many girls, with the support of their parents, continued their education, observing the Taliban dress code (burqa). But then the schools too were blown up.

In her essay in this volume, Shazia Irram describes how, under Taliban laws, women were allowed access to only the most rudimentary medical care (with few female health staff available) and could not venture out of their homes unless accompanied by male family members. Male doctors were not allowed to treat female patients. As it is, there were very few male doctors available, as most had fled due to threats from the Taliban. The minimal medical care that was available was extremely expensive. Thus, health facilities for women were declared the second-worst militancy-affected sector in FATA, says Irram. She paints a poignant picture of how many pregnant women were unable to reach the hospital in time, risking both the mother's life and the baby's. Not surprisingly, some parts of FATA had the highest child mortality rates in the country, as women had to depend on unqualified local nurses, working in homes without medical equipment.

Wrenched from home

One of the major consequences of the militarisation is the displacement of millions of people due to the conflict. It has been the biggest displacement in the history of the country. Since 2004, more than five million people have been displaced from FATA and parts of Khyber Pakhtunkhwa to safer places as a result of insurgency and military operations. The most recent wave is the displacement of more than one million people from North Waziristan where the military has launched its biggest operation yet. This has also resulted in the biggest displacement of the population.[1]

Unfortunately, the internally displaced persons (IDPs) have been completely forgotten by the government, fuelling further discontent and deepening their alienation. It has been more than five years since the operation in South Waziristan ended, but a large portion of the displaced population has still not been able to return home. Fighting has devastated the region, making it hard for people to start a new life. It will take years to rebuild and restore economic life there. Intense air bombing and heavy artillery fires have reduced major towns to mere rubble. Although the towns and the surrounding villages are now more or less under the control of the army, small bands of militants still lurk in the hills. With almost the entire

---

[1]http://www.internal-displacement.org/south-and-south-east-asia/pakistan/figures-analysis

population having been evacuated, the region has a deserted look; only soldiers are seen at their guard-posts on the hilltops.

Although the administration is optimistic about the displaced population returning to their homes in the districts cleared of militants, it will take years for complete rehabilitation of the devastated region. While the government claims that peace has been restored, a large number of IDPs in other tribal areas have been forced to return to their homes unwillingly. However, a significant number has chosen to settle in host communities, waiting for military operations to complete and true peace to return.

The displaced people face many social, economic, psychological and cultural problems. Access to health and education facilities in the camps is almost non-existent. This has exacerbated the plight of women and children who have been caught up in a conflict situation for over a decade now and are plagued by mental and emotional trauma. The psychological impact on the women displaced from homes and living in camps is much greater. Women live under severe stress, having lost their homes and several members of their family. Many of them suffer from depression, anxiety and other psychological ailments. Irram's essay shows how giving birth during times of conflict exacerbates 'psychological despondencies among women, increasing the risk for maternal deaths'. Many women in camps cannot go to a doctor for treatment due to social restrictions and poverty. Every third pregnant woman had a miscarriage during displacement due to exhaustion and the strains of the journey. Additional complications occurred upon arrival in the camps because appropriate medical care was not available.

Lack of education is a critical issue facing the displaced population. A decade-long armed conflict and mass displacement has had huge negative implications on the education system. According to UNICEF estimates, nearly 60 per cent of the total IDPs living in camps are children. Since the beginning of conflict in FATA region, hundreds of schools were damaged or destroyed, resulting in insecurity and trauma among children. Schools, particularly girls' schools, have been primary targets of the militant groups in FATA. Violent groups have targeted not only students but also teachers, females in particular. Furthermore, students and teachers face continuous opposition and threats of violence from militant groups, leaving them no option but to stay away from schools and other educational institutions.

The Taliban offensive was not confined to the tribal areas. Parts of Khyber Pakhtunkhwa also came under the Taliban influence before security forces drove it out. Once a relatively liberal region, dotted with ski resorts and fruit orchards and known for its dancing girls who performed at most wedding parties and other ceremonies, the Swat Valley is just 241 kilometres from Islamabad. Militant violence swept the lush green alpine territory in 2006, when a young, long-haired firebrand cleric, Mullah Fazlullah, organised a militia for the enforcement of sharia rule. Popularly known as Mullah Radio, because of his fondness for broadcasting his sermons, he and his associates had set up at least thirty-two FM stations in the region, broadcasting his jihadi messages round the clock. He was a formidable leader and developed a large following. Ironically, most of the listeners of his sermons broadcast on FM radio were women.

Because work was so hard to come by in the Swat Valley, a large number of men worked far away in the Middle East or in other parts of Pakistan, and Fazlullah understood that winning the support of the women in the area would be an effective strategy. He exhorted them to pull their daughters out of government-run schools, which he described as the 'centre of all evils,' and so thousands of girls were taken from school. 'Women are meant to fulfil their responsibilities inside their houses. Only in case of dire need they can come out in a veil,' he would say in his radio addresses.

Women donated their jewellery and savings to him and persuaded their husbands to grow beards and say their prayers regularly. They even supported Fazlullah's mandate that children should not be inoculated with the polio vaccine, which he claimed was un-Islamic. 'To cure a disease before its onset is not in accordance with sharia laws,' he declared. 'You should not send a single child to drink a drop of [the vaccine] anywhere in Swat.'

In a short time, Mullah Fazlullah's followers set up a parallel administration, establishing Islamic courts that imposed sharia law. They also began killing those who publicly opposed them. In the next two years they went on to kill more than 300 political workers. The systematic elimination of political opponents left only two options: surrendering to the Taliban's authority or fleeing to safety. Residents of Mingora, the main town in the Swat Valley, would often wake to bodies hanging from electric poles in the town's central square, in full view of the military, with a note of warning not to remove them until midday. Many of those executed by the militants were women; their bodies were thrown into the square, which became known as Zibahkhana Chowk, or 'Slaughter Square'.

Bakht Zeba, a former member of the Swat district council, virtually signed her death warrant when she criticised the Taliban for preventing girls from attending school. In December 2008, masked gunmen dragged her out of her house, brutally thrashing her before shooting her in the head. Educated women like Zeba were specially targeted. The names of those who had already been executed by the Taliban for violating their decrees, as well as those it planned to kill next, were broadcast every night, and terrorised residents would listen to the transmission to find out if any of their kin were on the dreaded list. Among those slain was a local artiste, a dancer known as Shabana. Her body was dumped in the square in the centre of Mingora town; the radio proclaimed, 'She deserved death for her immoral character.'

As Farzana Ali writes in her essay for this volume, compared to other Pashtun areas, society in the Swat Valley was traditionally more liberal, with fine arts and aesthetics taking up a large space within the cultural fabric. Artistic expression was institutionalised through customary forms, such as a mela or fair, where music concerts and dances used to be regular features. She explores the contrast between the customary way of life in the region and what became of it after the Talibanisation of Swat through the lives of the traditional dancers of the valley, who were once revered for their art.

Sectarian strife

Meanwhile, rising sectarian militancy is also a cause for serious concern in Pakistan, as Muhammad Zafar highlights in his essay in this volume. It presents a grave threat to the unity and stability of the country. Religious leaders, doctors, and other prominent public figures in particular have been targeted in this insane sectarian war, and even places of worship and religious gatherings have not been spared.

Sectarian violence is not new to Pakistan, but there has been a steep increase in such attacks in recent years, with the rise of violent extremism in the country. This massive escalation in sectarian terrorist actions highlights the growing nexus between Sunni extremist groups such as Lashkar-e-Jhangvi (LeJ) and the TTP.

Sectarian conflict in Pakistan took an organized militant form in the 1980s. It had its roots in the so-called Islamisation process initiated by the military regime then in power. The government's secular disposition gave way to a professed determination to Islamise society. The Islamisation of law, education and culture illustrated the Sunni sectarian bias of the Pakistani state. The official dissemination of a particular brand of Islamic ideology not only militated against Pakistan's diversity, but also bred discrimination against non-Muslim minorities. The political use of Islam by the state strengthened a clerical elite and created sectarian groups that aggressively pushed their militant ideas. This move towards the establishment of a Sunni-Hanafi state reflecting the beliefs of the dominant sect created a sense of insecurity among the Shia minority community. Moreover, the dynamic of exclusion and minoritisation, which had existed since the creation of the country in various forms, was sanctified by Islamisation.

As a result, the more orthodox and militant version of Sunni Islam grew in strength and public influence. The spread of jihadist literature from Afghan training camps to Pakistani madrasas in the 1980s fuelled radicalism among the students. Islamisation of education created a mass sectarian consciousness far beyond the confines of the madrasa, which resulted in a dramatic shift towards extremist Sunni orthodoxy and anti-Shia militancy. More extremist Sunni groups demanded a constitutional amendment to declare Shias a non-Muslim minority and excommunicate them from the realm of Islam.

The Shia community reacted strongly to the enforcement of the Hanafi laws by the military regime. Until 1979, Pakistani Shias were a politically moderate community and had supported secular political parties. But General Zia ul-Haq's Islamisation and the Iranian revolution spurred them into political activism. The Islamic revolution in Iran had inspired Shias everywhere. Tens of thousands of Shias gathered in Islamabad in 1980 to protest their marginalisation by the Sunni majority, the biggest show of strength by the Pakistani Shia community. It was also the period when a Shia political party known as Tehrik Nifaz-e-Fiqh Jafaria (TNFJ) or the Movement for the Implementation of Shia Jurisprudence was formed, a move reflecting the community's new-found assertiveness. As the only Shia Islamic state, Iran became the centre for spiritual guidance and political support for most Pakistani Shias. The military government and its Sunni allies perceived it as an Iranian conspiracy to export its revolution to Pakistan.

The divide, deepened by the actions of the state, such as the enforcement of Sunni Islamic laws under General Zia ul-Haq's military government, could never be bridged. Shia revolutionary idealism was followed by the emergence of militant Sunni sectarian organizations. Sipah-e-Sahaba Pakistan (SSP) or Army of the Prophet's Companions was formed in 1985 with a one-point anti-Shia agenda. SSP represented a state-sponsored and Saudi-backed movement against Pakistan's pro-Iran Shia minority. It sought to turn Pakistan into a Sunni state.

External factors contributed hugely to stoking sectarian conflict in Pakistan. The Iranian revolution evoked a strong reaction throughout the Muslim world. The spill-over effect of the Shia revolution worried many Arab rulers as well as the Pakistani military regime, which was trying to establish an Islamic system of a different kind. The rivalry between Sunni Arab states and Shia Iran was further heightened during the Iran-Iraq war. Money poured in from Arab countries anxious to counter the radical Shia Islam sponsored by Iran's revolutionary regime. In the process, Pakistan became the battlefield in an intra-Islam proxy war. Iran and Saudi Arabia supported their respective allies. Madrasas funded by Saudi Arabia, Kuwait and other Gulf countries, especially after the Soviet invasion of Afghanistan, became the centre of Sunni militancy, as well as recruiting grounds for sectarian organizations.

The sectarian conflict took a more violent turn with the formation in 1996 of LeJ. A breakaway faction of SSP, the new sectarian outfit believed in using terror tactics to force the government to accept its demand of declaring the Shia community a non-Muslim minority and establishing an orthodox Sunni Islamic system in the country. Although the number of its hardcore cadres had never been more than five hundred, the group has been responsible for most of the sectarian killings over the last decade. By 2001, LeJ had been involved in 350 incidents of terrorism. Most LeJ militants came from among the rural unemployed, particularly those in southern Punjab, but its highly secretive and mobile organization made it lethal. The rise of the Taliban in Afghanistan gave the Sunni sectarian groups a further impetus.

While Balochistan, particularly its capital, Quetta, has become the main centre of gravity for Sunni sectarian militancy in recent years, it is certainly not an isolated provincial phenomenon. The problem is much more deeply rooted and has links with terrorist networks operating in Punjab and other parts of the country. Although the rise of Sunni sectarian militancy is relatively new to Balochistan, the province has witnessed some of the most gruesome carnage in recent years. Sectarian militants have caused Quetta to be drenched in blood many times in the past, but the ghastly massacre of Hazara Shias is shocking even by Pakistan's bloody standards. It is a sinister attempt to systematically annihilate an entire community because of its faith. There have also been several incidents where Shia passengers have been pulled out from buses, forcibly had their IDs checked and then shot dead in cold blood in other parts of the province.

As Zafar explains in his essay, the Hazaras had originally migrated from Afghanistan to escape genocide. A close-knit community in Quetta, they are more educated than other local communities and many serve in the military and other government services. Their distinct Mongolian features make them easily identifiable targets of sectarianism. Their colonies have been attacked many times over the past ten years, leaving thousands of people dead. The massacres have forced thousands of Hazaras to migrate to other parts of the country or seek asylum in foreign lands. Pakistani security agencies have failed to stop slaughter after slaughter and to provide protection to their hapless citizens, leaving them at the mercy of the murderers. Though technically outlawed, sectarian outfits operate freely and openly promote their toxic worldview through hate literature.

Foreign funding of radical madrasas and sectarian outfits has contributed hugely in fuelling religious extremism in the province. Pakistani security agencies in the past had also propped up these extremist groups to counter Baloch nationalist groups, with disastrous consequences. It will take a massive effort now to dismantle those networks. But it has to be done to salvage the situation.

Initially, the upsurge in Sunni militancy was to some extent linked to Al Qaeda and the Afghan Taliban insurgents using the province as their base after the US invasion of Afghanistan in 2001. This connection came to light after the investigation into a series of attacks on Shia mosques and Ashura processions in Quetta between July 2003 and March 2004 that killed hundreds of worshippers. The probe showed that Dawood Badani, a close relative of Khalid Shaikh Mohammed, was the mastermind behind those suicide bombings for which responsibility was claimed by the LeJ.

But the recent tide of anti-Shia violence coincides with the emergence of tribal militias propped up by Pakistani intelligence agencies to counter the Baloch separatist movement in the province. Some of the government-backed armed outfits also draw their support from the networks of hundreds of madrasas in the region.

With donations from Gulf and Arab countries, most of those
madrasas are run by hard-line clerics having close ties with the
LeJ. This provides a deadly and unholy nexus of forces fighting
the Baloch separatists and those waging war against the Shia
community.

As in other conflict zones, Hazara women are bearing the brunt
of the violence. The targeted killing of male family members has
left them with no other choice but to stand on their own feet. This
was never easy, especially since their distinctive features are easily
recognisable, restricting their movement and the options available
for earning their livelihood. The conflict has also had a negative
impact on the education of girls, reducing the access of Hazara girls
to education. Fewer girls are now enrolling in the university after a
bus carrying Hazara female students was blown up by militants. The
lives of Hazara women have also been affected by migration of the
male members of the family to other parts of the country for work.
Many women are single-handedly taking care of their children.
Thousands of Hazara men have migrated to other countries, but it
is not easy for everyone to get asylum.

Far from the mainstream

For the past several years, Balochistan is facing a low intensity
insurgency by Baloch separatists. Since the province became part of
Pakistan some sixty-five years ago, Baloch nationalists have led four
insurgencies—in 1948, 1958-59, 1962-63 and 1973-77—which were
brutally suppressed by the state. Now a fifth is under way. Unlike
in the past, educated middle-class youth are leading the separatist
movement, rather than tribal leaders. An overwhelming majority
of Baloch nationalists had earlier rejected secession and struggled
for autonomy within the framework of the Pakistani federation. But
state repression has blurred the division, forcing many moderates to
ally themselves with the radicals. The policy of killing and dumping
the bodies of political activists has pushed increasing numbers of
people, particularly among the younger generation, into the fold of
separatist groups. According to Human Rights Watch, around 300

corpses of disappeared persons were discovered in 2011.[2]

This situation inspires little confidence in the idea that moderates are returning to democratic politics. Though most nationalist parties have returned to the mainstream and some of the fighters have surrendered, the situation in the province is far from being normal. An uninterrupted democratic process is the only way to restore the confidence of the people of Balochistan in the federation. The decision by nationalist parties to return to electoral politics despite the threat of violence is indeed a step forward in Balochistan's struggle for democratic rights.

---

[2]Human Rights Watch. 2011. 'We Can Torture, We can Kill, or Keep you for Years: Enforced Disappearances by Pakistani Security Forces in Pakistan'.

No Woman's Land

SHAZIA IRRAM GUL

'I died that day!' declares thirty-two-year-old Naseema in deep anguish. Her fifteen-month-old baby became yet another victim of the repressive Taliban rule in Pakistan's tribal areas. She was unable to get her sick baby to hospital because there were no men at home that day, and the Taliban had prohibited women from venturing out alone. Her baby daughter did not survive.

Naseema's story mirrors that of scores of women in Khyber Agency. Studies show that giving birth during times of conflict not only increases the risk of infant mortality, it also exacerbates psychological disorders and intensifies the risk of maternal deaths (Wazir and Irfan Uddin 2011). Of the women interviewed across refugee camps in Khyber Pakhtunkhwa, every third woman who was pregnant when driven out of Federally Administered Tribal Areas (FATA) had a miscarriage due to exhaustion and the strains of the journey.

FATA, a relatively unknown, rugged frontier bordering Afghanistan, became front page news after the US focused on the region following the terror attacks of September 2001. Pakistan's involvement in the 'War on Terror' came in the wake of its support to the Taliban fighting for power in Afghanistan. Many militant groups originally fighting in Afghanistan established bases in FATA, launching attacks on the US and its allies across the border and severely impacting the lives of FATA's residents. With a change in foreign policy, the Pakistan Army began an assault on certain militant outfits in 2001, which resulted in the displacement of the local population, making them flee to other parts of the country.

These internally displaced persons (IDPs) account for nearly a quarter of the 3.2 million displaced people in Asia. There have been 746,700 IDPs since 2004 (IDMC 2014). Of these, about 10 per cent live in camps while 90 per cent live with host communities in neighbouring Khyber Pakhtunkhwa and elsewhere (UNHCR 2012).

'People should know how we are suffering,' says a young woman displaced from Orakzai Agency in FATA. 'I was expecting to deliver a baby within a fortnight, when security forces ordered us to vacate the area for what they said would be three days only. But these three days have not yet passed,' says Zanib, 34. Her baby was born during her march to safety. Thousands of displaced women have suffered similarly, trekking down treacherous mountain paths with children, the sick and the elderly to safer areas and camps. They have lost everything and are filled with anguish and rage. They now share stories of how their homes were destroyed during bombing and they have little to go back to. One woman lost seven men in her family in a single day; they died during interrogation by Pakistani security forces. Her home is known as the 'widow house' in Khyber Agency.

Between a rock and a hard place, the women living in this troubled frontier land have been subjected to atrocities from armed men on both sides, and security personnel have not turned out to be their saviours.

'Uzbek [foreign militants] and [Pakistan Army] soldiers are the same to me. What did I do to be treated like this?' cries twenty-five-year-old Mehar Tabba, a widow who fled from her native town, Mir Ali, in North Waziristan when the Pakistan Army launched Operation Zerb-e-Azb on June 15, 2014 to flush out Taliban militants from this restive tribal agency. Nine months before the operation, the Pakistan Army had killed her husband for his suspected ties to the Taliban. Tabba is one of the 600,000 IDPs from North Waziristan Agency in FATA.[1]

The area has turned into a virtual war zone, with fatalities occurring on both sides. The words 'mortar', 'drone', jangi jeyyaz (war aircraft) and karrpeo (curfew) have become a part of daily

[1]FATA Disaster Management Authority, July 2014.

vocabulary. As noted by Dr. Farzana Bari, human rights activist and professor at Quaid-e-Azam University, the hostilities increased the number of vulnerable people: widows, orphaned children, and families of the Taliban abandoned by their men folk.

Militant justice

'For the past three years, before we fled, we couldn't work in our fields due to bombing, drone attacks and the frequent curfew. Our children are weak from lack of food,' says a woman who now lives in a camp for displaced people. The patriarchal tribal society did not permit women to freely access resources without male members of the family; with Taliban rule came additional restrictions on their mobility. In 2007, 90 per cent of Khyber Agency was under Taliban control, where it had imposed its own version of sharia. Dilbaro from Khyber Agency, now living in Jalozai Camp, was not permitted to work in the fields, had to close her shop and was prohibited from going to the market. She also couldn't take her children to the doctor or even carry out daily chores with ease because of the imposition of the burqa by the Taliban. She says, 'We fetched water from streams and tube wells and found it difficult to balance the water pitchers on our heads with our faces covered. We often got hurt.'

Women constituted 60 per cent of the workforce in the agricultural sector in FATA, which consists mainly of subsistence farming (Naseer 2014). Zanib recalls, 'Tirah Valley was our heaven on earth. After completing household chores we fetched water from the stream, harvested and cut the wheat crop and picked walnuts off the trees. We were very happy. When the Taliban came they turned the valley into a battleground, compelled us to wear burqas, socks and gloves and confined us to our homes.' In Khyber and Orakzai agencies under Mangal Bagh's sharia law,[2] women were prohibited from working in the fields.

---

[2] *The Express Tribune* reported in 2011, 'The man causing trouble is Mangal Bagh, a former bus driver turned warlord who heads a relatively small militia called Lashkar-e-Islam, which seeks to apply sharia, or Islamic law'. This militant organisation operates in Khyber Agency, Pakistan. Several Pakistani newspapers have referred to him as Haji Amir Mangal Bagh.

Zanib says that despite complying, they were often fired upon, or got caught in the crossfire between warring groups. Iran Bibi from Khyber Agency, who once owned her own cows, buffaloes, sheep and goats, said, 'They fire on women working on farms and have killed many who were cutting fodder for cattle. I sold my cows and buffaloes because I didn't have resources to feed them.'

Women also generated money by raising livestock and poultry, and through their intricate handicrafts. In some areas like Khyber Agency and North Waziristan, women do exquisite beadwork. As the security situation deteriorated, markets were often closed and men were not able to go out to work. Women started to make ends meet using small businesses run in their homes, such as selling groceries, fabric, vegetables and general items for female patrons. Middle-aged Rajmeena, also owned a general store, 'I was earning 2,000 [Pakistani] rupees per day and more during Eid.' As many as twenty to thirty shops in Rajmeena's locality were run by women. Dilbaro was also among those who had started up a small business selling clothing but had to shut it down after receiving threats from a local militant group.

In Orakzai Agency, women walked great distances to collect firewood and mazri (palm) from which they made a variety of domestic products. When the Taliban fighters took refuge in surrounding forests they would abuse the women and even beat them with whips, so they eventually stopped going.

While it retained control in FATA, the Taliban imposed an oppressive system of administration and justice based on existing traditional tribal norms. The Pakistani Taliban version of sharia was very similar [to that] given by Taliban in Afghanistan [especially] regarding women. This discourse was more tribal and customary in nature rather than Islamic.[3] The Taliban exacerbated an already bad situation as far as the women of FATA were concerned. The imposition of the burqa, child marriage and restrictions on acquiring education, were all aimed at maintaining complete control over women's lives.

---

[3]Prof. Khadim Hussain, analyst on FATA affairs, interview, December 2014.

The institution of marriage was also used by the Taliban as an instrument of force. Locals had to agree to marry off their daughters to Taliban militants out of fear. Tribal customs and traditions were exploited as very young girls and women were forced to marry militants. Naseema says that the Taliban would burst into private homes to ostensibly 'check the morality of the girls' and then force the parents to marry their daughters to the militants. She adds, many militants were drug addicts and involved in petty crimes so parents would never have willingly agreed to such marriages. The Taliban militants would also announce in the mosques that parents should contact them for the marriages of their daughters.

Thus, Shahi, Dilbaro's daughter, was forcibly engaged to a militant four years ago. He died in the fighting, and now his family insists that Shahi marry her fiancé's elder brother, who is already married, with five children. Appeals through the Jirga, the tribal council, have failed. A female is not permitted to participate in, or take a case to, a Jirga. Her case has to be conveyed through male family members. Women such as Dilbaro, who have no close male family members, cannot hope to get justice from a Jirga. Shahi is not the only victim, but most other families are too scared to share their stories.

The Taliban inflicted harsh punishments for perceived 'crimes'. For example, a man in Bara was lashed because his wife stepped out of the house accompanied by a boy under ten years of age. Haram, a woman at the camp, said she stood at her doorstep to answer queries posed by security forces personnel, and Taliban spies informed their superiors, who began threatening her and her husband. She added that in Tirah Valley, women have been beaten for stepping out of their homes without a mehram or escort. The strong patriarchal code has also influenced the behaviour of women themselves in the IDP camps. They feel dishonoured outside the protection of their homes. 'Whereas the women used shawls when visiting neighbours, they now ask for burqas,' says Yasmin Akhtar, regional manager of the NGO, Khawando Kor-Bannu.

Bad to worse

The Taliban multiplied the woes of women in FATA, which has a separate political administration based on Pakhtunwali, a code of tribal customary practices. Sarfaraz Khan, director of the Central Asia Area Study Centre at the University of Peshawar, explains, 'Most of the customary institutions, practices and interpretations of Pakhtunwali are highly gendered. They exclude women from social, political, judicial and public spheres.'

He points out that, even before the Taliban takeover and accompanying militarisation, 'FATA had one of the highest ratios of "missing women" in the world and also poor socio-economic indicators for women.' Cultural, traditional and social practices have excluded them from decision-making at the domestic level and also limited their access to education, with the exception of a few girls who attend primary classes in boys' schools. For most children, the only source of education in many parts of FATA is the mosque or religious seminary; girls go to a Quran teacher. Teenage girls help with household tasks and marry early. Polygamy is common, but the consent of women to this system is not sought. Extended families are the norm and women are responsible for the children's welfare, but have no say in any decision-making. Female doctors are rare, and nurses and lady health workers (LHWs) are few. In 2013, for instance, there were only 55 LHWs in FATA as compared with 2,515 LHWs in Punjab province, according to the government's records of the LHW programme.[4] Conditions in Basic Health Units and hospitals where women patients are treated are abysmal, say women who have used these services.

Under the Taliban regime, women were allowed access to the most rudimentary medical care, with only a few female health staff available. Even the few male doctors left—most having fled due to Taliban threats—were not allowed to treat female patients. Thus, the second-worst health facilities for women were declared to be in the militancy-affected sectors in FATA. According to a 2014 report

[4]Government of Pakistan, 'The Lady Health Workers Programme', 2008.

by the Human Rights Commission of Pakistan (HRCP), almost eighty hospitals were hit by militancy and military operations. Many pregnant women were unable to reach the hospital in time, risking the lives of both mother and child.

The 200-bed Agency Headquarters Hospital in Khar, Bajaur Agency, used to provide treatment to over 100,000 patients annually, with the help of 120 doctors and 100 paramedics. But it is now empty of both patients and doctors, who have mostly fled to Peshawar.[5] The little medical care available is extremely expensive. The child mortality rate is high in some parts of FATA,[6] as women have had to depend on diyas, or untrained birth attendants, to assist them in childbirth in their homes. The situation is not much better in other health-related areas. A woman from Bara narrated her experience with severe toothache. Instead of the dentist, her father (who had no medical training) examined her teeth and described their condition to the male dentist, who then prescribed treatment.

Fleeing from militancy did not reduce the anguish of these women, since life in the camps is also tough. Thirty-four-year-old Zanib has lived in Jalozai Camp for four years with her nine children and husband. When I met her, she was making mud bricks. 'The camp is terribly hot in summer and cold in winter; the extreme climate is killing. We cannot go home due to continuous fighting so we decided to build a room with mud bricks.'

Like the other women in the camp, Bakht Wari from Orakzai Agency is also unable to return home. She lives with her fourteen children in one tent. She says, 'There is no peace of mind, no security and above all, no proper facilities at the camp.' Among the multiple problems faced is that of accommodation. In Togh Sarai Camp, Hangu, a wedding was planned but the new couple could only manage a corner curtained off within the same tent housing the entire family. Separate tents are very difficult to get. The lack of privacy adversely affects marital and family relationships.

---

[5]FATA Directorate of Health 2012.

[6]FATA Directorate of Health 2011.

In this camp in Hangu, most of the tents are not suitable for the extreme weather conditions and water drips inside during heavy rain. An elderly woman from Orakzai Agency broke down while recalling the time when heavy rains flooded her camp. She spent the night without shelter along with her two infant grandchildren. A case officer told this journalist that tents often collapsed in heavy rain and that food and other possessions were ruined as a result.

'There is no food, water, electricity or latrine, and even the market is far away,' complains a fifteen-year-old girl in the Domail Sparka Wazir Camp in Bannu which houses 400 to 600 people displaced from North Waziristan. Boys and girls below the age of ten are barefoot, and no women are visible outside the tents, which are securely fastened with tarpaulin sheets. The mud paths between the tents are flooded, the smell of excrement fills the air and children's faces are pock-marked with mosquito bites. I enter a tent packed with six to eight beds and with clothing strung across the centre. A young girl named Khunaza greets me warmly. In fluent Urdu, she speaks of her painful journey via Afghanistan where more than 100,000 Waziristanis have taken refuge. An elderly woman, Abahi, tells of rumours circulating that foreign militants had taken refuge in their area, with the help of local militant commanders. She adds that clerics in North Waziristan had caused fear and insecurity. Abahi bemoans the transformation of her homeland: 'My lovely watan, once a peaceful place, turned into hell.' The toll on human lives has taken many forms, not all of them tangible.

Present tense, future unknown

Due to terror attacks, drone strikes, and military operations, the inhabitants of FATA have experienced severe trauma. As Dr. Khalid A. Mufti, a psychiatrist at Ibadhat Hospital, Peshawar, explains in a 2013 FATA Research Centre (FRC) report, 'More than 54 per cent of the population living in the conflict zone exhibit symptoms of acute psychological stress, and among local residents, particularly women and children, many suffer from psychological as well as physical abuse and trauma.' The displaced women have been caught in the conflict for over a decade now and are plagued by mental and emotional pain, including nightmares, which are typical symptoms of trauma.

The conversation of women in Jalozai Camp revolves around stories of recent bombings, firings and the killing of locals, as well as stories of their displacement. Each narrative begins and ends with loss: of home, family, livestock. Naleum Ali, a psychologist at the camp explains, 'These women invested their love and energy into maintaining their homes; their houses were a part of their ego and respect.' The severe stress imposed on these women due to the loss of their homes and loved ones is visible as they narrate their stories. 'The stress of a major loss quickly depletes energies and emotional reserves. Unresolved grief can lead to depression and anxiety, which is very common among these women,' says Naleum.

Camp residents also have to endure demeaning remarks from the local populace, which results in their keeping to themselves and not discussing their trauma. In addition, many women in Bannu who are from North Waziristan are reluctant to share their experiences of suffering, as they remain fearful of the Taliban. An elderly woman says, 'Anyone who criticised the Taliban was killed. We do not talk about them even in the camps because they spy on us and may later punish men from our families.'

The lack of a broad-based education has also added to the insularity of the tribal population. Due to internecine feuds and long-standing conflict in the tribal areas, most people could not go beyond a basic religious education. With a 2013 FRC report declaring the literacy rate for FATA women to be as low as 3 per cent and the destruction of hundreds of schools over the past few years, as well as the threatening and intimidation of female teachers and students, the situation is dire. According to figures provided by the FATA Directorate of Education, in 2011 alone, 505 schools were damaged and destroyed, while 108 schools for girls in FATA were dysfunctional due to threats from militants. A 2013 HRCP report adds that 120,000 female students in FATA were forced to quit school between 2009 and 2011 due to Taliban threats; many girls were also forced to join seminaries.

However, despite these difficulties, many girls, with the support of their parents and teachers, relentlessly pursued an education. One courageous teacher is Samia Zaib, 55, who is now principal of a school. She continued to teach while observing the Taliban dress code and wearing a burqa, until her school too was blown up by unknown assailants. Two years later, her school in Bara was shifted to Sirband, Peshawar but enrolment has fallen by half. Students and teachers have to submit to body searches on a daily basis while travelling from Bara to Sirband. Since students can't travel during curfew, they miss their exams. Concessions are not always made for students in conflict areas who have to sit for their exams again.

Military menace

Serious abuses, including indiscriminate attacks against civilians, targeted killings, curfew, airstrikes, demolished houses, routine house raids in search of militants and detention of locals, have fuelled displacement.[7] Shakeel Qadir, the person in charge of security in Khyber Pakhtunkhwa, says that army operations in FATA were necessary to 'stop infiltration of militants and establish the writ of law....The area was first evacuated and then army operations began.' However, the majority of women in the camps say that no advance warning of military operations were issued; only sometimes evacuation orders were given during counter-insurgency operations. In some parts of FATA, the destruction of homes during US drone operations is also reported to have led people to flee.[8] Most of the displaced women felt that army operations were the major cause of their displacement. As most people in FATA live below the poverty line, their displacement comes at great economic and social cost, especially to the women.

---

[7]This list is based on interviews with women in IDP camps between October and December 2014.

[8]Centre for Civilians in Conflict, 2012, p.24

The women reported being terrified by house searches, bombing and drone attacks. Iran Bibi from Khyber Agency said that even before displacement, the situation had been very tense because army tanks backed by gunship helicopters had started patrolling the area. 'The bombs gave us no time to rest,' she says. For many women, the presence of the army in FATA also caused untold hardship and misery as soldiers would enter private homes without notice, on search missions. A woman from Upper Tirah Valley said, 'The [male] security forces open personal belongings. We find this embarrassing and insulting.' A 2010 HRCP report states, 'People have also fled their homes as a result of aerial bombardments, arrests, house demolitions and military operations.'

Although the Pakistan Army has reclaimed control of most parts of FATA from the Taliban over the past three years, the inhabitants of the area have paid a high price in the form of detentions, deaths of suspects in custody, and indiscriminate attacks on innocent citizens. According to Amnesty International, 'Millions are locked in perpetual lawlessness in Pakistan's North Western Tribal Areas, where human rights abuses committed by the Armed Forces and the Taliban are beyond the reach of justice.' Many displaced women talked about their tragic experiences at the hands of the security forces and the Taliban.

In North Waziristan, according to *Mashriq*, an Urdu newspaper published from Peshawar, shells fired from helicopters and artillery hit the town of Mir Ali, and fourteen members of the Moski tribe, including ten women and a child, lost their lives. Many families from Mir Ali in the camp in Bannu told this writer that they had much to share about the killings of their loved ones, but were afraid to speak openly for fear of repercussions by the security agencies.

Very often, curfew would be imposed for long periods. Abahi, the elderly woman from North Waziristan, said she was a heart patient and had to endure pain for many days during a curfew because her son couldn't go out to buy medicine. People were also short of food and had to borrow from their neighbours or go without. Further, the families of daily wage labourers who could not work due to curfew suffered deprivation. Relatives had to take permission from the authorities to take anyone who became ill, was injured or died during curfew to the doctor or for burial. Often, permission was denied. Many women died during childbirth, as they could not access medical help during curfew.

Says Khunaza, 'Curfew also makes peoples' lives miserable. No one can feel our pain.' She speaks from bitter experience, as her mother suffered a stroke and was unable to access medical help because of the curfew. While Khunaza speaks, her mother walks around with a stick, trying to communicate through blurred speech that is incomprehensible. Khunaza says that her mother keeps trying to ask: will I get any treatment or not?

Pakistan experienced two waves of displacement in FATA, and recorded 140,000 newly displaced persons in 2013 alone. A significant number of these IDPs still remain in camps and other localities, even though their areas of origin have been officially 'de-notified'. This is due to security or economic concerns, and some are still waiting for government assistance to rebuild their houses before returning. The majority of the inhabitants in camps are women and children whose needs are different from the men. In Camp Togh Sarai Hangu, for example, women still lack even the basics, such as tents, clothes, food, etc. although they have already spent a year and more there. Further, like Mehar Tabba, many single women live in constant fear and anxiety about how to protect themselves and their children, how to make ends meet and how to ensure adequate shelter in case they are forced to spend a prolonged period in the camp. Sexual and gender-based violence[9] is a major problem, but apparently sexual harassment has decreased after the formation of a camp Grand Shura, and sector-wise Shura. (The Grand Shura is a ten-member committee of elected tribal elders in the camp.) 'The role and functioning of the Shura in terms of providing justice to victims is still traditional and customary,' says the Camp Coordinator.[10]

[9]The non-profit Centre for Excellence in Rural Development (CERD) psychologist in Jalozai Camp in an interview in September 2014.

[10]CERD, Camp Coordinator, Faysal Kamran in an interview in September 2014.

Many women-headed families struggle to cope, as their men have either been killed, or have moved out of the camps to earn a living. One twenty-one-year-old woman I met was caring for her five younger siblings and sick mother in Jalozai Camp while her father worked in Lahore. Living with continuous economic insecurity and being dependent on aid from others is painful for these self-respecting women. The constraints of their displacement, unemployment and an unreliable income, along with the challenge of managing all household needs with little or no support, have placed great pressure on them. These women are among nearly a million people who registered for aid after the army began its offensive in North Waziristan. Although there is enough food, many, especially women, don't receive assistance due to lack of identity cards. Those living in camps are generally considered most in need of assistance, but two-thirds of IDPs outside camps live below the poverty line and do not have adequate access to food, medicine, housing and basic services. Displaced families outside the camps worry about unfamiliar surroundings and how to manage utility bills and house rent.

Along with all the problems of daily survival in the camps, the women still fear the militants who have issued threats on FM radio, said a case officer of an international non-government organisation at Jalozai Camp, Nowshera. The women in camps revealed—on condition of anonymity—that they suffered sexual abuse at the camps. They were also subjected to constant physical and verbal abuse by their husbands. Many women in camps cannot go to a doctor for treatment due to social restrictions and poverty.

Reign of silence

The women of FATA are directly affected by the conflict, but there is a deafening silence when it comes to their participation in peace-building and conflict resolution strategies in Pakistan and specifically in FATA. This invisibility extends to all tiers, including during talks with militants, at the Aman Jirgas (traditional peace councils) or as part of the National Action Plan (NAP).[11] Not a single woman has been a delegate in the teams undertaking peace talks with the Taliban and other militant groups.

The Taliban's dogmatic views have made women's rights to education and free movement the main casualty in the current situation. The UN Security Council Resolution (UNSCR) 1325 recognized the need to increase women's role in peace-building in conflict-ridden countries, but Pakistan has not implemented Resolution 1325 as yet. On February 12, 2014, Pakistan's Senate (or upper house of Parliament) passed a resolution asking the government to protect the rights of women and minorities in the peace talks, but it remained ineffective as Article 247-B places FATA outside its jurisdiction.

This systemic exclusion of women has not kept pace with the changes taking place in gender roles. After displacement, women and girls have learnt new skills such as handicrafts, tailoring, how to market their products and to handle paperwork and finances. Many acquire an education to enable them to contribute to peace-making and rebuilding local economies and communities. 'These changes in gender relations reinforce women's role in peace talks and reconstruction processes, and as agents of change,' says Shakeel Qadir, lamenting that women's empowerment is not addressed during or in the aftermath of conflict. The lack of discussion around these issues is perhaps an outcome of the lack of media attention and the resulting absence of public discourse.

The outdated Frontier Crimes Regulations of 1901, which give dictatorial powers to the Political Agent, have remained a hurdle to freedom of expression in FATA. With militancy growing in the area and the deteriorating security situation since 2005, working conditions for journalists in FATA have worsened. Thirty-four journalists (mostly from FATA) were killed between 2008 and

---

[11]The NAP was implemented in January 2015, following the gruesome terrorist attack on a Peshawar school in December 2014, as a coordinated retaliation by the Pakistani government. Its aim is to drastically crack down on terrorism across northwestern Pakistan.

2014, according to a report by Amnesty International. With such insecurity, it is not surprising that the realities of the situation in FATA are not reported.

Although official and national media coverage in FATA is not universal, residents use a variety of sources to send and receive messages. At one time, there were ten radio stations in Malakand Agency, along with many others in Bajaur and adjacent tribal areas.[12] However, radio was also a medium to spread extremist doctrines. Mullah Radio of Maulvi Fazlullah in Swat is one example of how propaganda was disseminated by the Taliban. In the absence of the internet, cell phones and other modern means of communication, radio was used to influence the masses in these remote tribal regions. Unemployed youth in particular were very vulnerable to jihadist propaganda. Like the general population, women too initially subscribed to the propaganda, believing that the Taliban would bring in a new era of peace and plenty.

To counter the militants' FM radio stations, under a project financed by USAID in 2004 and 2006, four FM radio stations were established in Wana, Miranshah, Razmak and Jamrud respectively. The Wana radio station was blown up by militants in 2009. The remaining three stations continued their broadcasts despite technical and operational difficulties as well as threats to employees in Miranshah and Razmak. Intermedia, a global research consultancy, initiated a two-year project on Khyber Radio, which had its own news and current affairs programmes, with two female reporters covering news and information specific to women's health, and social and traditional life in FATA. Unfortunately, the reports were not crafted through the lens of gender.

On the other hand, national print media reports are limited to the achievements of the Pakistan security forces, attacks, encounters, displacement figures, sufferings and instances of shortage of food or assistance.

In local radio broadcasts from Peshawar, Kohat, Bannu and D.I. Khan, and even FATA, where there are three FM radio stations,

---

[12]Data on FM channels was provided in *Dawn* newspaper on 5 July 2007.

content is generally limited to news and current affairs programmes, although tribal women's issues are highlighted occasionally through programmes sponsored by NGOs. Their main goal however seems to be to publicise their own work rather than to analyse the real issues affecting women of this region.

International media such as Radio Mashaal, Dewa (Voice of America Pashto language service) and BBC have also gained a wide audience in FATA. Where national and local media fail to cover relevant issues, especially relating to women, international media attempts to fill the gap.

Media coverage of FATA women is also limited for other reasons. Journalists state that access to women is difficult due to cultural norms that limit freedom of movement and communication by women, security issues, and the influence wielded by stakeholders who do not wish certain facts to be disclosed. Male journalists say that they have to approach local, female NGO workers to interview women in camps on their behalf. A few female reporters do work for radio, but they lack training and experience and their reports need depth and focus or more follow-up on current issues. In this situation, the suffering of women remains invisible and unheard, as do their stories of resistance and fortitude under extreme stress.

Bibliography

Amnesty International Report. 2015. *The State of the World's Human Rights*. Amnesty International.

Centre for Civilians in Conflict and Columbia Law School. 2012. *The Civilian Impact of Drones: Unexamined Costs, Unanswered Questions*. New York.

Dawn. 2007. http://www.dawn.com/archive/2007-07-05 Published 5 July. Karachi.

Bari, Farzana. 2010. *Gendered Perceptions and Impact of Terrorism / Talibanization in Pakistan* Islamabad: Heinrich Böll Stiftung, Pakistan.

FATA Directorate of Education. 2011. Available at http://data.org.pk/blog/the-war-on-education Accessed in June 2016.

FATA Directorate of Health. 2011. Available at https://fata.gov.pk/Global-fac.php?iId=378&fid=47&pId=327&mId=178 Accessed in June 2016.

FATA Research Centre (FRC). 2013. *A Seminar Report on IDPs of FATA: Issues and Challenges*, published April 30. http://frc.com.pk/wp-content/uploads/2013/06/IDP_SEMINAR_REPORT.pdf Accessed in June 2016.

Georgy, Michael. 2011. 'Bus driver-turned-militant takes on Pakistan again' in *The Express Tribune* (Reuters). Published October 27. Available at http://in.reuters.com/article/idINIndia-60147720111027 Retrieved in June 2016.

Government of Pakistan. 2008. Ministry of Health, PHC Wing, National Programme for Family Planning and Primary Health Care, *The Lady Health Workers Programme*. Available at http://www.who.int/pmnch/countries/ali_akhtar_hakro_Pakistan.pdf. Accessed on 8 January 2016.

Haider, Mateen. 2014. 'War's Human Cost: UNHCR Global Trends 2013' in *Dawn*, Published June 20. Karachi.

Human Rights Commission of Pakistan (HRCP). 2010. *Annual Report*. Available at http://hrcp-web.org/hrcpweb/annual-report-2010/ Accessed in October 2015. Lahore.

——2013. *Annual Report*. Available at http://hrcp-web.org/hrcpweb/annual-report-2013/ Accessed in June 2016. Lahore.

——2014. *Annual Report*. Available at http://hrcp-web.org/hrcpweb/annual-report-2014/ Accessed in June 2016. Lahore.

Internal Displacement Monitoring Centre (IDMC) Report. 2014. Available at http://tribune.com.pk/story/708406/nearly-a-quarter-of-million-people-displaced-in-pakistan/ Accessed in June 2016.

Kamal, Asad. 2014. *Impacts of Violence on Demographic Dividend of FATA*, Available at http://frc.com.pk/wp-content/uploads/2014/01/Research-Paper-8.pdf Accessed in June 2016. Islamabad. FATA Research Centre.

Khan, Sarfaraz and Samina. 2009. *Patriarchal Social and Administrative Practices in the Federally Administered Tribal Areas (FATA), Pakistan: A Case for Gender Inclusive Reforms*. Peshawar: Central Asia Area Study Centre University of Peshawar.

Naseer, Moona. 2014. *Daily Times*, http://dailytimes.com.pk/opinion/16-Feb-14/fata-women-and-the-question-of-taliban-sharia Accessed in June 2016. Lahore.

Wazir, Mehran Ali Khan and Irfan Uddin. 2011. 'Impact of War on Terror on Maternal Mortality in FATA,' in *TIGAH: A Journal of Peace and Development* (Volume V, June 2014). Islamabad: FATA Research Centre.

From Ghungroos to Gunshots

FARZANA ALI

On a cold winter night in January 2009, the anguished cries of two women broke the silence and rudely awakened the residents of Banr Bazaar in Mingora, the main town of the Swat Valley. No one dared to come out of their homes during the night curfew. They later learnt that a group of men had gained entry to the home of Shabana, a twenty-five-year-old dancer, and dragged her out to the accompaniment of ominous chants that it was time for the dumm, the lowest of the low, to die.

The young woman's mother begged the leader of the group to spare her daughter's life and swore she would ensure that Shabana would never dance again. But to no avail. The men dragged Shabana by her hair through the town, with her wailing mother running after them. She was brutally battered with rifle butts and then shot at point-blank range; her bullet-ridden body left in the square: a gory warning that dancing was in defiance of the Taliban's will. Green Square, where Shabana met her gruesome end, has now been renamed Khooni Chowk (Bloody Square).

The next day, on January 3, 2009, the Taliban commander Maulana Shah Dauran broadcasted a warning on one of their FM radio stations: his men had killed Shabana and if any other girls were found performing in the city's Banr Bazaar they would be killed 'one by one'. He went on to warn the local population that the militant organisation would not tolerate 'un-Islamic vices'. This was at a time when the Taliban had effectively taken over Swat. The tinkling of ghungroos (musical anklets) and the mellifluous

notes of the rubab (lute) had inexorably given way to the staccato
burst of gunshots.

According to Shabana's father, Qamar Gul, the Taliban barged
into their home intending to punish his daughter for performing
at a wedding ceremony in nearby Mardan. Some men knocked on
the door and made inquiries about a dance party. Assuming they
were potential customers, Qamar Gul courteously invited the men
inside to wait while Shabana got dressed. 'As soon as she came into
the room, the four men shouted: "Let us start!" They seized her at
gunpoint and declared that they were going to slit her throat,' he
recounts, still terrorised by the memory.

Shabana's family is desperately poor; she was the only bread-
winner. After her brutal murder, her family fled Swat and returned
only when peace was restored in the city after August 2009. Her
mother died three months after Shabana. When she ran to free her
daughter from the clutches of the Taliban, a sharp piece of glass
pierced her foot, which became badly infected. Still in deep shock
and grieving over the fate of her daughter, she sought no medical
care and died an untimely death. Shabana's father too is very ill. Her
brother drives an auto-rickshaw to earn a little money. The family is
able to survive only because of the support offered by the residents
of Banr, most of whom are blood relatives.

While Shabana's killing was one of the more visible atrocities
committed by the Taliban, its rigid clampdown has badly affected
the decades-old culture of Banr Bazaar, where music and dance
were a part of daily life. The female dancers of this area, who had
learned the art from their mothers and grandmothers, were forced
to give up their profession. One of them is also named Shabana, and
happens to be a cousin of the slain Shabana. Born in Banr Bazaar,
she followed in her mother's footsteps and made a career out of
singing and dancing. However, when the extremists took control
of Swat in 2007, she was forced to abandon not only her profession
but also her ancestral home.

Shabana is loath to remember the night when the Taliban
dragged her cousin out of the house and killed her at 'Khooni

Chowk'. When I met the younger Shabana in August 2014, she recalled, 'Before Shabana's killing, we received letters telling us to wind up our business. We had to hang signboards in front of our houses refusing entry to visitors. Letters were addressed to male members of every family asking them to get the girls married. Eventually, some families stayed on while others left the area. Taliban wanted us to give up our profession, calling it a sin. We said it may be a sin to you, but to us it's the profession of our ancestors. How can we leave it? What else will we do after giving up this profession? Our men have no businesses or jobs. They are uneducated. How will we earn a living? But the demands of the Taliban only escalated.'

The rigidity of the Taliban and its condemnation of joyous expressions of culture is in complete contrast to the openness and diversity that once marked the Swat Valley.[1]

Vale of tolerance

Swat is one of the most beautiful valleys of Pakistan, and was known as a tourist paradise. Terraced fields, startlingly green rice paddies, abundant orchards redolent with fruit, and views of snow-capped mountain peaks can be seen at every turn of the road.

This valley was earlier part of Afghanistan, but the 1893 Durand Line agreement brought it under the British Empire. In 1915, a Jirga (tribal council of elders) declared Swat a sovereign state and in 1917 Mian Gul Abdul Wadud became its first ruler. In 1926, he was granted the title of Wali (ruler) of Swat and was provided an annual privy purse. With the end of British rule in the Indian subcontinent, and the creation of Pakistan in 1947, the princely state of Swat acceded to Pakistan while maintaining internal autonomy. This autonomous status continued until 1969 when the states of Dir, Chitral and Swat were formally merged into Pakistan.

Archaeological sites dating back over 5,000 years are testimony to Swat's immense religious and cultural diversity. Historical evidence

---

[1] The Swat Valley spans about 3798 sq km and is a part of the Malakand division, which comprises Malakand, Buner, Swat, Shangla, Upper Dir, Lower Dir and Chitral, and forms part of the Khyber Pakhtunkhwa province.

indicates that Swat was one of the areas where Buddhism flourished during the time of Emperor Ashoka (268-232 BCE), and when people converted to Islam around 1100 AD, religious influences from both these major faiths continued to hold sway. This picturesque valley was once the home of the Hinayana sect of Buddhism and a regional centre of a Himalayan civilisation that extended from Tibet to Kashmir.

The valley is primarily inhabited by different tribes of Pashtuns, an ethnic community residing in the border regions of Afghanistan and Pakistan. They are divided into tribes, sub-tribes and clans. Their language is Pashto, and the living code is called 'Pakhtunwali', an ancient self-governing tribal system that regulates nearly all aspects of Pashtun life.

When the Yousafzai Pashtuns from Afghanistan conquered the Swat Valley in the sixteenth century, they turned it into a centre of Pashtun culture. Since the Yousafzais did not practice an extreme form of Islam, Buddhist, Hindu and Sikh archaeological sites were never damaged or destroyed, as happened when the Taliban ravaged neighbouring Afghanistan.

The Yousafzai Pashtuns were open-minded, and their own dances and folk songs were influenced by the region's Buddhist past. Indeed, Swat was the only place in the Pashtun belt where even girls from the families of professional singers, dancers and musicians could choose a career in the performing arts. Today, the Swat Valley can still feel justly proud of the remarkable contributions of a host of Pashto folk singers such as Zarsanga, Khan Tahsil, Qamru Jan Bibi, Gulnar Begum, Hidayatullah, Akbar Hussain, Mashooq Sultana, Ahmed Gul Ustad and Akbar Hussain, who perfected their art and harmonised it with modern musical trends.

An enduring aspect of Swat's culture is the traditional folk dance which is performed at weddings and other cultural ceremonies. The renowned artistes from the Valley have been associated with their professions for many generations, the most famous of them from Banr Bazaar in Mingora city. Swat's soil has proven to be fertile for poets and singers through the ages and society has always held them in great regard.

In the 1960s, during the regime of the Wali of Swat, Mian Gul Abdul Haq Jehanzeb, Banr Bazaar was home to more than 100 artistes' families. They were all patronised by the Wali of Swat, who was himself married to a dancing girl. Female dancers of that generation still remember him for the respect he gave to their art. Jamal Shah, 45, a harmonium player from Banr Bazaar refers to the time when the Wali Sahib allotted a specific area to the artistes of Swat that later came to be known as Banr Bazaar. 'That was a very peaceful time for the artistes of Swat; people honoured them. Many girls of Banr Bazaar were married into reputed Pashtun families. The dancers were free to dance at any marriage ceremony.'

Linguistics professor and cultural critic Khadim Hussain provides an insight into Swat's current problems, and those of the dancers' community. 'The society that evolved in the former state of Swat was at variance with the social and cultural practices in most parts of the province inhabited by the other Pashtun tribes. The social organisation remained inclusive to a large extent,' he points out. Fine arts and aesthetics occupied an important place in the cultural fabric of the community and artistic expressions were institutionalised. Indigenous cultural expression also flourished in the customary melas (fairs) featuring music concerts and dances.

Enter the extremists

These activities continued even after the merger of Swat with Pakistan, although state patronage was replaced with social and group patronage. But two developments—one in the late '80s and the other in the early '90s—coupled with the prevailing social, cultural, class and gender frictions, have largely defined the critical situation in recent years.

Firstly, a petition in the Peshawar High Court in 1989 sought to declare unconstitutional the Provincially Administered Tribal Areas (PATA) Regulation of 1975—a legal framework distinct from the rest of Pakistan. Secondly, the Tehrik-i-Nifaz-i-Shariat-i-Muhammadi (TNSM), a conservative Islamist group, formed in 1992 by Sufi Muhammad, a Jamaat-e-Islami renegade, who managed a madrasa in Kambar, Dir, began the radicalisation that followed in the valley.

The first event was indicative of peoples' desire to get rid of the discriminatory legal regime, while the second evidenced a shift in religious authority in the valley as the TNSM attracted extensive support, especially in the upper reaches of Swat. The discourse of power, ideology and control was reconstructed, reflecting the growing socio-cultural friction in the Valley. The mode and scale of the conflict may also be understood by observing the patterns of ideological persuasion, social contagion and territorial expansion by the TNSM and the Swat chapter of Tehrik-e-Taliban Pakistan (TTP).

The Pashtun era before 1917 had particular legal, social, cultural and political frameworks. The influence of these frameworks continued, despite the changing dynamics from 1917 to 1969, when Swat was a semi-autonomous state, first within British India and then in Pakistan. The status of the clergy, shifts in religious authority, socio-cultural dynamics in evolutionary perspective, gender dynamics and legal battles must also be understood in the context of Swat in order to comprehend the complete picture of the present conflict. Emerging geostrategic and institutional factors served to exacerbate these conflicts between 1989 and 2008 and brought the region to its current crisis.

After militarisation and the insurgency in Swat, cultural and artistic space was taken over by rigid religious doctrine. Fine arts, especially dancing, were construed to be evil and socially and culturally unacceptable. Those involved with dance and music were persecuted and forced to leave the Swat Valley, in stark contrast to the period of patronage under the Wali. Osman Ulasyar of the Suvastu Arts and Culture Association, an art lover from Swat, remembers the time when female dancers from Banr Bazaar used to perform at every festival. 'There used to be a three-day celebration at Eid-ul-Fitr and a seven-day celebration on Eid-ul-Azha. Music, comedy shows, skits, dancing were all part of the traditional celebrations,' he reminisces.

Ulasyar also elaborates on the steady takeover of the Swat Valley by religious extremists, and laments that no action was taken against these non-state actors. In 2007, a pirate (illegal) FM radio station launched by the militants to preach religious bigotry across the Swat Valley was led by Mullah Fazlullah, a thirty-two-year-old lift operator turned Taliban commander, and son-in-law of Sufi Muhammad of TNSM. 'Fazlullah in his daily inflammatory broadcasts discouraged girls' education, called polio immunisation un-Islamic, and equated musical expression with obscenity,' says Ulasyar.

Fazlullah exploited the presence of the US-led NATO forces in Afghanistan and prevailing injustice in Pakistani society to urge people to wage jihad against the so-called 'infidels.' He also demanded the promulgation of Islamic sharia law throughout the Malakand region. In their radio broadcasts, he and his second-in-command, Maulana Shah Dauran, described dancers, musicians and singers as 'friends of Satan', responsible for the moral degradation of society.

Immediately after these broadcasts came bomb attacks on music shops, followed by the ban on singing and dancing by the militants. 'We can say that 2006 to 2009 was an era of barbaric activities in Swat. During this period not only were many lives lost, but there was a devastating impact on our civilisation and culture. Our hujras (community meeting places) were destroyed, and our ceremonies were bombed. Artistes were not allowed to perform any cultural activities,' Ulasyar said.

Musicians and singers from Banr Bazaar were left with no choice but to publish advertisements in local newspapers, declaring, 'We the residents of Banr Bazaar want to inform people that we are not associated with the dancing profession. We have left it forever. Please do not contact us in this regard.' They went on to pledge to live a 'pious life' according to the Taliban's version of Islam and sharia. In order to save themselves from the wrath of the Taliban, they put up signboards and banners declaring, for example, 'Aaj se Nachgaana band: Meherbani is silsiley mein dastak na dein' (From today, there is no more music and dance. Please do not knock on our doors). The public distancing from professional music and dance seemed to be their ticket to survival.

According to Ulasyar, the Taliban insurgency completely changed the cultural narrative of the Yousafzai Pashtuns of Swat, for whom artistic pursuits had been an integral part of the social fabric for hundreds of years. The insurgency not only destroyed basic infrastructure in the valley, it also obliterated an old socio-cultural order based on mutual coexistence.

Abaseen Yousufzai, Dean of the faculty of Pashto at the Islamia College University, Peshawar, blamed the government for its failure to provide protection to the Banr Bazaar community. According to him, militancy not only destroyed the livelihoods of the residents of Banr Bazaar, but also had a negative effect on culture. Yousufzai said, 'Music is part of our culture and these artistes are our assets, and when someone tries to stop them from performing, these actions amount to changing our tradition and values. They want to transform local cultural values.'

For almost half a century, Banr Bazaar represented the finest traditions of art and was the pillar of the Pashto music industry. Many singers like Gulnaz and Ghazala Javeed came from Banr Bazaar and earned fame all over the country. When the militants captured Swat, their first targets were musicians and artistes. They publicly burned music and CD shops, threatened the artiste community and kidnapped and murdered some artistes. Anwar Gul, harmonium player and close companion of Pashto singer, Sardar Yousafzai, was shot by militants; famous Pashto singer Gulzar Alam escaped a gun attack; and after Shabana's death, a local singer, Ghani Dad, was gunned down in Swat.

Due to fear of these militants, many of the artistes changed their profession or escaped from Swat. They did not get any protection from the government. By August 2009, following the 'Operation Rah-e-Rast', also known as the 'Second Battle of Swat', the military wrested control of the Swat Valley from the Taliban. However, the government did not take any constructive steps for the rehabilitation of those who returned. While the rise of religious militancy in the region heralded the death of the traditional culture of Swat, the government's indifference to the defenceless community of artistes proved to be the final nail in the coffin.

After Shabana was publicly executed in 2009, the fate of the dancing girls of Swat was sealed when, instead of providing protection to one of the most vulnerable segments of society, the authorities yielded to the demands of the Taliban. According to a BBC report,[2] Malakand Commissioner Mohammed Javed told their correspondent that the agreement to remove the dancing girls and close businesses during prayers was reached between him and the TNSM chief, Sufi Muhammad, in March 2009.

A palpable fear forced the inhabitants of Banr Bazaar to perceive their profession differently. Gone was the pride in their culture, replaced by trepidation and dread. This is evident from the words of artistes who, for understandable reasons, were not willing to talk in front of the media. Kainat, 22, a singer from Banr, says, 'The musicians were in a constant state of terror. Gone are the days when we used to participate in live concerts in Swat till late at night. Open air performances are a far cry. We can now perform only indoors and that too is very rare.'

Muskan, 21, whose grandmother used to dance in town melas, says, 'The burden of the whole family's expenses is on my shoulders. I dance out of necessity, not for pleasure. I wish I had been born into another life. We have no respect in society. Everyone wants a house, a husband. I would love to have children. Even if I marry into a dancer's family, I would never want my daughters to dance. I have seen the circumstances we had to face, so why would I want that for my daughters?'

These statements describe life today in an austere Banr Bazaar, where every dancer's attitude towards dance has changed. The dignity enjoyed by their mothers and grandmothers has now turned into shame. Although people still come to their homes, they enter

---

[2]http://news.bbc.co.uk/2/hi/south_asia/7924232.stm

not as connoisseurs of art, but as mere customers. Banr Bazaar, which once housed more than a hundred dancers' families, was at one stage left with only twenty-two.

The abnormal normal

Life is back to 'normal'. But for those who have lived in Banr Bazaar for many years it is not the same. Artistes did return to Banr after peace was restored in Swat, but there is a big difference. Now, music parties are held behind closed doors. Dancers perform, but only for those who they are personally acquainted with. The doors of Banr are not opened to unfamiliar knocks. Musicians still play harmoniums and tablas, but are reluctant to disclose their identities due to fear of repercussions. Shops selling music and movie CDs and DVDs have reopened, but for those like Sana Ullah Khan, whose shop was destroyed by the extremists in 2007, business is not the same. There is a pall of intimidation, and it is not a job he enjoys anymore.

Says musician Jamal Shah, 'Our work was badly affected during the time of the Taliban from 2007 to 2008. Everything was closed. Even the government was not in our favour. We all left Swat.' Many families returned to Banr with the hope of making a fresh start. However, they were disappointed at finding no clients because of frequent curfews and the army's hold over Swat, and again thought of leaving the place for good. Jamal Shah also abandoned professional music and started working as a driver in Mingora. That is the only way he knows how to earn money now.

Religious sanction

From a position of admiration and appreciation, how did the dancing girls of Banr Bazaar come to be subjected to such treatment? The search for an answer leads to sixty-five-year-old Zamurd, a dancer of the time when Mian Gul Abdul Haq Jehanzeb was the Wali of Swat. Living in a small two-room house, Zamurd said her community had seen much better times. She recalls 'In our time artistes had respect. When the Wali married girls from Banr, it sent a very positive message about our profession.'

Discussing the distortions that crept in after the attempt to suppress culture, she said, 'When militants imposed restrictions on dancers and musicians, it was in the name of Islam. This changed the norms of society and people accepted it as if they were listening to holy sermons. But after militancy ended, surprisingly the customers' demands turned more towards the flesh trade than dancing. The real cultural essence of our dance was lost in the ashes of militancy.'

Banr Mohalla, initially known for performing arts, has also emerged as a hub for the sex trade in the last two decades. As a result, dancing girls from this area became persona non grata and were prohibited from interacting with other women of the area. However, some elderly women from Banr are now teaching the Quran to children from adjacent areas.

Historians have also documented the change in Banr culture pointed out by Zamurd. Ulasyar says that it seems that vulgarity in dress, as well as in the dance itself, is appreciated more by the majority, rather than dance as an art. Before the Taliban took control of Swat, the Muttahida Majlis-e-Amal (MMA) government was in power during 2002-07 in the North West Frontier Province (now known as Khyber Pakhtunkhwa). Religious extremism was allowed to grow during this period, with the MMA government sharing the same conservative views about culture and art. During the MMA regime, cultural activities were banned in the province, dance and music were prohibited and the Nishtar Hall, a flourishing cultural centre in Peshawar, was closed down.

Ulasyar blames the provincial government not only for its active crushing of cultural activities, but also for its abysmal neglect of the local culture of Swat. According to him, the government has consistently created hurdles in the development of local culture, rather than promoting it. All activities in accordance with culture and tradition should be encouraged and supported. Cultural clubs should have been set up at divisional and district levels and the state should have set up institutions to support such art forms, he says.

Peshawar-based women's rights activist Rukhshanda Naz, who is also executive director of the Legal Aid and Awareness Services and member of Takrah Qabailee Khwenday (TQK), an NGO that works for the development and rights of tribal women, says, 'For common people it is difficult to understand why their culture was declared un-Islamic and why a few religious extremists were imposing "Arab Culture" in the name of Islam. Nevertheless, poor village women were trapped by religious figures because a large number of women considered them as "saviours". Consequently, in a short span of time, many people were influenced by religious extremism and a handful of religious militants forced a progressive majority to accept their agenda.

In that period, women were the prime targets of public victimisation as a strategy of creating terror and fear. The most vulnerable group was of women engaged in arts and dancing. Increasing religious extremism transformed the tolerant society in Swat to one accepting of cultural conservatism. It also enabled religious extremists to promote their agenda by using religion to cover criminal activities. Shabana's case was one such example: before killing her, the Taliban snatched money and jewellery from her family. Many other criminal groups adopted the same modus operandi. All the while, the state remained a mute spectator and failed to protect its own citizens. To some extent, conservative elements within the state machinery were in favour of such moves. As such, there was an unwritten approval for targeting dancing girls and local artistes in the name of religion.

A critical aspect of the situation was that the Taliban had no alternative economic options for women who were forced to give up dance and music. Dancing girls were a soft target to manipulate and wrest control over their resources.

Due to the atmosphere of fear, many government employees, especially from the police, resigned from their jobs and published advertisements in local newspapers announcing their disassociation from the government. A sample of such an advertisement in the Azadi newspaper: 'I Sher Khan, s/o Shahi Room, resident of Mingora, Swat, want to inform through this notice that from today I have no relation with any government organisation. I have resigned from my post. Now I want to live my life according to Islamic rules and I request the government to announce sharia in Swat.' Another one goes: 'I Aqleema Bibi, w/o Mohammad Ali, resident of Khawaza Kheela, Swat, have resigned from the post of Lady Health Worker. I was posted in Maglore, but now have no connection with the government job.'

And the music died

The plight of musicians in the militancy-affected areas of Khyber Pakhtunkhwa and FATA can be judged from the simple fact that between 2008 and 2013, eighteen people were reportedly killed for their direct involvement with dance and music. These figures are from the study, 'Effects of repression and militancy on musicians and artists of Swat Valley' compiled by the Pakhtunkhwa Cultural Foundation (PCF) in 2014. Most of these were women, which shows a combination of changing religious and cultural trends, as well as the shrinking public space for women in general and female singers in particular. Some of the reported examples are:

- On October 16, 2008 famous Pashto singer Gulzar Alam escaped a gun attack near Bacha Khan Markaz, Peshawar.
- On December 15, 2008, Anwar Gul, harmonium player and close companion of Pashto singer Sardar Yousafzai, was gunned down by militants.
- In January 2009, TTP militants stormed into the home of Shabana in Mingora city and killed her in the town square.
- In April 2009, four months after Shabana's death, a local singer, Ghani Dad, was gunned down in Swat.
- On April 27, 2009, the young singer Shamim Aiman Udas was allegedly shot dead by her brothers inside her flat in Peshawar.
- In January 2010, Pashto singer Kamal Mahsud died under mysterious circumstances due to burn injuries in Islamabad. Mahsud had left South Waziristan due to the fear of militancy after the Inter-Services Public Relations (ISPR) of the Pakistan Army distributed his music album free of cost among the tribal people. The music album was part of the war propaganda against the militants.

- On March 14, 2010, a young dancer, Afsana, whose family fled Swat due to fear of the Taliban, was shot dead in Peshawar.
- Adnan Abdul Qadir, a final-year student of BS Civil Engineering at University of Engineering and Technology, died from a severe beating by the Islami Jamiat Talaban (IJT) on March 19, 2010, for listening to loud music.
- On November 27, 2010, Quetta-based Pashto singer Yasmeen Gul died in her home in mysterious circumstances
- On June 18, 2012, the popular singer Ghazala Javeed was shot dead by her husband.
- On June 22, 2013, Shazia, a Pashto performer in Nowshera district suffered critical burns when she was allegedly attacked by a TV producer who was forcing her to marry him.
- In July 2012, prominent singer Saima Naz was seriously injured when her brother opened fire on her in Peshawar.
- In November 2013, unidentified gunmen opened fire on Pashto singer Spogmai in Peshawar. She was injured and her mother was killed.

All these cases were reported in the media. The culprits responsible for some cases of the crimes were arrested, but most were released due to insufficient proof or as a result of an agreement between the two parties. The numerous murders of artistes are evidence that although the army has wiped out the Taliban from Swat, extremism is still part of the social fabric of Khyber Pakhtunkhwa.

Today, society has become so violent that many people indulge in pillaging and murder under the guise of being the Taliban. Sometimes local people or even relatives were involved in killings within the artiste community. With the writ of the state weakened, such violence continues to take place with impunity and culprits are rarely brought to book.

Of the nearly one hundred families of dancing girls, half have returned, but they are living under fear and do not meet visitors. Most women have stopped dancing and have started singing instead. One of them is Neelo, who, like many performers in the region, goes by a single stage name. 'Dancing was also a good profession but singing is better. Many people give respect to singers. But they don't have respect for dancers like during the Wali's time. I want to marry a man who not only respects me but can also give me a peaceful life without any fear. I want to live in a secure home without any unknown knocks. I feel insecure when I am dancing in front of people because they are not admirers but just customers,' she says, adding that she would like the next generation to be educated, learn the scriptures and keep away from this art. Even her brothers advise her to get married and leave the dancing profession. Both the brothers have two daughters each, but they haven't taught the girls to dance.

A visit to Banr Bazaar reveals a sombre mood, tainted by a pall of gloom. More than 3,000 Pakistani infantry personnel were sent to Swat to confront Taliban forces. Although most have now been withdrawn, there are several permanent check-posts manned by three or four army personnel each, while many more patrol the area during curfew. The presence of heavily armed men, inducing a sense of apprehension even in the most lion-hearted, has a dampening effect on the practice of dance and music for which this locality was once famous. Religious extremism has changed the perception of society towards a traditional cultural and artistic space, which has now been replaced by doctrinaire faith. A pervasive fear has descended on lanes that were once alive with the sounds of music, ankle bells and laughter. What will it take to bring back the tinkle of ghungroos?

Bibliography

BBC News. 2009. 'Swat "dancing girls" must leave'. Available at http://news.bbc.co.uk/2/hi/south_asia/7924232.stm Accessed in February 2016.

Buneri, Shaheen. 2011. 'Dancing Girls of the Swat Valley', *World Policy Journal*. Vol. 28 Issue 3. Durham, NC: Duke University Press.

Buneri, Shaheen, Muhammad Arif and Rameez Hassan Zaib. 2014. *Music and Militancy in North Western Pakistan (2001-2014)*. Peshawar: Center for Peace and Cultural Studies.

Footprints of Militarisation

SYED ALI SHAH AND SHAISTA YASMEEN

Toorkhail Syedan village, close to the Afghan border in Balochistan, sometime in the 1970s. The mud walls of about seventy houses reverberate with lilting Pashto music and the tinkling laughter of young girls. It is Eid, and women are dancing to the beat of the darya, a hand-held drum. Little boys grab at their flowing veils, delighted to play with the colourful dupattas. These happy occasions are now fast fading memories.

Global geopolitics intervened to irrevocably change daily life in these frontier villages. In the early 1980s, the impact of the Cold War between the US and the erstwhile USSR directly shaped the socio-political base of Balochistan in general, and Pashtun-dominated areas bordering Afghanistan in particular. The smuggling in of arms and drugs and the propping up of radical Islamists to counter the Soviet invasion in Afghanistan had a far-reaching impact on this impoverished part of the world.

Almost overnight, women were marginalised; an ultra-masculine Kalashnikov-and-heroin culture permeated Toorkhail Syedan and other parts of northern Balochistan. Women were strictly veiled and prohibited from singing and dancing in public during weddings and festivals. The popular folk dance, Attan, was now organised only by young women and girls without the presence of men. 'Even the rare occasions for pleasure were finished,' said an elderly woman who requested anonymity.[1] They were also stopped from going outside

---

[1] The strong tribal culture prohibits women from speaking to men outside the family. Many of those who did manage to speak would rather remain anonymous.

the boundary walls of their homes unless accompanied by male family members. 'We miss the old days,' says Bibi Amna, 60, now a grandmother. Like Amna, elderly women speak about the 'golden days' when there were no restrictions.

In a village close to Toorkhail Syedan, a clergyman stopped women from traditional dancing and destroyed their daryas. As the villagers watched their daryas being broken, something in them too broke. 'After that scene of destruction, we preferred not to dance anymore,' said another elderly woman.

The withdrawal of Soviet troops brought no respite to the beleaguered province that is now wracked by two conflicts. The first conflict is north of Quetta—the provincial capital, bordering Afghanistan—caused by the influx of Afghan Taliban from across the porous border following the US-led 'war on terror,' and the establishment of their bases to launch attacks on Western and Afghan troops on the other side. This has further radicalised the region, bringing in its wake sectarian hostilities that also play out the rivalries of powerful neighbours—Shia Iran and Sunni Saudi Arabia. Brutal attacks against the ethnic minority Hazaras—Shias with distinct Mongolian features—are commonplace.

The second conflict, simmering south of Quetta in the swathe stretching up to the Arabian Sea, in the ethnic Baloch and Brahui areas, is what well-known author and columnist Ahmed Rashid calls the longest civil war in Pakistan's history. This is the insurgency led by Baloch nationalists who seek autonomy and control over the province's rich resources like oil, natural gas, copper, gold and lead, among other minerals.

Gas from Balochistan powers Pakistan's development, but 59 per cent of the urban areas of the province have no access to the commodity, while its availability in rural areas is even less (Firdous 2014). Big multinational corporations are in the fray for mining contracts in the province. Balochistan also has the longest coastline in Pakistan, with the strategic deep-sea port of Gwadar being developed by the Chinese. Gwadar forms a gateway to the Strait of Hormuz and energy-rich Central Asia. But the insurgents allege that the Baloch population has not benefitted in terms of jobs and that the demographics of the port town are changing, with an influx of people from other provinces coming to take up residence and employment.

The province is the largest in Pakistan, covering nearly 44 per cent of the landmass, but has the smallest population, which, according to preliminary results of the 2012 census, was only 13.61 million. The province seems to be caught in a vicious cycle, with the roots of unrest lying in poverty and lack of development, and the violence, unrest and militarisation in turn keeping Balochistan from achieving its development potential. The province is the least developed among the four federating units of Pakistan in terms of social and economic indicators.

Overall, 56 per cent of Balochistan's population suffers from multidimensional poverty.[2] The province's Human Development Index (HDI) value in 2010 was 0.391, an increase of a mere 0.064 from 0.327 in 2004. Among the three components of HDI— education, health and income—the income index for Balochistan had declined to 0.409 in 2010 from 0.487 in 2004.[3]

And the people are, quite literally, up in arms about the abysmal state of affairs.

Driven to desperation

Author and veteran journalist Zahid Hussain writes, 'Baloch nationalists have led four insurgencies—in 1948, 1958-59, 1962-63 and 1973-77—which were brutally suppressed by the state. Now a fifth is under way, and this time the insurgents are much stronger. Unlike the past, the educated middle-class youth, rather than tribal leaders, are leading the separatist movement.'[4]

---

[2]The Oxford Poverty and Human Development Initiative describes multidimensional poverty as made up of several factors that constitute poor people's experience of deprivation—such as poor health, lack of education, inadequate living standards, lack of income, disempowerment, poor quality of work and threat of violence.

[3]UNDP Pakistan report on *Area Development Programme Balochistan*

[4]*Dawn* 2013

Education is much valued, and despite extreme privation, women are determined to study. Farkanda Aslam, associate director of the Institute for Development Studies and Practices (IDSP), Quetta, says, 'The difference between rural and urban areas is that women can get an education and work in the latter, while in rural areas, the families are often driven to the streets, having lost their earning members.' Many Baloch women and children can now be seen begging on the roads, she adds.

Sharing a sense of the prevailing insecurity, she says, 'People here are not sure if those leaving home will ever come back. If there is a blast, people start contacting family members. When we get out of our houses, we feel fear, or if some search operation is taking place in the evening, we feel really insecure.' People here are psychologically disturbed, she adds. Crucially, 'if some members from a family are missing, it exerts immense economic pressure.' Aslam is herself the head of her family, supporting her elderly parents and widowed sister-in-law. 'The impact of militarisation is more on women than (on) men. Women are more affected if there is a military operation in the area. Women die and the media gives no coverage to these issues,' she says, giving the example of Nushki, a town and district southwest of Quetta, where houses were demolished in one such operation and only women died, as there were no men at home. Women can't even talk about their issues, as this will open them up to severe threats, she added. At least the media should highlight their stories, she says.

Silencing the media

Says Nargis Baloch, a journalist from Makran, who has been working for the *Daily Intekhab* for twenty-seven years: 'Earlier when I was asked to travel to far-flung areas for reporting, I would have no fear travelling there alone and staying at community centres. I don't fear traditional or societal constraints, but I am scared of the different terrorist and extremist groups and military involvement.' She says, 'As a journalist, you need to watch what you write, how you write and what terms you use against or for such entities... With so much restriction in reporting, a journalist feels fed up sometimes. I fear that anything can happen at any moment—my family or my home can come under attack.'

It is little wonder then that the impact of militarisation, particularly on women, is little talked about or reported in the media. Says Fatima Iqbal Khan, who heads the Humanitarian Educational Work And Development (HEWAD) organisation, 'If we look at the national electronic media, it doesn't talk about issues faced by Balochistan. The only media which does talk about women's issues is radio.'

A recent radio programme produced by Kalim Ullah Baloch of the Pakistan Broadcasting Corporation (PBC) in Turbat interviewed Rizwana, 26, a local resident. She studied till Grade Eight and got married at sixteen years of age. She was never allowed to step out of the house, except to attend wedding ceremonies of relatives. Says Baloch, Rizwana's story is the norm in his area, where women are no longer even allowed to question why so many restrictions are placed on them.

No more spring

Spring in the villages of Balochistan was an opportunity for women to step out of their mud-walled houses and enjoy bountiful nature. Groups of women, from the elderly to the young, used to freely roam in the plains, mountains and valleys to gather the mushrooms and bushki (greens) that proliferate during spring. 'Now my daughters are frightened to go outside the village for celebration of the spring festival,' says Bibi Jan from Toorkhail Syedan. Women used to sing traditional songs during their hunt for naturally cultivated flowers, vegetables and mushrooms. However, that is no longer the case.

In Quetta, Rukhsana Ahmed Ali, Chairperson of the Society for Empowering Human Resource (SEHAR), says, 'I am from the Hazara Community. Twenty years back, our community was very strict about women going outside homes. Women are still facing the same problems. Their mobility in the society is an issue for family and husbands. Their urge to take part in various social activities is a challenge. I feel sectarianism is responsible for all these issues for there is no acceptance of other schools of thought. And these security issues are also affecting the activities of women,' she adds.

Salma Javed, a gender specialist from the Aurat Foundation in Quetta, says, 'The good thing is that now we are witnessing an increase in the number of women in politics, educational institutions and NGOs. At the same time we are experiencing an increase in threats. Due to the current safety and security situation, women's mobility is hindered. For example if they are going to the Combined Military Hospital, there are pickets in different positions, which cause a lot of delay in reaching the place. Even in hospital, we park our cars outside the premises which causes delays,' she adds.

Women have few options which they can avail of, whether in educational institutes or hospitals. She points out that Balochistan University is in Sariab Road, which has been the scene of many targeted killings and blasts. 'I have been working for eighteen years in the social sector. Despite facing difficulties, I work for the community. I witnessed bomb-disposal staff at a distance of three feet from where we were stuck and couldn't go back. Every time a motorbike passes, we feel threatened,' she says. She points out that the majority of women professionals, including social workers, journalists and educationists, have had to flee the province.

Displacement from Balochistan is a major issue. Accurate figures are difficult to obtain because of the inaccessibility of conflict zones. Nevertheless, the Internal Displacement Monitoring Centre (IDMC) said in its 2008 report that conflict in Balochistan has led to internal displacement of at least 84,000 people, including an estimated 26,000 women and 33,000 children. It says that at the height of the insurgency, some 40,000 troops were dispatched to the region and estimates the number of people displaced at that point was as high as 200,000.

Most of those displaced from the hinterland live in sub-human conditions in refugee camps in the districts of Quetta, Nasirabad and Jaffarabad without proper shelter, food and medicine. The IDMC report says local people in the areas where IDPs are living are not allowed by intelligence agencies of the Pakistan Army to help the displaced. It says that the army prevented the Edhi Centre, a local charitable organisation providing medical assistance to the IDPs, from setting up medical centres. It also says that UN agencies and NGOs have been denied access to the internally displaced in Balochistan.

Violence, abductions and acid attacks

Attacks against women have become frequent and take many forms. In Quetta, Nelofar Abadan, an elderly woman belonging to the minority Farsi community was abducted by armed militants on March 8, 2012, ironically on the evening of International Women Day. She was kept in captivity till December 21, 2012, when she was set free. The family confirmed payment of a ransom for her release but gave no further details. Nor did any militant group claim responsibility for the kidnapping. This incident caused panic among the women of minority sects in Quetta.

'As a girl I used to bicycle down the streets of Quetta,' says Roshan Khursheed Bharucha, who is related to Nelofar Abadan. Bharucha is no ordinary woman. She was a provincial minister and senator during the regime of former military dictator Pervez Musharraf. 'It is ironical that we are locked in our houses even in the twenty-first century,' she laments. 'At one time, Quetta was free from religious, sectarian, ethnic and regional conflict. All communities enjoyed cordial relations. We used to freely roam around without fear,' she says.

Farkanda Aslam of IDSP says that a number of acid attacks took place in Qalat, Quetta and Khuzdar. These have been politicised as a religious issue, but happen because the attackers don't want women to venture out, she adds.

Two motorcycle-borne assailants sprayed acid on the faces of four women in the market on Quetta's Sariab Road on July 22, 2014. The women were shifted to the Bolan Medical Complex (BMC) Hospital in a serious condition. No arrests were made.

This incident was followed by an acid attack in the Mastung area of Balochistan in which two women were injured and the assailants managed to get away. Acid attacks took place in Quetta a few days before the Muslim festival of Eid-ul-Fitr. In the aftermath, most women stayed away from shopping in the area. Pamphlets warned that 'women roaming without men would be our target'. Cosmetics shops and other shopping centres wore a deserted look after such warnings. Though no acid attack has taken place in Balochistan since then, the horror of previous attacks still resonates in the province.

The victims suffer in silence. Thirty-five-year-old Fatima (not her real name) lies on a bed in Quetta's largest medical facility, the BMC Hospital. Clothed in traditional Balochi dress, she speaks in measured sentences to narrate her ordeal. 'I was shopping for Eid when suddenly somebody sprayed acid on my face,' she says, her voice breaking.

The other victims, including two teenage girls, were also admitted to BMC's Burn Ward. Surrounded by their grief-stricken parents and frightened family members, the acid attack victims had covered their faces. Fatima was 'fortunate' as only 3 per cent of her face was damaged in the attack. 'Now I pray for immediate recovery,' she says, asking whether 'the treatment will bring back my identity'. The acid had burnt through her shawl and clothes.

The chief minister of Balochistan, Dr. Abdul Malik Baloch ordered an inquiry into the acid attacks. 'Such barbarians will not be spared,' Balochistan's Home Minister, Mir Sarfaraz Bugti, said in a statement issued to the press, declaring that there was no room for such kinds of incidents under Islam or under Baloch traditions and norms.

However, violence against women has been constantly rising in Quetta and other parts of Balochistan. Most cases go unreported due to fear and intimidation. Journalists, too, take extreme care when it comes to reporting violence against women in the strictly-veiled society. People are cautious even on social media and try to avoid controversies while commenting on women's rights. Nevertheless, despite the conspiracy of silence, some shocking news appeared on TV screens and the front pages of leading newspapers in September 2008.

Two women were reportedly buried alive in Balochistan's troubled Naseerabad district, infamous for tribal disputes. The news made headlines in electronic and print media, prompting public anger. Civil society, the media and human rights activists mounted pressure on the government to apprehend the accused. The matter was probed and the guards of an influential tribal chieftain who had committed the heinous crime, allegedly at the chieftain's behest, were arrested and later convicted. The details of the killings are still shrouded in mystery and the real culprit in the case seems to be still at large. A senator from Balochistan, while commenting on the tragic fate of the women, said, 'It was our tradition'.

The Naseerabad and Jaffarabad belt is also known for 'honour' killings. 'As many as seventy-five women were murdered on the pretext of so-called "honour" in different parts of Balochistan,' the women's rights organisation Aurat Foundation (AF) Balochistan said in its annual report for 2014. 'The data showed a surge in violence as compared to the previous year, when forty-five women were killed in the name of "honour". Most of the cases took place in the Nasirabad and Sibi divisions,' it said. Haroon Dawood, the executive director of AF, commented, 'Balochistan has seen a 24 per cent rise in incidents of violence against women as compared to the past.'

Six women were kidnapped and four were gang-raped in 2014 in Balochistan, the AF report said. Most of the rape cases go unreported. Fear of disclosure, damage to social status and possible disputes with the perpetrators' tribe appear to be the underlying reasons behind under-reporting of rape in the province.

The murder and attempted rape of a seven-year-old Hazara girl made headlines in November 2014. The incident took place in the heart of Quetta. The body was found in a garbage bin a day after she went missing from her residence. Her father, who works as a watchman in a government department, lodged a complaint. It was only after pressure from political parties and women's and human rights activists, that the police arrested the culprit.

Unfair deal

While the Constitution of Pakistan has guaranteed fundamental rights irrespective of creed, gender, colour, faith, race, etc., since 1973, the state has failed to guard the rights of citizens, especially women, in Balochistan. Mere lip service has been paid by political parties, human rights and women's rights groups regarding the rights of women.

The Balochistan cabinet has no woman minister, despite the reservation of 33 per cent of the seats for women legislators in the assembly. Similarly, there is no woman in any key executive post in the province. 'Women are ignored in policy-making issues regarding women,' says Raheela Durrani, a legislator from the ruling Pakistan Muslim League (PML). Most of the women legislators are from Quetta, rather than the remote areas of the Balochistan, and belong to relatively well-off and influential families. Yet, women legislators cannot use their funds on their own and have to bow to the directions of the male political leadership.

Women are not free to vote for candidates of their choice. Political parties gather women's national identity cards and then divide them among the candidates. In spite of clear orders on the part of the Election Commission to give women the right to vote, political parties dominated by religious and tribal mores do not allow women to exercise their constitutional and fundamental right.

Says Captain Dr. Ruqaya Saeed Hashmi of the Pakistan Muslim League (Quaid-e-Azam Group), PMLQ, 'There is token participation of women in the Provincial Assembly and [an] example of it is that they cannot speak in the assembly or utilise development funds given to them.' She speaks from experience—she says she has not been able to do anything in the thirteen years she has been an assembly legislator.

The combination of militancy, religious fundamentalism, poverty, tribal disputes and social barriers seems to be the underlying reason that deprives women of their rights in Balochistan. Women lack access to education and health facilities since the government always has to be focused on maintaining law and order, rather than dealing with gender inequality.

Ghost schools

Statistics paint a bleak picture, with less than 2 per cent of rural women educated and only 26 per cent overall female literacy in the province, say sources in the education department. The Balochistan Millennium Development Goals Report of 18 May 2012, released by the Government of Balochistan and UNDP, says that while the net primary enrolment ratio for the province was only 44 per cent (against a target of 100 per cent in 2008/2009), the Gender Parity Index for primary education was an abysmal 0.58 in the same period.

Education is a right denied to many children across Pakistan, but the state of literacy, particularly of females, is dismal in Balochistan. Women have no access to schools in remote areas of Balochistan. The provincial government has declared acquisition of education compulsory and necessary under Article 25-A, but it is yet to be translated into action.

Most girls are enrolled in primary classes, but drop out as they get older, since access to secondary schools is a problem. According to officials, the dropout rate is as high as 70 per cent, with the highest being in Dera Bugti. Saboor Kakar, secretary of education for Balochistan, believes militancy, poor governance and poverty are the root causes of such low female literacy.

Co-educational schools and colleges exist in the Makran belt, but the emergence of new militant organisations that have warned girls of dire consequences if they attend schools has prevented females from enrolling, plunging Balochistan to the lowest rank in female literacy in Pakistan. In Panjgur, Makran district, private co-educational schools were targeted and threatened by militants in May 2014. Parents were also intimidated into not sending their girls to school. The chief minister of Balochistan, Dr. Abdul Malik Baloch stated that 2.3 million children were out of school, most of them girls.

Many girls' primary, high and middle schools exist only on paper in Quetta and thirty-one other districts of Balochistan. According to sources in the education department, there are more than 7,000 'ghost' teachers and more than 5,000 ghost schools. In Quetta, the high fees charged by private girls' schools also restrict parents from sending their daughters to school.

Attacks on institutions of learning in an attempt to dissuade young women from university education are also disturbing. The April 2010 targeted killing of Nazima Talib, assistant professor of mass communication at the University of Balochistan, seemed to be a direct warning against the pursuit of higher education. The Baloch Liberation Army (BLA) claimed responsibility for the murder, which instilled fear in faculty members across the province. The HRCP and other rights groups condemned the killing and demanded enhanced security for academic staff who are particularly vulnerable.[5]

In another horrific incident, on June 15, 2013, at least twenty-five people, including the deputy commissioner of Quetta, fourteen students of a women's university and four nurses were killed when a bomb tore through a bus. This was followed by a suicide attack and a gun-battle in the BMC hospital, where the injured students were taken for treatment. The banned outfit Lashkar-e-Jhangvi, a Sunni militant group, claimed responsibility for the attack. Some reports suggested that the intended targets of the bus bombing were possibly Shia from the Hazara ethnic minority. However, due to an earlier change of route, the bus carried a more ethnically mixed group and has been described as 'the wrong target' of the perpetrators.[6] The attack put fear into the minds of young women and their parents, leading to a drop in enrollment particularly by the Hazara community.

Health crises

Dr. Ali Nasir Bugti, provincial coordinator of the Balochistan government's nutrition program announced at a press conference in March 2014 that the maternal mortality rate in the province was much higher than that of other provinces of the country. He said 785 mothers out of 100,000 lose their lives during pregnancy in Balochistan as compared to 272 in the rest of the country.

---

[5]*Pakistan Observer,* 2010.

[6]*The Economist,* 2013.

Maternal deaths account for 35 per cent of the mortality among women of reproductive age (Pakistan Demographic and Health Survey, [PDHS], 2007). In 2012, the maternal mortality ratio (MMR) was estimated at 996 per 100,000 births (Sathar, Wazir and Sadiq 2014); the infant mortality rate was 97 per 1,000 births; and the under-five mortality rate was 111 per 1,000 births (PDHS 2013). The ratios currently translate into an annual death toll of nearly 3,000 women, 28,600 infants and 4,000 children (aged 1-4), primarily due to conditions that could easily be prevented with basic healthcare.[7]

There are few gynaecologists in the remote areas of the province, and the majority are concentrated in Quetta. Most pregnant women are treated by traditional, unskilled birth attendants. 'Increasing militarisation has forced skilled birth attendants to flee from rural parts of the province,' says Rukhsana Kasi, a well-known gynaecologist. Kasi names the worsening law and order situation in the province as one of the reasons for the increasing maternal mortality rate. Since 2008, there has been a spate of killings and kidnappings of doctors from Quetta and other parts of Balochistan. Most of the doctors were released by their captors after receiving heavy ransom amounts from their family members. These untoward incidents forced doctors to quit rural areas of Balochistan and left patients at the mercy of quacks.

Rukhsana Kasi points out that during pregnancy, multiple vaccinations are required. But in Balochistan, there are no trained officials to administer these medicines in 247 out of a total of 627 Union Councils,[8] says an officer of the health department who declined to be named. Most of these Union Councils are located in the least developed, militancy-hit remote districts of Balochistan.

Captain Dr. Ruqaya Hashmi of PMLQ says that there are six divisions and thirty districts that lack Basic Health Units which are usually set up by the provincial government for basic health care

---

[7]The Evidence Project. 2015

[8]The Union Council is the basic unit of local government. Each Union Council serves a population of 10,000 to 15,000.

in urban centres. People from far-flung areas approach the Civil Hospital, but even that lacks facilities. She alleges that the health department does not have proper data on the maternal mortality ratio (MMR) as women can't travel to Khuzdar or Mastung for data collection. 'Whenever they are doing something, they quote data collected by international organisations,' she adds.

Dr. Cecilio Tan, who has been coordinating the international humanitarian aid organisation Médecins Sans Frontières' medical projects in Balochistan since 2013, says some of the reasons for the high MMR are poverty and illiteracy. Conflict and political instability play a role in maintaining this high rate, he adds. On an average, women give birth to six to eight children and very often have their first baby at the age of sixteen.[9]

Dr. Mahadeem of Quetta's Civil Hospital said in a recent radio interview that mobility was the biggest issue as far as MMR was concerned. 'Many pregnant women lose their lives while travelling to the hospitals to deliver. They are either carried on bullock carts or tractors and the rough road journey is at times too much...they sometimes die on their way to hospital or give birth to still borns.'

According to the National Nutrition Survey (NNS) 2011 conducted by Aga Khan University, the nutrition problem in Balochistan is alarming when compared to the rest of the country. 'We are in a state of emergency when it comes to malnutrition among women and children,' says Dr. Bugti. NNS 2011 indicates that the prevalence of chronic malnutrition is 52.2 per cent and maternal anaemia is 47.3 per cent.

Dr. Bugti said infant mortality rates were high in Balochistan, elaborating that, out of 1000, a total of 158 children died at birth as compared to 103 in other parts of Pakistan. In view of the alarming malnutrition and anaemia among women and children, the Balochistan Assembly in January 2015 unanimously adopted a resolution to protect children. 'Most of the children in Balochistan are underweight and malnourished,' said Provincial Health Minister

---

[9]*Dawn* 2014.

Rehmat Baloch at the same press conference. The World Food Program in collaboration with the provincial health department has already launched a nutrition program in nine districts of Balochistan. 'We are providing cooking oil, biscuits and other food items to malnourished children and women suffering from anaemia,' Dr. Bugti said.

High rates of anaemia among women contribute to the lack of resistance to disease. Women in the province also suffer from tuberculosis, hepatitis B and C and breast cancer. The latter is proving to be fatal, since no proper or timely detection and care is available, especially in rural areas. According to a report by the Free and Fair Election Network (FAFEN), a coalition of thirty civil society organisations in Pakistan, two-thirds of the BHUs run by the Balochistan government have no female staff. In their absence, self-medication in remote villages puts the lives of women in peril.

What seems to be unfolding in Balochistan is a humanitarian crisis of huge proportions having its roots in militarisation, and impacting women in all spheres of their lives. There is very little knowledge or information about this in the rest of the region or even the world. It is a story that needs to be told.

Bibliography

Barbero, Igor G. 2014. 'Natal Neglect in Balochistan', in *Dawn* published on 14 September. Lahore.

Economist, The. 2013. 'Cruel beyond belief' available at http://www.economist.com/news/asia/21579886-no-honeymoon-nawaz-sharif-pakistans-terrorists-cruel-beyond-belief published on June 22. Islamabad.

Evidence Project. 2015. *Reducing Maternal and Child Mortality In Balochistan* Policy Brief. Available at http://evidenceproject.popcouncil.org/wp-content/uploads/2015/11/Reducing-Maternal-and-Child-Mortality-in-Balochistan_Policy-Brief.pdf Published in September. Accessed in June 2016. Islamabad.

Firdous, Iftikar. 2014. 'Deprived Province: 59% of Balochistan without natural gas' in *The Tribune*. Published May 26. Available at http://tribune.com.pk/story/713135/deprived-province-59-of-balochistan-without-natural-gas/ Accessed in June 2016.

Hussain, Zahid. 2013. 'Battle for Balochistan' in *Dawn*. Published on 25 April. Available at http://www.dawn.com/news/794058/the-battle-for-balochistan Accessed in June 2016. Lahore.

Internal Displacement Monitoring Centre (IDMC). 2008. 'Internal displacement due to conflict in Pakistan'. Available at http://lib.ohchr.org/ HRBodies/UPR/Documents/Session2/PK/IDMC_PAK_UPR_S2_2008_ InternalDisplacementMonitoringCentre_uprsubmission_INDIVIDUAL. pdf Accessed in June 2016.

Pakistan Observer. 2010. 'HRCP Condemns Killing of University Teacher in Quetta' published April 29. Available at http://pakistanobserver.blogspot. in/2010/04/hrcp-condemns-killing-of-university.html. Accessed on 8 February 2016.

Rashid, Ahmed. 2014. 'Balochistan: The untold story of Pakistan's other war' in BBC News. Published Feb 22. Available at http://www.bbc.com/ news/world-asia-26272897. Accessed in June 2016.

Sathar Z.A., Wazir, M.A., and Sadiq, M. 2014. 'Prioritizing family planning for achieving provincial maternal child health and development goals.' Islamabad: Population Council.

UNDP Pakistan. 2013. 'Area Development Programme Balochistan' Available at http://www.undp.org/content/dam/pakistan/docs/CPRU/ Project%20Briefs/ADPB.pdf Accessed in June 2016.

Daring to Dream

MUHAMMAD ZAFAR

Nargis Ali Changazi, a bright young student from the Hazara community, cherished dreams of becoming a journalist some day. 'It is a great feeling to be a storyteller in a society where it is taboo for women to do such jobs,' says Nargis, who desired to tell the 'untold tales' of her people. On June 15, 2013, the young woman witnessed her dream literally blown into little bits in a massive explosion in front of her.

On that fateful day, she was walking towards her bus in a parking lot in the Sardar Bahadur Khan Women's University in Quetta, the provincial capital of Balochistan in southwest Pakistan. An ordinary day at the university suddenly turned into a nightmare when the bus was blasted to smithereens by a suicide bomber. So intense was the explosion that she fainted, even though she was at the other end of the parking lot. When she came to, she broke down upon seeing blackened bodies and her friends and colleagues lying in pools of blood. Nargis does not clearly remember what happened in the following days. 'For three months, I could not sleep because of the explosion,' she says. Even a year-and-a-half later, girls' piercing screams of agony resonate in her ears. Twelve young women lost their lives in the blast; several more were permanently injured; the psychological trauma is immeasurable.

According to Nargis, around 60 per cent of the female students in her university abandoned their education mid-way. 'One reason was the blast and the second was the indifferent attitude of the Women's University administration,' she said. The administration decided that, in the interests of security, a bus could not carry more than five female students of the Hazara community. Even though the authorities claimed that they had stepped up security, these young women's parents were forced to make their daughters quit their university education as they were afraid of taking any more risks. From more than 100 female Hazara students enrolled in the University of Balochistan (UoB) before targeted killings began in 2001, the current figure is a dismal twenty students.[1]

Nargis and her friend, both first-year students of journalism, had to give up pursuing a university degree following the deadly attack, which also caused deep trauma to their psyches. Yet, Nargis continues to speak on behalf of Hazara women. Appearing at a landmark hearing in September 2012, at the Supreme Court of Pakistan's Quetta Registry, in a case regarding enforced disappearances and law and order in Balochistan, Nargis deposed before the then Chief Justice of Pakistan, Iftikhar Chaudhry. She highlighted the Hazara community's security issues, with special reference to the problems that Hazara women faced in accessing education. She pointed out that security personnel could not give them protection in the Hazara-majority settlements like Marriabad and Hazara Town, where militants were able to strike at will. 'We have talented boys and girls in our community. We need education but we don't have any university or even a campus in our area,' she said, adding that talent was being wasted because of the lack of opportunities for higher education.

Indeed, getting an education is not just difficult for Hazara women in Balochistan; it is a matter of life and death. Sectarian tensions have deeply impacted their lives and without adequate steps from the government, there is likely to be further deterioration in the status of Hazara women.

But the situation was not always as bleak. Khaliq Hazara, Chairman of the Hazara Democratic Party (HDP), remembers a time when Hazara girls formed the majority of students in every

---

[1] UoB information centre

college and university. Despite the difficulties the community faced as a minority, the education of girls was deeply valued.

Birth of sectarian strife

The Hazaras, a minority community of Shia Muslims originating from Bamiyan and Mazar-e-Sharif provinces of Central Afghanistan[2], have been fleeing sectarian persecution for about eight decades. Migration spiked after the installation of the Taliban regime in Afghanistan in 1996. Many families are still divided between the two countries and several are still struggling to get citizenship in Pakistan. The Hazaras purchased land in the Marriabad area in Quetta valley, named after the Marri Baloch tribe of Balochistan. Hazaras remain somewhat isolated from the rest of the population and avoid cross-sect marriages. They are also easily recognisable on account of their distinct Mongolian features, which makes them vulnerable to attacks. They are often targeted when they travel outside their neighbourhoods. Their places of worship and peaceful processions were attacked on several occasions by suicide bombers. Some see this as sectarian violence and religious intolerance, while other analysts such as veteran journalist Siddique Baloch, and senior journalists Shahzada Zulfiqar and Saleem Shahid, who are based in Balochistan, consider it a proxy war between Saudi Arabia and Iran to spread a more fundamentalist version of Islam.

The unprecedented rise in massacres and targeted killings has restricted the movements of the group in their neighbourhoods of Hazara Town and Alamdar Road, located near the foothills of the Quetta valley. These incidents have also forced them to flee from Balochistan and shift to metropolitan cities in other provinces.

In the past decade, the Hazaras have been subjected to suicide bombings at their mosques, processions and passenger buses and on several occasions they were forced off buses, lined up and killed,

---

[2]According to the National Census, 1998, the population of Balochistan consisted of 70 per cent Baloch, 20 per cent Pashtun, and 10 per cent 'other' communities including Hazara, Punjabi, Urdu, Sindhi and Seraiki speaking communities.

following their identification as Shia Muslims. The Hazaras term these targeted killings 'genocide', because women, children, young and old Hazaras alike are killed in an attempt to decimate their population. The banned Sunni supremist group, Lashkar-e-Jhangvi (LeJ), has claimed responsibility for the attacks.

However, before 1979, the province did not witness sectarian hatred. Certain broader political processes, fuelled by the geopolitical vested interests of various international and national players have led to the current quagmire.

The 'Afghan War', when the now-defunct Soviet Union invaded Afghanistan to defend the Saur Revolution—the name given to the communist People's Democratic Party of Afghanistan's takeover of political power from the government of Afghanistan in 1978—and the Iranian Islamist (Shia) revolution coincided in 1979. Pakistani strategists believed that the next target of the Soviet Union would be Pakistan, as the Red Army was aiming to control the crucial Gwadar sea-port in Balochistan. This port has been the focus of world powers on account of its strategic importance as a warm-water port that never freezes throughout the year. Secondly, it is located at the mouth of the Strait of Hormuz, which sees the passage of 30 to 40 per cent of the world's oil from the Persian Gulf states. Faced with the USSR's desire to gain control over Gwadar and the coastal towns and ports of Makran, the Pakistani strategists' agenda became to block the Soviet advance beyond Afghanistan. Hence, Pakistan had to ally itself with the US's crusade against communist expansionism. The war was fought with US brains, Saudi Arabian and United Arab Emirates' money and proxy militias from Pakistan's Federally Administered Tribal Areas (FATA), which are populated mainly by the Sunni, Hanafi, Deobandi and Wahabi sects. They were chosen as the main combatants as they resided on both sides of the Afghanistan-Pakistan border (Lodhi 2011).

In the wake of the Afghan War, 3.5 million Afghan refugees entered Balochistan and Khyber Pakhtunkhwa. Most of these refugees were Sunnis, and since they were unemployed, they served as a human resource for banned outfits and became conduits for the transfer of arms and ammunition.

By the 1980s, Salafi teachings (a rigid view of the sharia preached by Wahab Najdi of Saudi Arabia) had penetrated Pakistani society, and gained support at the highest levels. President Zia ul-Haq banned the Shia procession during Muharram. According to Bostan Kishtmand, spokesman of the Hazara Democratic Party, during Zia ul-Haq's regime, twelve policemen and fifteen Hazaras were killed on July 6, 1986 and curfew was imposed.

In the 1980s, with Iranian funding, the Hazara community formed the Tehrik Nifaz-e-Fiqh Jafaria (a movement to implement the sharia laws of the Shia sect). Even though the Shias are in a minority, and in no position to impose their fiqh (the Islamic jurisprudence of a particular sect), Sunni groups felt threatened. In reaction, Sunnis formed groups such as the Sipah-e-Sahaba (army of the companions of Holy Prophet BPUH) of Salafi-trained Sunni jihadis. The sharp polarisation resulted in hate literature from both sides.

Abdul Khaliq Hazara, chairman of the first Hazara political party, the Hazara Democratic Party (HDP) established in 2003, terms the religious extremism in Pakistan the result of rivalry between Saudi Arabia and Iran. 'Both countries are fighting a proxy war in Pakistan on a sectarian basis for the last thirty years. After the Iranian revolution, all the migrants who came to Pakistan are still here. The "Kalashnikov culture" should be abolished and the government should not support any armed or militant group in Pakistan. A particular mindset in the Pakistani state is deliberately encouraging religious extremism and the killing of innocent people in the name of a sect or religion,' he said, pointing out that in the absence of a policy to control these elements, the state is moving backwards.

Peace heroes

Amidst the sectarian polarisation and violence, women have been the most vulnerable. Hazara women have been caught in a conflict raging for the past decade, with over 2,000 brutally murdered. Now women are taking the lead not only in fighting for their survival but in defending their community. Many unsung women heroes are putting up a brave resistance, which is rarely mentioned in mainstream media or public discourse. This writer has interviewed about a hundred such women grapple everyday with the difficulties of daily existence under highly adverse circumstances with little support from the government.

Facing targeted killings and bomb blasts, along with the migration of male members, which has left them with no one to provide a livelihood, women have taken matters into their own hands. Although group activities are not evident on a mass scale, individual stories of Hazara women speak volumes about how they have had to undergo a paradigm shift as a consequence of the loss of the male members of their families. While women in other conflict zones of Pakistan may be facing a similar plight, the issues of Hazara women are complicated by the fact that they are easily recognizable by their distinct physical features. They cannot move freely through public spaces to seek a livelihood, both because they are constrained by tribal codes and because their features make them easily identifiable targets for discrimination and violence.

Dr. Ruqaiya Hashmi, 65, was born to a poor switchboard operator in the Quetta Electric Supply Company (QESCO). She matriculated from Mission Road Quetta Girls High School and went on to complete her MBBS from Dow Medical College Karachi in 1976, becoming the first woman doctor in the Hazara community. She was keenly interested in politics during her student days and joined the National Student Federation (NSF) in 1976 and entered mainstream politics in 1985. Dr. Hashmi also has the distinction of being the first woman from her community to join the Pakistan Army as a captain and serve in it for eight years. She left the armed forces as the rules prohibit family members from being politically active, and her husband and his father were active in politics.

'I was a poor girl and wanted to be famous in politics, and started social work in my student life,' she said. Her father's aim was to educate his children so that they could make a name for themselves in society. She went on to marry Saeed Hashmi, son of Iqbal Shah

Hashmi, a prominent leader of the Muslim League and a great supporter of Quaid-e-Azam, Muhammed Ali Jinnah. Dr. Hashmi worked for women of the Hazara community from 1988 until 1997, while her husband was a Member of the Provincial Assembly (MPA) and Senator, using his office to give opportunities to Hazara women for education and scholarships. She was critical of the Zia ul-Haq government, during whose regime religious parties in Pakistan were created and the process of Islamisation was irrevocably launched. This increased the problems for Shia Muslims in Pakistan.

The increased polarisation hit home as well. The hardest days in Ruqaiya Hashmi's life were when she had to face community sanctions. 'In 1976, when I married a Sunni man, my community closed the graveyard and Imam Bargah (congregation hall) to my family for two-and-a-half years.' She added that, following the ban on her father entering holy places, her father-in-law told her to win the hearts of the people of their community. He opened a free clinic for the Hazara community in which treatment and medicines were provided gratis. Since she lives in a male dominated society and belongs to an oppressed community, she faces difficulties in making her voice heard. 'It's hard to be recognised in a male-dominated society,' Dr. Hashmi says, adding that even now she faces a lot of difficulties, since swimming against the tide is always a challenge.

Staying strong

The conflict has created severe mental health issues for Hazara women. They remain traumatised for years after every attack and targeted killing. Staff at a psychiatrist's clinic in Quetta say that a number of Hazara women visit the clinic on a daily basis. Many are depressed and ill. The suicide attacks of January 10, 2013 and February 16, 2013 were some of the deadliest attacks on the Hazara community, killing more than 200 and injuring hundreds more. Yet, women must stay strong and pick up the pieces, rebuilding their broken lives with grit and determination.

Bibi Fatima, 40, lost her husband, Muhammad Raza, when he

fell victim to a suicide attack on the Yauom-e-Quds[3] rally in 2010 in a busy market at Mezan Chowk of Quetta. Bibi Fatima currently lives in a semi-constructed house, work on which ceased after her husband's death. 'After the death of my husband, pushing the wheel of life is no less than a war for me,' she says with tears welling from her reddened eyes. Earning a meagre livelihood by washing dishes in several houses in the neighbourhood, her daily wages are spent on basic needs for her house and eight dependent children. Her eldest step-daughter was married last year to her cousin. With the construction of her house yet to be completed, she and her children live in a basement which was being built as a storeroom. 'Now I don't have money to complete the construction work of my house and I am compelled to live like this. However, I thank God that it's our own house and not a rented one,' she says. Bibi Fatima said that her husband was a skilled artisan and would earn a livelihood by making water carriers from used tyres.

Her children study in schools in Hazara Town, where fees are exempt for children of shaheeds (martyrs). The Shaheed Foundation helps them, sometimes with cash of about 10,000 Pakistani rupees per month and sometimes with ration and food items. 'We want peace and calm here in our society where people can move freely without any fear,' says Fatima, adding that they have a right as Pakistani citizens to move freely. However, for more than ten years, the Hazaras have been too fearful to go out to even visit the main bazaar of Quetta.

Hazara Town is indeed an isolated ghetto. It has a population of 200,000 persons and 20,000 houses. There are no government colleges and not a single branch of any bank. 'We are scared to go out from our area for higher education and also for drawing our salaries from banks,' said Mohammad Hussain, a young student from Hazara Town.

Khaliq Hazara wants to set up small-scale industries for members

---

[3]Yaoum-e-Quds is observed on the last Friday of the holy month of Ramzan every year, to commemorate the arson on the Al Aqsa Mosque in 1969 in Jerusalem.

of the Hazara community, especially women, to develop their skills so that they can earn a livelihood to meet their daily needs. This is crucial for the women of the community, who do not generally migrate.

Political parties, such as Majlis Wahdatul Muslimeen led by MPA Agha Mohammad Raza, have arranged skill-sharing seminars in Marriabad for women from families that have been attacked to develop their skills in handicrafts, sewing, etc. so that they have the ability to earn. Talks are on with the government to set up a technical training centre for women where they can earn a diploma or degree. 'The small industry unit is on board and they will provide the machines and skilled teachers,' he says. Yet, these skills do not benefit women on a large scale, as they only stitch clothes for neighbouring houses within the town, instead of working on a bigger scale, with more organised marketing.

Those that did not flee

The Hazaras have been on the run for decades. Ruqaiya Hashmi's grandfather migrated from Afghanistan about 100 years ago, fleeing religious persecution, and worked as a labourer on the Sukkur Barrage in Sindh. Hashmi says that the wave of Hazara emigration from Pakistan in the 1970s was in search of a better future. That was a period when Europe needed skilled labour, which the Hazara community could provide, and they migrated legally. But now, she says, the situation has changed and people are migrating because they fear for their lives. The fear of getting killed in Pakistan has been a major impetus for migration since 2001. Women and children face additional difficulties, as only 10 per cent of the predominantly male emigrants get asylum. After leaving from Quetta, the men no longer remain in contact with their family members. This exacerbates the difficulties for women; there are at least 200 houses in Hazara Town where women live alone with their children.

Since families cannot migrate together to foreign countries, women are left behind to bear the brunt of seeking employment and education, while also bearing the pain of the targeted killings of their children. 'I wish the entire family could make it together. I do not care if it is a developing country with lesser economic opportunities,' says Yasmin, a woman whose husband is seeking asylum in Australia. She says there is a huge vacuum in her life. 'My life will be complete only after I am with my husband,' she adds. She manages to cope with the moral support of other women whose husbands are abroad. Many adopt precautionary measures to save the lives of family members, while others live in constant fear.

Dawood Changazi, a well-wisher of his community, maintains data on migration. He identifies two phases of migration of the Hazara community—one from 1998 to 2000 and the other from 2011 to 2014. 'Around 60,000 people of the Hazara community have migrated to Australia solely to seek asylum. Around 40 per cent are women and children and 60 per cent are men,' he says. The usual route is from Pakistan to Indonesia and then to Malaysia. From there, the migrants, who have no legal documentation, sail by boat to Australia. According to a 2015 report of the Human Rights Commission of Pakistan, more than 200,000 people from the tiny Hazara community have migrated from Quetta from 2001 onwards. Previously, entering Australia and getting nationality was relatively easy as Hazaras could get asylum on humanitarian grounds. But now, rules have been tightened. The Australian government has passed a law restricting such immigrants to the islands of Manus and Nauru from July 19, 2013.

A private school teacher recounted the story of a family of nine members that migrated to Australia two months earlier, in search of a better future. The road to Australia is not easy even for male members and it becomes more difficult when women travel through these risky routes. The desire to reach the destination exposes them to various dangerous situations, and many fall victim to human trafficking, death or other disasters.[4] More than 300 people, many of them Hazara, were killed when their boat overturned at sea near Indonesia in 2012, said Dawood Changazi.

---

[4]http://www.hazarapeople.com/hazara/hr/hrras/

Families sometimes pay a heavy price to go to Australia, taking loans or selling their property, which renders them insecure financially. Iftikhar Hussain, a tailor, stated that only a single member of his family reached Australia, despite spending 800,000 Pakistani rupees. 'Sending him to Australia has impoverished the entire family and we are unable to feed and educate our women and children now,' he said.

Khaliq Hazara, HDP President, said that women sell their jewellery and property to migrate to safer places. Hajira Bibi, 40, is one of the few Hazara women who dared to embark on a dangerous journey to ensure a life free from fear for her children. Her husband, like hundreds of other Hazara men, was brutally killed in targeted attacks on the Hazara community. Hajira decided to go to Australia not only for refuge but for a better future for her four children, the eldest of whom was seventeen years old. Due to financial problems, Hajira Bibi had to choose the risky Malaysian-Indonesian route to Australia, leaving behind her four children in Quetta. After she left Quetta in 2012, her family has not heard from her.

Some asylum seekers also migrate to Iran and to cities within Pakistan. Around 8,000 to 10,000 Hazaras have migrated from Quetta to Iran since 2012, which Changazi terms as the 'deadliest year for the Hazara community' during which major blasts and targeted killings took place in Quetta. At least 70 per cent of these migrants are students.

Helping themselves

In the absence of aid from both the federal and provincial governments, NGOs have stepped in to provide services. Nimso, which means 'help' in Hazargai, is an organisation set up in 2010 to work for the education of Hazara children in Marriabad and Hazara Town. Nimso president, Abdul Ali, said that the frequent deadly attacks from 2010 to 2012 prompted philanthropists of the Hazara community to establish an organisation to give free education to surviving families. At a fund-raising conference in 2012, members of the community made generous contributions amounting to 5.6

million Pakistani rupees. The organisation supports 400 families, providing books, school uniforms and shoes.

Shaheed Foundation is an independent organisation which helps the families of those who have died in targeted killings and bomb blasts. It provides rations and other support to 250 families to the tune of 1.8 billion Pakistani rupees per month. The foundation encourages community support through donation boxes in several locations in Hazara Town.

Political representatives of the community are also doing their bit. The Khair-ul-Amal Foundation for community development, set up by MPA Agha Mohammad Raza in 2000, provides living quarters in Yateem Khana, Imambargah and the Marriabad area of Quetta. Funds are generated through donors in Pakistan, as well as in other parts of the world. Raza is also trying to set up a sub-campus of the University of Balochistan in Koh Murdar. He spent 1.5 billion Pakistani rupees from his Public Sector Development Projects (PSDP) fund so that Hazaras can access higher education closer home. Raza is aware that this separate space is not a permanent solution for the Hazara community, which will have to move out of its own ghettos in search of jobs in other parts of the city.

Security for whom?

The mandate of the Pakistan Army is constitutionally limited to the protection of international frontiers. The army is called out only when required under the provisions of the Aid of Civil Administration Act, and the rules of Public Administration, 1973. For the most part, it is the paramilitary and police that have a visible presence in Balochistan.

Predominantly Hazara neighbourhoods have already been sealed off by paramilitary troops and police, and Hazara community members inform the police of their travel routes and schedules before embarking on any journey. 'Security has been increased and measures are being taken, such as the deployment of frontier corps, barricades and strict checking. Convoys led by security men to the pilgrimage sites and subsidised air tickets for the Hazara community to safely travel to Iran and Iraq, avoiding risk of road travel are measures that can end this sectarian violence,' said the Chief Minister of Balochistan. His assurances, however, are challenged by the HDP chairman, Khaliq Hazara, who maintains that targeted killings are still on the rise.

The Home Secretary, Akbar Hussain Durrani, is satisfied with the performance of law enforcers in recent months. 'The police was not trained to combat terrorism in the past but now they are being trained by senior officials of Pakistan's army, which will help to address the issue of targeted killings in Quetta and other conflict-ridden areas of Balochistan,' Durrani said. 'The bike-mounted police force has been introduced in Quetta and the police force, a civilian force, will soon replace the paramilitary troops.' According to Durrani, many perpetrators of violence have been arrested, and investigations are underway. In February 2015, Usman Saifullah Kurd, a leader of Lashkar-e-Jhangvi, who was involved in several suicide bombings and in the targeted killing of Shia Muslims, was killed during a raid carried out by security forces in the Quetta valley.

Misbah Iram, resident of Hazara Town, laments the retaliatory violence: 'Angry protestors from the Hazara community often attack the Sunni neighbourhood immediately after any attack on their community,' she said, adding that her brother had survived two murder attempts by angry mobs. 'The majority of people love each other and we have been living together for decades. The killings of Hazara people and the reaction of angry Hazara men are fuelling the hatemongers,' she concludes.

The Capital City Police Officer (CCPO) of Quetta points out that there is a need for awareness among the people that sectarian violence is not justified at any level, saying, 'It is a political issue and every stakeholder needs to play a role in ending targeted killings.' He also advocates an inter-faith dialogue between the two sects to address the challenge through other channels of conflict resolution. Given the sensitivity of the issue and deep schisms between the communities, it has been difficult for anyone to play a positive role in bringing about religious harmony. Police officials feel that there is a need to address this issue with more religious people playing a role. 'It is not a law and order issue. All we need is to hold open talks between two sects and spread tolerance,' said one highly placed police officer who did not want to be named.

Waging peace

'Media coverage of the crisis remains inadequate, with a focus only on violent incidents,' observes Shahzada Zulfiqar, a senior journalist based in Quetta. Zulfiqar, who is also the president of the Quetta Press Club, says that killers enjoy complete impunity. 'The banned Lashkar-e-Jhangvi spokesperson had threatened journalists in Quetta of dire consequences if they gave any kind of coverage to Shia Muslims,' he reveals, providing a context to the silence on the Hazara issue. 'Under tremendous pressure, media in Quetta is not reporting independently,' he says in a severe indictment of the state of freedom of expression. According to journalists in Quetta, the Lashkar-e-Jhangvi had warned that 'Coffins for journalists are also ready if they continue to portray Shiites as innocent victims.'

The Hazara Democratic Party (HDP) and other Shia organisations are also not happy with the role of the media. However, they admit that media persons themselves are also victims.

Balochistan Union of Journalists (BUJ) President Hamad Rind said that as many as forty-two journalists have so far been killed in Balochistan and not a single murder has been properly investigated. 'The writ of law does not exist in Quetta. People do not have a sense of security. The government and law-enforcing agencies have failed to play their constitutional role to ensure the protection of the people,' says Shahzada Zulfiqar. Senior journalist Saleem Shahid says that the media in Pakistan can play a positive role in society and can change the mindset of the people if its own protection is ensured.

Right moves

Dressed in immaculate white karate gi, uniformed disciples fold their right arms above their foreheads and thrust their left arms forward, open-palmed with fingers held firmly together. Their poker faces and agility are captivating. It is not just facial features that the Hazaras of Quetta seem to have in common with Hollywood superstar Bruce Lee; some can also pack a punch like the maestro. Hazara youth in Quetta have taken up self-defence training, taught by sensei Ghulam Ali Hazara. Though mere kicks and punches are no match for the heavily-armed militants and suicide bombers who have obliterated thousands of Hazara lives, the boost in self-esteem that comes with martial arts training can be crucial in combating fatalism and depression.

Twenty-year-old Shahida is one of the girls being trained at Ali's academy. She has won several national-level competitions and remains unbeaten till today. Now she is aiming for international accolades. Shahida says she came to the academy in 2006 to get her brother admitted, but developed an interest in martial arts herself. 'Martial arts are important for us, for our self-defence, as Hazaras are being targeted every day,' says Shahida. The third-year college student admits that she often misses classes at college to attend national camps to train for events. 'I am also training girls here at the Ghulam Ali Sports Complex to make Hazara women strong, confident and capable of self-defence,' she says. Another student, Rehmatullah, who started martial arts training in 2006, when he was just eleven, says, 'I want to work for my people who are living under immense pressure in Quetta. I have won ten titles at the national level and want to be a champion like my teacher Ghulam Ali Hazara.'

Fatima Batool, who has been learning to land kicks and punches for the last two years, says, 'I want to serve my country at the national and international levels.' She won a bronze medal at an event of the DG Rangers in Karachi and is hoping the sport will pick up in the near future. 'We are facing a lot of problems due to the law and order situation, as our events have been cancelled and lots of great talent is being wasted as a result.' Another student Nag Bakht, who started training two years after being inspired by Chinese and Hollywood movies, shares similar aspirations, 'I also want to be an Olympian.' That Hazara women can dare to dream amidst a tenuous existence is itself cause for hope.

Bibliography

Ali, Tariq. 2009. *The Duel: Pakistan on the Flight Path of America*. New York: Simon & Schuster Pocket Books.

Hazara People International Network. 2012. http://www.hazarapeople.com/hazara/hr/hrras/ Retrieved in June 2016.

Human Rights Commission of Pakistan. 2014. *State of Human Rights in 2014*. Lahore: HRCP.

Lodhi, Maleeha. 2011. *Pakistan Beyond Crisis*. Oxford: Oxford University Press.

NEPAL

Introduction: The Maoist Conflict and Women

DEEPAK THAPA

Despite being the oldest nation-state in South Asia with an unbroken history traceable directly to the mid-eighteenth century, Nepal entered the modern era very late. A century-long oligarchy under the Rana hereditary prime ministers, ruling in the name of a figurehead monarch, kept Nepal cut off from the rest of the world until 1951. Following the departure of the British from India in 1947, the Ranas lost their long-standing patrons, and an armed insurrection led by the Nepali Congress (NC), with support from a newly-independent India, easily succeeded in bringing an end to Rana rule.

The promise of a democratic era that the historic change signified was, however, soon belied. Instead of a constituent assembly (CA) to draft a democratic constitution, the years between 1951 and 1959 saw the country beset by extreme political instability. A reinstated and re-empowered monarchy gradually entrenched its hold on political power, while the numerous political parties that had emerged vied with each other for influence with the throne.

After nearly a decade of unstable politics, the first general election was held in 1959. The NC emerged victorious with a massive mandate and its leader, B.P. Koirala, became prime minister. However, this exercise in popular democracy was cut short in December 1960 by King Mahendra, who dissolved parliament, arrested the prime minister, outlawed political parties, and declared a state of emergency. This royal intervention ushered in three decades of direct rule by the king under the Panchayat system, or party-less governance through a form of 'guided' democracy.

Proscribed by law, the political parties remained active nonetheless, either in exile in India or clandestinely within Nepal. Among the more notable political actions of this period was an abortive armed uprising by the NC in 1962; a short-lived armed uprising by the communists in 1971; and a number of non-violent movements. The latter included a student-led movement in 1979 that resulted in a national referendum to choose between a multiparty system and the existing Panchayat form of government. In a vote believed to have been rigged, the latter prevailed.

Meanwhile, Nepal's communist movement had undergone a number of splits and regroupings. And, by the close of the 1970s, one strand, the Communist Party of Nepal (Fourth Convention), or CPN-Fourth Convention, had become the most prominent of the factions, while a strong contender for that distinction was the Communist Party of Nepal (Marxist-Leninist), or CPN-ML.

In the spring of 1990, taking their cue from the peaceful revolutions that had swept the former Soviet bloc in Eastern Europe, Nepal's political parties of all hues also came together to launch a popular movement against the Panchayat system. In less than two months of occasionally violent confrontations with the police, the parties were able to wrest concessions from the king, including the restoration of multi-party democracy and the relegation of the monarchy to a constitutional role.

A new, democratic constitution was drafted and general elections held in 1991. The NC came back to power but this time, the scale of its victory was much smaller, with new challengers in the field. Primary among them was the Communist Party of Nepal (Unified Marxist-Leninist), CPN-UML, which had evolved out of the CPN-ML, along with the CPN-Unity Centre, representing a major fragment of the original CPN-Fourth Convention. The more radical CPN-Unity Centre had pressed for a constituent assembly to frame the new constitution, failing which it continued to remain semi-underground, despite taking part in the parliamentary elections through its political wing, the United People's Front.

The NC was soon caught in infighting and the government, led by Girija Prasad Koirala, resigned in 1994. The mid-term election saw a hung parliament and, as the largest party, the CPN-UML formed a minority government. But Nepal's first communist government lasted only nine months before being replaced by an NC-led coalition.

On the far-left spectrum, the CPN-Unity Centre split once again, and while one faction opted to continue with parliamentary politics, the other stood against it. It was the latter that re-named itself the Communist Party of Nepal (Maoist), CPN-Maoist, in 1995 and began preparations for armed struggle. In February 1996, the Maoists presented a charter of forty demands to the government with the warning that if these were not fulfilled by a given date, they would be 'forced to adopt the path of armed struggle against the existing state power' (Thapa and Sijapati 2004). The government did not consider the matter with any seriousness, and neither, it seems, did the Maoists expect any meaningful response, because four days before the deadline, they attacked public installations, including a police station, in a number of places around the country, signalling the beginning of the 'People's War'.

Understanding the insurgency

The Maoist insurgency resulted from many factors intersecting at a particular juncture in Nepal's history. In the words of sociologist Chaitanya Mishra, the causes of the Maoist insurgency are manifold, including 'poverty, illiteracy and low level of educational attainment, unemployment and underemployment, inter-household economic inequality...and caste, ethnic, regional/spatial and gender oppression and inequality' (Mishra 2007). The unhealthy competition between the two main contenders for power—the NC and the CPN-UML—for much of the early 1990s, and their inability to adopt a more socially and economically inclusive approach to governance was also a contributory factor. Not only did they fail to gauge the level of expectations brought about by the changes of 1990, but they also did not demonstrate any attempt to, for instance, relieve the rural peasantry from exploitative working conditions.

The early post-1990 democratic period was ridiculed by CPN-Maoist supremo, Pushpa Kamal Dahal 'Prachanda', thus: '[J]ust by displaying the signboard of democracy any country does not become democratic. In Nepal for a long period there has been a feudal state with an autocratic monarchy. After the 1990 historic people's movement, the character of the state has remained autocratic and feudal in essence, although in form it gave the appearance of democracy' (Maoist Information Bulletin 2003). Hence, even as historically marginalised sections of society, namely, women, Dalits (former untouchables), Janajatis (indigenous peoples) and Madhesis (people with origins in and generally inhabiting the Tarai plains), saw in the re-establishment of democracy an opportunity to seek redress for centuries of domination in all aspects of public life by hill-origin 'upper-caste' males, the Maoists found it easy to cast themselves as champions of these groups.

There was also a strong economic argument to which the Maoists appealed quite successfully. When the Maoists began their armed insurrection in 1996, nearly half the population (42.5 per cent) lived in poverty, a condition resulting from three main factors: unsatisfactory aggregate growth output; inequitable accrual of benefits, leading to further disparities in income and assets; and unequal distribution of assets compounded by the widely divergent socio-economic status among different groups due to both geography and caste-, ethnic- and gender-related biases (Panday 2000). It was in this situation that the Maoists stepped in with rhetoric such as that given below.

> This state...has handed over the whole economy of the country to a dozen families of the foreign compradors and bureaucratic capitalists. Whereas these handful of plunderers have become billionaires, the real masters of this country and the national property, the toiling masses of Nepal, are forced to eke out a meager existence of deprivation and poverty. The sons and daughters of Nepalese peasants and workers reeling under unemployment and poverty are compelled to lead a

miserable life of dishonor and neglect in India and different parts of the world to earn their daily bread (*The Worker* 1996).

Politics as usual

In the years after 1990, belying popular expectations of deeper structural changes, the ruling parties, particularly the NC, viewed the regime merely as a change of guard. In an attempt to expand its organisational base after the fall of the Panchayat regime, these parties even began inducting individuals who had been part of that system,[1] bringing back to power some of the very individuals who for many represented the oppressive state. But, perhaps the most serious error was the manner in which successive governments responded to an incipient revolt. Their heavy-handed approach had the unintended effect of turning more and more victims of police brutality and their families against the government. At a time when the Maoists were propagating an alternative conception of the state, it was a mistake to rely solely on force without any attempt to counter the rebels' message either ideologically or through progressive action.

Yet, the Maoists would perhaps still have found it difficult to achieve the heights they did, had it not been for the strong base they had cultivated over the decades, particularly in the midwestern region of the country. In particular, the sparsely populated and wholly under-developed districts of Rolpa and Rukum provided a safe haven to the party, and also allowed it to successfully challenge the state and gradually consolidate its hold over the rural countryside.

After the CPN-UML came back to power in 1997 as a coalition partner in government, it tried to resolve issues politically, and the Dhami Commission[2] set up to 'search for solutions' is noteworthy

---

[1]One survey showed that 40 per cent of the NC leaders at the village and town levels had previously been part of the Panchayat system while the corresponding figure for the UML was 10 per cent (Hachhethu 2002).

[2]So called after the committee chairperson, Prem Singh Dhami, a CPN-UML member of parliament at the time.

for recommending socio-economic reforms similar to those demanded by the Maoists, acknowledging the brutality of the police and for emphasising the need to bring the CPN-Maoist into the constitutional process. But the frequent changes in government in the second half of the 1990s ensured that the findings of the Dhami Commission report could not be implemented (Thapa and Sijapati 2004). Instead, there was another sustained police campaign in 1998 which was widely reviled for its brutality. And, as it was unable to quell the insurgency, the campaign only served to further strengthen it by turning more people against the state.

Following its victory in the third parliamentary election of 1999, the NC was once again at the helm of government. But the Maoist uprising had still not reached the heights it would just a couple of years later. Neither, it seemed, were the people in general alarmed by it, as can be gleaned from an opinion poll conducted that year. The highest concern mentioned was reserved for lack of development (28.6 per cent), inflation (27.6 per cent), unemployment (18.4 per cent) and corruption (7.1 per cent), and only 4.7 per cent mentioned peace and security (Sharma and Sen 1999).[3] Prime Minister Krishna Prasad Bhattarai initiated contact with the Maoists and incremental progress was being made, but he was ousted by Girija Prasad Koirala, whose arrival on the scene led to concentrated attacks on government installations by the Maoists, including the overrunning of a district headquarters for the first time ever, in September 2000.

Then, in a surprising development in February 2001, the Maoists called for a conference of all political parties, organisations and representatives of mass organisations in the country; the election of an interim government by such a conference; and guarantee of a people's constitution under the leadership of the interim government. Since the demand for a CA was conspicuously absent from the list, the new proposal was viewed as a sign of the Maoists' willingness to eventually join mainstream politics. But, despite

---

[3]It is instructive that unemployment, inflation and corruption remained the three top concerns in another survey conducted in 2001 (Himal Association 2001).

some concessions from the government, the fighting continued unabated until the June 1, 2001 royal palace massacre that wiped out the entire family of King Birendra and brought into the picture his brother, Gyanendra, as king.

Royal takeover to the CPA

A month later, Koirala resigned, seemingly because of lack of support from the army to move against the Maoists, and Sher Bahadur Deuba of the NC took over. Deuba promptly announced a ceasefire which was reciprocated by the Maoists and negotiations began. After five years of increasingly bloody conflict, the country received a reprieve as the ceasefire held while the Maoists began to hold their meetings openly. This was also around the time that the rebels expanded their operations across the country.

It soon became apparent that the talks were heading for an impasse, given the divergent positions of the two sides, mainly on the issue of the CA. Five months into the ceasefire, in November 2001, fighting broke out again with the Maoists launching surprise attacks across the country, including, for the first time, against the army. The raids on army camps resulted in a considerable haul of armaments which was to provide the bulk of the Maoists' firepower in a conflict that rapidly accelerated.

The country was placed under a state of emergency with the suspension of most civil liberties, and an anti-terrorism ordinance adopted almost immediately to allow government security forces greater leeway in tackling the Maoists. The impact of these measures soon became clear with the number of deaths rising exponentially. Whereas in the nearly six years of the 'People's War' just 1,700 people had died, in just the year that followed the intensification of the conflict after November 2001, nearly 5,000 lost their lives, with close to two-thirds of them killed by the state (see Figure 1). Although the relaxation of the emergency six months later and increased scrutiny by the international community reduced the number of killings, the death toll continued to remain much higher than in the previous period.

Figure 1: Number of Deaths, 1996-2006[4]

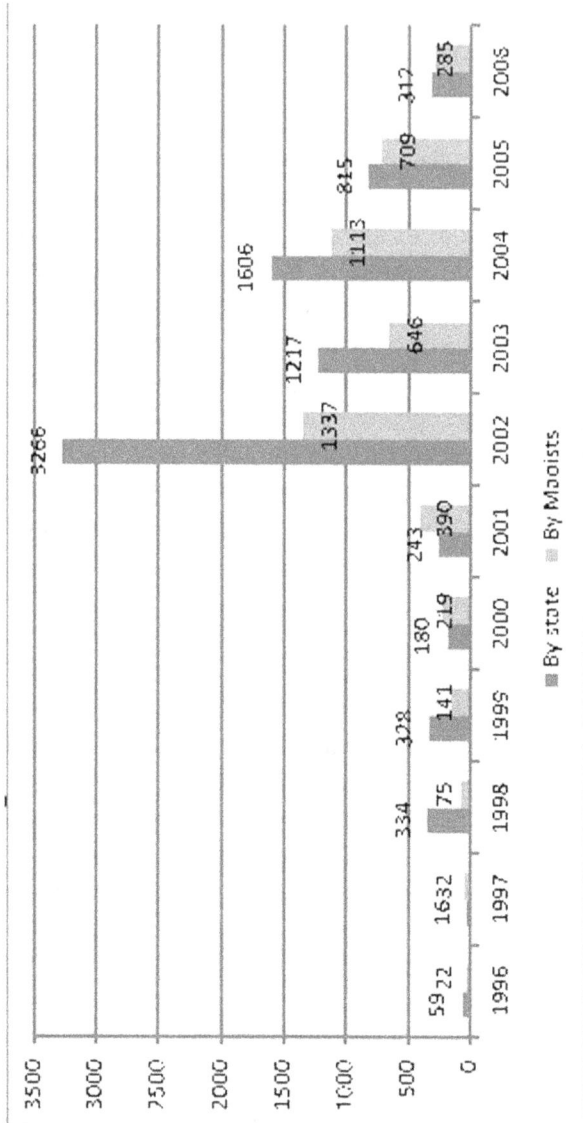

Source: *Human Rights Yearbook 2007*

---
[4]The number of deaths in 2003 is considerably smaller because of the ceasefire that lasted more than six months.

In June 2002, the perennial internal tussle within the NC came to the fore once again and, preceded by Deuba's dissolution of the parliament a month earlier, resulted in a vertical split in the party. In October 2002, after Deuba recommended that the parliamentary elections scheduled for November that year be postponed, citing the unfavourable security situation, King Gyanendra dismissed the elected government and appointed a cabinet of independents— politicians and technocrats. The major political parties ignored the call to join the government to give it an 'all-party' look and instead began street protests. This was the beginning of the rift between the palace and the political parties that was soon to have serious repercussions for the monarchy itself.

Meanwhile, the fighting raged on and the Maoists even assassinated the chief of the Armed Police Force, a formation that had been specifically created to tackle the insurgency. But, in a surprise move just days later, the government and the Maoists declared a ceasefire and the beginning of a new round of talks. The negotiations however, did not move in any fruitful direction, mainly because of the inability of the two sides to even begin discussing the main political demands that revolved once again around the question of a CA. Negotiations continued, even through a change in government, but the talks soon faltered and hostilities began anew in August 2003.

Ongoing street agitations forced the king once again to try and assuage the political parties and in June 2004, he reappointed Deuba as prime minister. Leading his own faction of the NC and with the CPN-UML as coalition partner, Deuba's specific mandate of starting talks with the CPN-Maoist and holding parliamentary elections within a year remained unfulfilled as the Maoists demanded direct negotiations with the king. And, on February 1, 2005, Gyanendra dismissed Deuba once again and assumed full executive authority.

The king promised that he would give the highest priority to reactivating multiparty democracy in the country within three years, with the implementation of effective reforms by restoring peace and security. Since Gyanendra had the full backing of the army, the people and political parties were initially cowed. The reaction from the international community was sharp, with India, the US and the UK all announcing the suspension of military aid that had begun in 2001. Soon, the political parties and civil society began their protests anew against a king who appeared quite inured to the anti-monarchy sentiments that were increasingly being echoed in the streets. The political parties formed the Seven-Party Alliance (SPA) against the king and also initiated direct talks with the Maoists. With the help of the Indian government, in November 2005, the two forces forged an agreement that identified the king as the main obstacle to both democracy and lasting peace. The SPA agreed to a CA, long demanded by the Maoists, while the latter agreed to join electoral politics.

Despite misgivings about the intent of the Maoists, the agreement held and in April 2006 the country was gripped by mass agitations, the likes of which had never been witnessed before. After nineteen days of protests, the king conceded defeat. Girija Prasad Koirala became prime minister yet again and declared before the reconstituted parliament that 'this meeting of the House of Representatives vows and decides to hold constituent assembly elections to draft a new constitution'. A ceasefire had by then been declared by both the Maoists and the new government.

In November 2006, the SPA and the Maoists signed the Comprehensive Peace Agreement (CPA), effectively ending the 'People's War'. The CPA, which resulted from months of deliberations, laid down the broad parameters to guide the political process until a new constitution was drafted. Among the major points agreed upon in the CPA were the election to a CA by mid-June 2007 under a mixed electoral system; the issue of the monarchy to be decided by the first sitting of the CA; an interim constitution to be promulgated and an interim legislature-parliament formed, along with an interim government that would include the Maoists; Maoist arms to be stored in cantonments under UN supervision; and the socio-economic transformation of the country to begin.

These arrangements were not universally welcomed. In

particular, it led to violent protests in the southern Tarai belt with Madhesis believing that their aspirations had been disregarded. Their prolonged agitation also spawned a number of armed groups that often used the political cover of fighting for Madhesi rights while engaging in overtly criminal activities such as kidnapping and extortion. Janajati groups, too, led protests seeking redress of their own demands. Through a series of agreements, the government was able to bring almost all agitating groups on board for the April 2008 election to the CA, which amounted to perhaps the most singular achievement of the Maoist movement.

Emerging as the largest party in the CA, the CPN-Maoist formed a government with the CPN-UML as the major coalition partner. Through a series of missteps, it gradually engendered disenchantment among those who had supported it. Political disagreements over a number of issues meant that a new constitution could not be drafted and when a second CA was elected in 2013, the CPN-Maoist had been pushed to a distant third place by the NC and the CPN-UML, a situation somewhat mirroring their respective standings in the 1991 parliament.

Women in the Maoist conflict

'A... "given" in Marxism-Leninism is a political theory whose organisational imperative—the vanguard party—can be inimical to the interests of women. Women's interests are assumed to be a subset of class interests...what is good for the working classes is thought to be good for women. As a result conceptions of women's interests that are not directly subsumed to class frequently remain only indirectly articulated' (Kruks et al 1989).

Despite the much-publicised claim that women made up between 30 and 40 per cent of the Maoist fighting force (International Crisis Group 2005), the above critique holds true for Nepal's Maoist movement as well. There is either no mention or, if at all, only in passing, of women's issues in many of the party documents published during the insurgency. Most telling is that the only reference to women in the famous forty-point demands heralding the Maoist declaration of war is limited to just one point: 'Patriarchal exploitation and discrimination against women should be stopped. Daughters should be allowed access to paternal property' (Thapa and Sijapati 2004).

As Prachanda (2004) predictably iterates, '...the issue of women's emancipation is inseparably linked with the issue of emancipation of the whole society', emphasising once again the need for a radical overhaul of the entire socio-political system for women to enjoy rights at par with men. He is rather dismissive about the Nepali women's rights movement, and sees its endeavours as leading women away from the 'revolutionary struggle for their genuine emancipation'. In fact, Prachanda believes that programmes geared towards skills development and literacy campaigns are part of a conspiracy led by 'foreign imperialist capital' to 'deprive women of the consciousness of historical necessity of the country' (Prachanda 2004). One of the top Maoist women leaders, Comrade Parvati (1999),[5] rails against women activists in a similar vein: 'They grumble against commoditisation of women but dare not protest against beauty pageants etc. They condemn revolutionary violence but condone state violence.' But it was the same rights activists who were justifiably outraged when the Maoists failed to name a single woman in either of the teams that surfaced to negotiate with the government in 2001 and 2003. As one of them wrote in an open letter to the Maoist leadership, 'We never expected our male-dominated government to involve women in the peace process, but we thought you were going to be different.'[6]

A prominent feature during the first half of the decade of the Maoist conflict had been the use of the media by the CPN-Maoist to express its views. Until forcibly closed by the government in November 2001, following the end of the first ceasefire and the

---

[5]The nom de guerre of prominent Maoist leader Hisila Yami.

[6]Aruna Uprety cited in Pettigrew and Shneiderman 2003.

imposition of a state of emergency (after which it went underground while also continuing an active online presence), its mouthpiece, *Janadesh*, functioned as a regular newspaper. The weekly was not only a vehicle to propagate party doctrine but also served as a platform for ordinary Maoist cadre to express themselves. Although the contributions were generally of questionable literary quality, the thrust of the sentiments is clear as in this poem by 'Kopila': 'What use is this one life if you are to be a slave?/ Compare your life with a tethered animal.'[7]

The section called 'Recollections' was highly popular among its readers (Hutt 2012). While much of the content dealt with personal impressions about the insurgency, it also allowed for fighters to remember someone they cared for. Take, for instance, this piece entitled 'A couple of paragraphs in honour of Great Martyr Kavita' by Shanti,[8] in which she describes an event that occurred on July 15, 2004, when a group of Maoists were surrounded and captured by 'royal American executioners' [i.e., soldiers from the Royal Nepalese Army]. Comrade Kavita is raped and tortured by the soldiers but she resists and taunts them, saying: 'I am a loyal soldier of the revolution. Shoot me if you have the guts.' She was killed half an hour later by the 'bloodthirsty dogs'. Shanti concludes: 'At present, Comrade Kavita's physical self may have turned into soil but her thoughts continue to live, and have laid the foundation for the birth of thousands of revolutionaries.'

With end of the conflict in 2006, there was a sudden burst of writing by both Maoists and their sympathisers. This included political biographies of some of the leaders, collected works, expositions of Nepal's social and political problems, etc., but more common was the body of literature based on the conflict-era experience. As Hutt notes, 'by late 2010 over 350 books of poetry, fiction, songs, essays and memoirs had been written, either by Maoist or pro-Maoist authors or by others using the conflict as their

---

[7] *Janadesh*, Year 14, Number 30, July 5 2005.

[8] *Janadesh*, Year 14, Number 27, June 14 2005.

subject matter' (Hutt 2012).[9] Women were somewhat represented, with around half-a-dozen women authors figuring among the writers of some forty-three book-length memoirs (Hutt 2012), including perhaps Tara Rai's most famous one, entitled *The Diary of a Guerrilla Girl*.

Maoist propaganda aside, there have been significant representations of women's perspectives on the 'People's War'. Among the first to appear was in 1998 when a group of Nepali women journalists toured Rolpa and Rukum. Their stories in the Nepali-language media, some of which were synthesised in the seminal piece 'Where There Are No Men: Women in the Maoist Insurgency in Nepal' (Gautam et al 2001), provided a first-hand account of life in general in the shadow of the conflict. For a long time, the only Maoist view on women in the conflict came from Comrade Parvati in 'Women's Participation in People's War in Nepal' (1999) and 'The Question of Women's Leadership in People's War in Nepal' (2003), both of which explained how women participated in the conflict as well as provided an indication of the limitations they faced. But, from the outside, there have also been a number of scholarly critiques of the role of women in the war as well as its impact on them, some of which have been cited here. These appeared both while the fighting was on going and thereafter, and are too extensive in volume and content to be dealt with here with any sense of justice.

Joining up

In a surprisingly frank exchange with a reporter in 2000, Prachanda says that although as communists, they were aware of 'the woman question', it was not taken up with any seriousness within the party, and women's participation in the party was indeed negligible (Onesto 2000). His party saw the potential of involving women in the 'People's War' only after the fighting had actually begun (Onesto 2000; Comrade Parvati 1999). And it took five years more, until

---

[9]Hutt cites information provided by Kailash Rai.

2001, for the party to seriously consider the contribution of women in the 'institutionalisation of continuous revolution and their role in preventing counterrevolution' (Comrade Parvati 2003), something that is presumably a given for men.

Amongst the enduring images to come out of Nepal's decade-long Maoist conflict is one from the early 2000s showing four village women attired in everyday lungi and tops, long-barrelled guns slung on their backs, and lower faces masked by kerchiefs as they stare at the camera. This and other similar photographs were subsequently overtaken by the seemingly more sensational ones of women in the combat fatigues of the Maoist People's Liberation Army complete with automatic weapons. The earlier image, however, stands out for its ability to depict the appeal of the Maoist movement to a cross-section of Nepali society and the ease with which these women had simply picked up the gun aiming for a better future.

All three essays from Nepal in this volume revolve around the theme of wanting to create a more just society. Although the individuals portrayed in the essays have been moved by certain aspects of their lives to join the Maoists, the common thread is the strong desire for change for the better. But, before that is to materialise, each struggles in her own way with the fact that they are women and fighters as well. Despite the different trajectories of their sometimes tragic journeys, a common feature in their stories is of having to prove themselves much more than their male comrades, and, yet, also having to face discrimination even at the height of the conflict. The injustice of their treatment becomes even more pronounced with the advent of peace, as age-old traditions, the breakdown of which had so swayed the women, reassert themselves even among the Maoists, pushing women back into a role of subservience. Women, thus, are forced to witness the dream of revolution wither away, while at the same time continuing the struggle against oppressive societal norms they had thought were a thing of the past.

The involvement of women appears to have been gradual, and different reasons have been provided for women's attraction to the

Maoist cause. Two strands, however, stand out: a desire to change
the socio-cultural, economic and political status quo; and a strong
motivation to take revenge on government security forces. The first
is summed up by a journalist who toured the Maoist strongholds
in 1999: 'For many women, the "People's War" offers an immediate
escape from an oppressive situation where they can't go to school,
may be forced into an arranged marriage and are expected to spend
the rest of their lives devoted to husbands, in-laws and children'
(Onesto 1999). The tearing down of debilitating social norms was
indeed a strong reason for women to join the Maoists and it is a
theme that recurs in writings about women in the 'People's War'. As
a one-time combatant said, 'We hoped to dismantle the old society
and replace [it] with a new progressive society that respects equal
rights of women.'[10]

Maoist leaders are careful to point out that the level of patriarchal
discrimination is not necessarily the same for all groups. Comrade
Parvati makes the distinction that the 'People's War' has 'helped
Indo-Aryan women to break the feudal restrictive life imposed by
the puritan Hindu religion by unleashing their repressed energy.
It has given meaningful lives to Tibeto-Burman [i.e., Janajati] and
other women who are relatively free and have greater decision-
making rights' (Comrade Parvati 1999). 'Meaningful lives', however,
turns out to be no more than a vacuous phrase, for it contributes
nothing to a better understanding of what drove Janajati women to
provide the substantial bulk of the Maoists' female fighting force,
at least in the initial stages.

On the other hand, there seems to be an excessive focus on the
control over their sexuality made possible by women's participation
in the 'People's War'. Prachanda says it outright when he holds
that Magar women from Rolpa and Rukum enjoy greater [sexual]
freedom: 'Women can easily divorce, and if a woman remarries, the

community does not look at her like she is a bad woman' (Onesto 2000).

In one of Comrade Parvati's oft-cited articles (2003), she details the extent of women's involvement in the Maoist movement: 'Several women' in the Central Committee of the Party , 'dozens of women' at the regional level and 'hundreds' in the district levels, and 'several thousands' in the area and cell levels in the Party, 'many' women commanders, vice commanders in different sections within the brigade, platoons, squads and militia, 'four women out of 37 members' in the United Revolutionary People's Council, and '1,500 women's units' in the western region alone, meaning that the 'total number of women membership in the women's mass organizations is six hundred thousand'. Even ignoring eyewitness accounts that doubt if the extent of women's participation was ever that high,[11] it is instructive that amongst the examples to emphasise how emancipated Maoist women cadre are, most turn out to be merely in juxtaposition to their relationships with men. Thus,

> 'Com. Shilpa…had a heroic death while laying an ambush against the reactionary armed forces in May 2002. She dared to denounce and divorce her husband who had reneged against the revolution after being captured… There is an increasing trend of widow remarriages… The definition of the family of martyrs has now been extended to those wives of martyred comrades who have remarried without forsaking the revolutionary cause. This has indirectly helped widows of martyred men to remarry without feeling guilt. Take the example of Com. Shilu, the commander of the historic women jail breakers in Gorkha in March, 2001. She has remarried another comrade after losing her husband Bhim Sen Pokharel who got martyred…'

Of course, there is no doubt that many women from marginalised groups, having felt the brunt of double discrimination of gender

---

[11]See, for instance, Thapa 2004.

as well as caste/ethnicity, had joined the Maoists to change their conditions. A former female combatant explained her motivation in these terms: 'I belong to a marginalised lower caste and poor family. My family has to work for rich people for more than sixteen hours a day but still we do not have enough food at home... I thought it's all because of the exploiting system of the state; therefore, I joined PLA to fight against the system, and to establish a new state with equal distribution of all resources to all' (Khadka 2012).

The second theme, of vengeance, is linked to two aspects. One is the experience of losing loved ones at the hands of the security forces.[12] Given the indiscriminate violence the security forces indulged in from the very beginning, there was no shortage of women and girls who wanted to find a way to deal with their loss. Comrade Parvati explains that her party has been channelling such grief by 'consciously trying to transform their bereavement into a source of strength, to avenge the killers' (Comrade Parvati 1999). As a woman Maoist said: 'Whenever the army enters the village, we get a few new women joining the militia...they don't just eat and take away the chickens and food the villagers have, they also torture women and even rape them...those poor people do not have any place to go to seek justice. So they come and join the party, in order to retaliate' (Sharma and Prasain 2004).

Rape by government troops figures prominently when dealing with the issue of women and the Maoist conflict. Comrade Parvati (Hisila Yami 2007) provides an account of how the security forces used rape as 'an instrument of state repression' in Rolpa. 'In Rolpa alone, [in] village after village there were cases of mass rape on Maoist cadres, sympathizers and simple villagers'. Lohani-Chase (2008) writes about being surprised by a police officer's open admission that government troops indulged in systematic rape, which served to boost the recruitment of women into the Maoist cause. In the words of the officer, women were attracted to the Maoists out of a 'sense of revenge as many security officers (army

---

[12]The experience of Anoopam in the article by Sewa Bhattarai is one such example.

Figure 2: Number of Women Killed by the Nepali State, 1996–2006

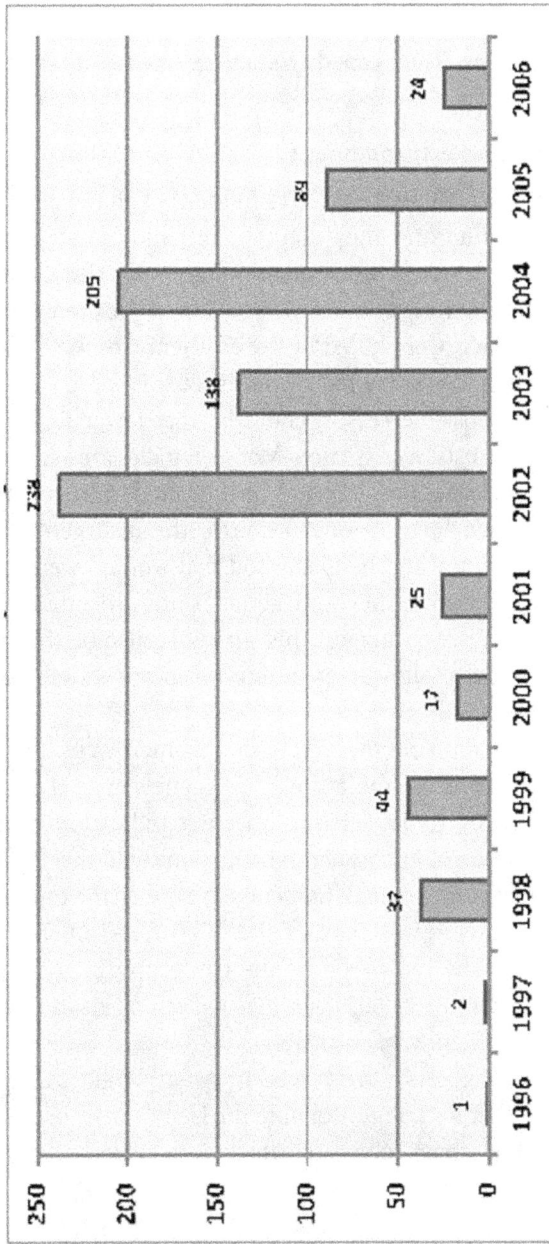

Year	Number
1996	1
1997	2
1998	37
1999	44
2000	17
2001	25
2002	234
2003	138
2004	205
2005	89
2006	24

Source: *Human Rights Yearbook 2007*

and police) indeed acted in excess and brutally with women during search operations. They raped women in front of their brothers and fathers'.

Engagement and estrangement

Women comprised 8 per cent (1013 in total) of all the dead during the Maoist conflict and they died at the hands of state security forces in much larger proportions than men. Of those who died during the decade-long conflict, 61 per cent of the men and 81 per cent of the women were killed by government troops.[13] There has been no discussion about what accounts for this somewhat glaring disparity. One possible reason could be that fewer women were killed by the Maoists because non-Maoist females are generally less politicised and, hence, less likely to be subjected to 'people's action' for any perceived form of opposition to the insurgents. On the other hand, discounting the likelihood that women were killed in larger numbers because they were at the frontline of attacks—since there is no evidence to suggest this—it could also be that rape by government troops followed by killing was more widespread than is generally believed.

What is indisputable though, is that women were involved in substantial numbers in the Maoist insurgency, even if not to the extent claimed by its leadership. The first indication of a more realistic estimation of female combatants came with the registration and subsequent verification of fighters who entered the cantonments that had been set up as part of the 2006 CPA. Of the 32,250 individuals initially registered by the United Nations Mission in Nepal, 61 per cent (or 19,602) qualified as combatants. Only 20 per cent (3,846) of them were women.

The Maoist fighters were placed in twenty-eight camps while they waited either for integration into the Nepali army or a financial package to allow them to voluntarily re-join civilian life. It took a

[13]All figures based on data available in *Human Rights Yearbook 2007*, inseconline.org.

full five years, until November 2011, for the major political parties, which included the Maoists, to finally come to an agreement on their future although it was not one that found favour with the vast majority of the cantoned fighters. Fewer than 1,500 opted for integration and the rest took voluntary retirement, with cash packages ranging from 500,000 to 800,000 Nepali rupees. The number of women choosing to join the Nepali army was only 105.[14]

Life for ex-combatants who chose the retirement package has been difficult. Apart from a feeling of betrayal by their party for its apparent capitulation to the Nepali army, their own reintegration into society has been far from seamless, for reasons ranging from hostility from society to feeling at a loss about the future, given that many had spent a large part of their productive youth either fighting or in the cantonments (Martin Chautari 2013). It has generally been worse for women fighters, particularly when they were expected to resume traditional subservient roles within the household, despite participating as equals during the conflict. Coming from a background where sexual boundaries had somewhat been erased to celebrate the valour of men and women equally (Bleie 2012), this experience was deeply unsettling for many. As a former fighter put it, 'I and my husband were discharged at the same time, and came to his house together. We had [the] same daily task in [the] cantonment but when we came home, my husband totally changed. I had to work at home and farm from 4 o'clock in the morning to 11 o'clock at night but my husband used to talk about war experiences with other people outside the house. I could not tolerate that. As a result, we got divorced...' (Khadka 2012).

There was also the issue of societal attitudes and stigma towards women who had lived away from home along with men.[15] Further, there were cases of marriages among Maoist cadres cutting across

---

[14]http://e.myrepublica.com/2014/component/flippingbook/book/1018-republica-26-september-2012/1-republica.html

[15]www.irinnews.org/report/88806/nepal-reintegration-challenges-for-maoist-female-ex-combatants.

caste and ethnic boundaries that had been actively encouraged by the CPN-Maoist. But after the fighting ended, these same 'revolutionary' unions had great difficulty being accepted by their respective families. As a Brahmin woman who had married a Dalit comrade-in-arms recalled, her decision had been appreciated even by Prachanda. Her husband was slain during a battle and after being discharged from the cantonments she was accepted neither by her husband's family nor by her own. 'I felt abandoned...[by] both families and society,' she said (Khadka 2012).

There have been some advances made by the Maoists in promoting women to leadership roles compared to the other parties. That had become partly evident in the villages of Rolpa and Rukum even in the early years of the conflict, with the absence of men leading to greater engagement of women in local politics (Gautam et al 2001). Most strikingly, in the 2008 CA election, the CPN-Maoist had seventy-six women CA members (while the NC had thirty-eight and CPN-UML had thirty-six). The significant presence of women in the CA was mainly due to new electoral rules that decreed that 50 per cent of the seats in the proportional representation part of the election had to be reserved for women. But even in the directly elected (first-past-the-post) section of the election, the CPN-Maoist was able to get twenty-four women elected, far above the other two parties—of all the seats won by the CPN-Maoist, women accounted for 29 per cent as opposed to 0.74 per cent and 0.33 per cent for the NC and the CPN-UML. But by the time of the 2013 CA election, the number of Maoist women candidates directly elected went down to just one[16] (or 0.3 per cent of the total), and while this could have resulted from the fact that the Maoists were soundly defeated in the latter election, given the party's past record on the question of women's leadership, the earlier rosy picture appears to be more of an exception than the rule. After all, it has been pointed out that when, in 2001, the Maoists established

---

[16]This sole winning candidate, Onsari Gharti Magar, is now the Speaker of the Legislature-Parliament, the first woman to hold that position in Nepal.

'people's governments' in twenty-one districts, not a single one was led by a woman. Further, in the 'Magar Autonomous Region', the same region where Prachanda had pointed out that women are so liberated, the party found no woman capable of being included in the 'government' there (Manchanda 2005).

In conclusion, it would not be wholly incorrect to state that, as with similar movements elsewhere, Nepal's Maoist leadership mobilised women towards the particular objective of overthrowing the state, with the promise that it would best fulfil their particular interests. In the immediate aftermath of the success of the 2006 movement, there seemed to be some significant progression towards that goal as well, with, for instance, the passage in 2006 of the 'Act to Amend Some Nepalese Acts to Maintain Gender Equality' or the amendment to the Civil Service Act in 2007 to provide for reservations in government service for women. The progressive vision of the CPN-Maoist may have become diluted by now and the party may have forgotten the women warriors it used to be so proud of, but these are achievements that have grave and positive implications for the future of Nepali women. The majority of the embittered former women combatants may not be aware of or even care about such matters, but had it not been for their contributions to the Maoist insurgency, it is very unlikely that these measures would have been possible. That perhaps can remain their only consolation.

Bibliography

Bleie, Tone. 2012. *Post-war Moral Communities in Somalia and Nepal: Gendered practices of Exclusion and Inclusion.* Tromsø: Centre for Peace Studies, University of Tromsø.

Comrade Parvati. 1999. 'Women's Participation in People's War in Nepal', *The Worker*, 5 October.

——2003. 'The Question of Women's Leadership in People's War in Nepal', *Monthly Review*.

Comrade Kopila. 2005. *Janadesh*, Year 14, Number 30. Published on July 5. Kathmandu.

Comrade Shanti. 2005. 'A couple of paragraphs in honour of Great Martyr Kavita' *Janadesh*, Year 14, Number 27. Published on June 14. Kathmandu.

Gautam, Shobha, Amrita Banskota and Rita Manchanda. 2001. 'Where There Are No Men: Women in the Maoist Insurgency in Nepal', in *Women, War and Peace*, Rita Manchanda (ed). New Delhi: Sage.

Hachhethu, Krishna. 2002. *Party Building in Nepal: Organisation, Leadership and People*. Kathmandu: Mandala Book Point.

Himal Association. 2001. *Political Opinion Survey Nepal 2001*. Kathmandu: Himal Association.

Hutt, Michael. 2012, 'Reading Nepali Maoist Memoirs', *Studies in Nepali History and Society*, 17:1, June 2012, pp. 107-142.

IRIN News. 2010. 'Reintegration challenges for Maoist female ex-combatants', April 14.

INSEC. *Human Rights Yearbook 2007*, inseconline.org.

International Crisis Group. 2005. *Nepal's Maoists: Their Aims, Structure and Strategy*. 27 October.

Khadka, Sharda. 2012. 'Female Combatants and Ex-combatants in the Maoist Revolution and their Struggle for Reintegration in Post-War Nepal' (Master's thesis). Tromsø: Centre for Peace Studies, University of Tromsø.

Kruks, Sonia, Rayna Rapp and Marilyn Young (eds). 1989. *Promissory Notes: Women in the Transition to Socialism*. New York: Monthly Review Press.

Lohani-Chase, Rama. 2008. 'Women and Gender in the Maoist People's War in Nepal: Militarism and Dislocation' (PhD dissertation submitted to the Graduate School-New Brunswick Rutgers, The State University of New Jersey).

Manchanda, Rita. 2005. 'Women's Agency in Peace Building: Gender Relations in Post-Conflict Reconstruction' in *Economic and Political Weekly*, 29 October.

Martin Chautari. 2013. 'Political Risk and Ex-Combatants', Policy Brief, No. 9, August.

Maoist Information Bulletin. 2003. 'Chairman Prachanda Answers to an US Paper', No. 7, December 15.

Mishra, Chaitanya. 2007. *Essays on the Sociology of Nepal.* Kathmandu: FinePrint.

Onesto, Li. 1999. 'Women Warriors' in *Revolutionary Worker*, No. 1032, 28 November.

——. 2000. 'Red Flag Flying on the Roof of the World: Inside the Revolution in Nepal: Interview with Comrade Prachanda' in *Revolutionary Worker*, No. 1043, 20 February.

Panday, Devendra Raj. 2000. *Nepal's Failed Development: Reflections on the Mission and the Maladies.* Kathmandu: Nepal South Asia Centre.

Pettigrew, Judith and Sara Shneiderman. 2003. 'Women and the Maobaadi: Ideology and Agency in Nepal's Maoist Movement' in *Himal Southasian*, January.

'Prachanda'. 2004. 'Problem of Women's Emancipation and the Need of Today' in *Problems and Prospects of Revolution in Nepal (A Collection of Articles by Comrade Prachanda and Other Leaders of Communist Party of Nepal [Maoist]).* Kathmandu: Janadisha Publications.

Sharma, Mandira and Dinesh Prasain. 2004. 'Gender Dimensions of the People's War: Some Reflections on the Experiences of Rural Women' in *Himalayan 'People's War': Nepal's Maoist Rebellion*, Michael Hutt (ed). London: C. Hurst & Co.

Sharma, Sudhindra and Pawan Kumar Sen. 1999. *General Election Opinion Poll: How Voters Assess Politics, Parties and Politicians.* Kathmandu: Himal Association.

Thapa, Deepak and Bandita Sijapati. 2004. *A Kingdom under Siege: Nepal's Maoist Insurgency, 1996-2004.* Kathmandu: The Printhouse.

The Worker. 1996. 'Appeal of the C.P.N. (Maoist) to the People', Vol 2, June.

Yami, Hisila. 2007. *People's War and Women's Liberation in Nepal.* Kathmandu: Janadhwai Publication.

A Deft Defence

DEEPAK ADHIKARI

On a clear moonlit night in autumn, around 800 Maoist cadres led by Nanda Kishor Pun 'Pasang' marched towards a training camp of the Armed Police Force (APF) in Bhalubang, a small town in Dang district that serves as a gateway to the midwestern region of Nepal. They had trekked south for several days from their stronghold in Rolpa, venturing boldly into enemy territory.

Two days earlier, on October 11, 2003, a rebel attack on an APF camp further west in Kusum, Banke district, had gone horribly wrong. Plans for the attack were leaked, and two dozen Maoist rebels—including a company commander and vice-commander—were killed and an equal number injured. Undeterred, the guerrillas were targeting the strongly fortified base of the APF. The attack on Bhalubang was all the more important because it followed a seven-month ceasefire that had broken down in August after soldiers of the then Royal Nepal Army killed nineteen unarmed Maoists in the village of Doramba in Ramechhap district (Adhikari 2014: 82).

A feisty platoon commander in her early twenties, going by the nom de guerre 'Kushal Rakshya', led the first assault with sixteen guerrillas. At midnight, they surrounded the camp and opened fire. As two other assault groups advanced from the banks of the Rapti River, the APF troops activated landmines. Kushal Rakshya saw her comrades fall one by one; others perished in a hail of gunfire as they tried to penetrate the layers of barbed wire that surrounded the camp. The death of her comrades filled her with vengeance. She threw her rifle aside and grabbed a dead rebel's M-16 and began firing. 'I wanted to win the war at any cost, but I also wanted to make sure none of our combatants was injured. I was single then, but my soldiers had wives and children,' she recalled.

As the battle dragged on into the night, the number of wounded increased, and at around 2:30 a.m., she was shot in the leg. Her fellow guerrillas helped her to limp to the makeshift medical post at the rear of the battlefield.

At noon the next day, the state security forces struck the medical camp where she and dozens of wounded were being treated. Escaping with the help of 'volunteers'—men and women recruited by the Maoists—it took three days to reach relative safety in the jungle at Ratmate that straddles Dang and Rolpa. But it was not secure for long—the government troops attacked the next day. Terrified Maoist fighters pleaded with Kushal Rakshya to allow them to retreat. She was the only commander and one by one, her comrades fled the jungle hide-out. Hours later, she heard gunshots nearby. During a brief lull Kushal Rakshya and a fellow fighter crawled through the shallow waters of the stream, dodging gunshots. Jittery and panic-stricken, her comrade started crying.

Kushal Rakshya realised that remaining under water was safer than hiding under trees. The two removed their bandages and plunged into a pool below a waterfall. Soon, they were attacked with 81-mm mortar guns. Kushal Rakshya knew how to swim, but her companion didn't. She handed her a log to keep afloat. A little later, two guerrillas returned to carry Kushal Rakshya's companion to safety. She was left behind because there was an unofficial policy according to which wounded guerrillas from the same command were prioritised for rescue (the party later amended this policy).

Alone and desperate, Kushal Rakshya feared for her life, debilitated by a profusely bleeding leg, hunger and exhaustion. She pleaded with an elderly shepherd for help, but he was reluctant, fearing a backlash from security personnel, who had already killed one of his goats. 'Please save me,' she cried. 'Please carry me to my home in Rolpa. Please, my mother is waiting for me.' He changed his mind and helped her limp along the trail to a secure place. Hours later, he came back with his wife, a wicker basket and some clothes. At the couple's small shed, she was fed and clothed. Three of the seven bullets that hit her were still lodged in her leg, and her wounds began to fester. She spent nights crying in pain and her hosts joined her in empathy, creating a chorus that echoed through the hills.

Three days later, the shepherd ran into some party members at a local pharmacy. When he told them about a wounded rebel, they followed him to the shed, surprised to find her alive. After hurried first aid, she was carried off on a bamboo stretcher.

Who was this gutsy warrior and where did she come from?

Joining the ranks

Kushal Rakshya grew up in a large well-to-do ethnic Magar family in the hamlet of Korchabang in Rolpa district, the pampered youngest of six sisters and three brothers. Their paddy fields ensured sufficient food for the family; their mud and stone house served as a shelter for Maoist leaders.

Hers was a childhood that resembled a normal coming of age in the hills of rural Nepal. She used to set out at six in the morning, walking for an hour to reach the Yug Pokhara Secondary School. From her own accounts, Kushal Rakshya emerged as a fearless, confident and precocious child. 'I was a class monitor in school, so even boys used to be scared of me,' she recalled.

The Magars are the third-largest indigenous group, accounting for about 7 per cent of country's population. Though they are spread across the country, the mountainous region that extends from Mount Dhaulagiri to the Kali Gandaki river basin in midwestern Nepal is their stronghold.

The Maoists' association with the Magars ran deep. The Magars had already been subjected to state suppression for their support of radical communists, including the legendary leader Mohan Bikram Singh, whose foray into the region in the mid-1950s radicalised many local youth. Several communist agitations led to a strong foothold in the region. The state did everything in its power to suppress political dissent. In 1995, the Nepal Police launched

'Operation Romeo' in Rolpa district, arresting more than 300 locals, and forcing villagers to flee. Rolpa had been a stronghold of the Samyukta Jana Morcha Nepal, a Maoist front organisation. Krishna Bahadur Mahara, a former school teacher and Barman Budha Magar, a popular local leader, were elected in the parliamentary polls in 1991 (de Sales 2010).

In 1994, when Kushal Rakshya was eleven years old, she dropped out of school for two years due to a serious injury. When she returned following medical treatment in Kathmandu, the Maoist 'People's War' had gripped her mountain village. 'Everyone in our family had joined the Maoists, even the children. There was great police repression,' she said.

On April 23, 1999, when she was sixteen, Kushal Rakshya and her friend 'Sapan Shila', who was twenty-one, joined over a hundred young men in a military training session in Hanning, a hamlet of Rolpa. Until then, only two other women, known by their noms de guerre 'Samjhana' and 'Nabina', who would go on to become legends among fighters, had joined the Maoist army. Kushal Rakshya was a ninth-grader and active in the student organisation of the Maoist party. While her family had plans to send her to an English-medium school in Dang, the young student was all set to join the rebel army.

From her home in Korchabang, Kushal Rakshya trekked with Sapan Shila for three hours to a Maoist redoubt higher up in the hills. First they were trained in the use of lathis (batons). A week later, Maoist commanders taught them how to use the khukuri, a traditional curved knife. A month later, a Maoist commander who went by the name of Prakash taught them how to use guns. 'I closed my eyes and fired a shot,' she recalled. As part of the training, she was given a backpack weighing 5 kilograms and was ordered to run for 3 kilometres through the forest. 'We were tired, running through the trails and even considered quitting!' she recalled.

Then came the inevitable step of cutting their hair. Kushal Rakshya didn't feel very different, as her hair was already cropped. At home, she used to be called 'Kanchho', a term of endearment reserved for the youngest son. In comparison, her friend Sapan

Shila's hair was long and thick; she cried when she had to part with her tresses.

She was given a small backpack and books in Nepali on Marxism, Leninism and Maoism and biographies of Karl Marx, Frederick Engels and Jenny Marx. She had not carried anything from home. When Kushal Rakshya joined the force, the Maoists had yet to form the People's Liberation Army. But by the time she signed up, the police had unleashed a brutal search and kill operation codenamed 'Kilo Sierra 2' in more than a dozen districts, driving villagers into the Maoists' arms. In early 1998, a year before the launch of the ten-month-long counter-insurgency operation, Prime Minister Girija Prasad Koirala had offered an olive branch, but the rebels had turned it down. The state responded by launching the crackdown, killing 500 people and arresting thousands. Kushal Rakshya and hundreds of young people were part of the wave that swelled the Maoist ranks after the operation. She and others were organised into Ladaku Dals or fighting groups, consisting of eleven members each.

Their drafting was followed by an advanced training six months later. In Sukedaha village of Rolpa, Kushal Rakshya was happy to be one among seventeen women and 250 men who had gathered for a month-long military training. They were given combat fatigues and arms training, including advanced training on the use of a rifle. Early every morning, they ran up and down the hills as part of the daily drill. They attended classes on military theory and discipline and were taught the virtues of a good soldier. 'We took practical lessons on how to launch an attack and detonate landmines and how to take cover when under attack,' she recalled.

Kushal Rakshya was yet to take part in battle. That moment came on February 19, 2000. She was part of a temporary company led by Pasang to attack a base camp of the Nepal Police in Ghartigaun of Rolpa district. It was only during training in Sukedaha that she had heard enemy gunfire. Now the battle was closer and her cousin 'Gulab', who had earlier trained her to use arms, was also among the force. They launched the attack through assault groups in seventeen areas. She and Sapan Shila were in the second assault. The Maoists found thatches nearby and used them to set houses on fire. They blasted grenades, killing seventeen of the security forces, including an inspector. Later, for the first time ever, she saw the bodies of her fellow comrades: Sankalpa and Sandesh. 'We were worried because we didn't know what was going to happen next. But it also gave us a sense of purpose. We would quickly salute the fallen comrades and vow to fulfil their dreams,' she said.

Taking on the Royal Army

By 2001, the Maoists had defeated the Nepal Police and were inexorably drawn into the war with the Royal Nepal Army. In June, King Birendra and several members of the royal family were killed in what came to be known as the Palace Massacre. A month later, the government and rebels agreed to cease offensive actions against each other and peace talks began in August. The truce was tenuous at best because there was no ceasefire code of ethics. Under the pretext of peace talks, both sides prepared for the inevitable war. In September 2001, in Kureli village of Rolpa, the Maoists convened the first national assembly of the newly launched People's Liberation Army (PLA) and named Pushpa Kamal Dahal 'Prachanda' its supreme commander.

The government and the Maoists each waited for the other to blink. On November 23, 2001, the rebels ended the four-month ceasefire by carrying out their most audacious operation yet by attacking the army in Ghorahi, the headquarters of Dang. Scores of soldiers and a number of policemen were killed in the strikes, and seventy Maoist comrades were freed from jails. Prime Minister Deuba announced a state of emergency; civil rights were suspended and the Royal Nepal Army was mobilised for the first time since the Maoists launched hostilities five years earlier. The Maoists were declared 'terrorists.' The war rapidly escalated, and more than 100 people were killed in the next three days.

Kushal Rakshya was one of fifty soldiers of the newly formed PLA who descended along the steep hills, negotiating rock strewn paths and streams, to the Dang Valley to carry out the PLA's biggest attack on Ghorahi, the town on the valley's eastern edge (Chalaune 2009:17). From the village of Sirpa in Rolpa district, she accompanied her long-time companion Sapan Shila and Sapana, a section commander. Carrying a backpack with 150 rounds of bullets and a .303 rifle slung over her shoulder, she was determined to perform her duty as a section vice commander. 'A gun gave us strength to overcome fear. Even the combat fatigues boosted our confidence,' she said, recalling that whenever she returned home in civilian dress, she feared that security forces might kill her. 'While in battle, I was motivated to kill the enemy because not doing so meant risking my own life,' she said.

With the attack on Dang, she returned to the military life she cherished. She had recently been a bodyguard for Hisila Yami, Maoist leader and wife of Baburam Bhattarai, the party's ideologue. After the couple left for India, she had been redeployed to the Maoist army. 'I was looking forward to the attack. The mood was upbeat and we three women encouraged one another to fight and accomplish our goal,' she recalled. Experienced fighters like Kushal Rakshya were much sought-after among the Maoists because for the first few years, the party had very few women combatants. Among a group of twenty or thirty combatants, hardly two or three were women. Kushal Rakshya said the new recruits in the PLA entered with typical patriarchal mindsets. 'Most leaders of our party were well aware of women's issues and treated us on equal terms, but new recruits viewed women as inferior. After several months however, they changed their views and began to respect women,' she recalled.

Kushal Rakshya was a member of one of twenty-four assault groups under Pasang, which were responsible for launching an attack on the main gate of the heavily fortified Royal Nepal Army base with six barracks, three communication posts, and fourteen sentry posts as well as bunkers and trenches. They confronted around 250 soldiers under the command of a major. By 3 a.m. they had captured a huge cache of arms; dozens of soldiers had surrendered and the barracks had been reduced to rubble. The Maoists had several trucks on standby to transport the cache of plundered arms. She boarded one of the trucks as they drove to Dahaban in Rolpa district. En route, she and other fighters learned to fire light machine guns (LMGs) and the more portable sub-machine guns (SMGs). At noon, when she made it to the shelter, she was greeted with news of loss: Sapana and her husband Bijog, also a commander, had been killed in the battle.

Kushal Rakshya is born

While the death of her close companion was devastating, the Dang attack became memorable in other ways. It was here that the young combatant, officially named Purna Pun and popularly known as Bina, renamed herself. Like most Maoist guerrillas, she was an avid reader of books by Russian and Chinese writers such as *Mother* by Maxim Gorky and *Shining Red Star* by Li Xintian. Inspired by protagonists who had two first names, she decided to follow suit.

'After the attack on Dang, I named myself "Kushal Rakshya" which translates in English to Deft Defence,' she said. Her friend Rewati Gharti Magar, who until then was called the unappealing name Chhahari (Shade), named herself 'Sapan Shila' (a variation of Sahanshil, meaning Tolerant). The underground party's policy dictated that any new entrant could adopt a new first name without a surname. Although assuming a fresh identity was in tune with the party's vision of a new, revolutionary path, in practical terms, it was also for security reasons: once they adopted new names, state security forces, which relied on old records, would be unable to trace them.

The loss of women commanders like Sapana was acutely felt. Both male and female leaders of the party highlighted the fact that over 40 per cent of the PLA guerrillas were women (Yami 2004). While it is nearly impossible to verify this claim because most of the battle-hardened soldiers were transferred in 2005 to the party's wings such as the Young Communist League, the party struggled to fill its senior military positions with women. At each post-battle review, Kushal Rakshya fought for a greater role for women. 'We discussed how many rounds a fighter fired, what his/her responsibilities were and whether or not he/she fulfilled them. I made it a point to raise the issue of senior positions for women,' she said.

War involves tough jobs, such as laying ambushes and mines and commanding military posts. Most male guerrillas, according to her, were of the view that women were incapable of such 'masculine' tasks. 'But we proved them wrong. We excelled in everything, be it training or drills. In the first major battle in Dang in November 2001, we displayed courage and military acumen, dispelling misconceptions about us,' she said. After the battle of Dang, women carried out reconnaissance missions, gathered intelligence reports and took charge of the safety of large numbers of troops. 'Even within the PLA, we had to fight for our rights,' she said.

She recalled the battle of Ghartigaun where she was one of 800 Maoist fighters deployed to tackle the state security forces. Her assault group was given a .303 rifle, but it was commander Sangam who had authority over it. She got a chance to fire it only after the end of the battle. 'Even our commanders thought that if women were in a majority, the opponents would humiliate us.' she said. 'But their perceptions changed after we fought alongside them. We demonstrated that we were equally strong.'

Many women fighters either left the PLA after marriage or were not given higher responsibilities. The two pioneering women guerrillas Nabina and Samjhana only fought until late 2001. When the government mobilised the Royal Nepal Army against the Maoists, the two had already left the party. This made Kushal Rakshya, who once headed a women-only Maoist platoon, one of only a few women commanders.

To make matters worse, Sapan Shila was killed on September 17, 2003, in an attack on a training camp in Bhabang area of Rolpa district. She had risen to the level of company commander and was one of the fifty Maoists killed in the attack by security forces. Kushal Rakshya heard the news that very day. In shock, she refused to eat. Her mind was flooded with memories of their time together. 'Sapan Shila was my closest friend. I still miss her. Her death was devastating. I lost an intimate friend and fellow fighter,' she said.

Kushal Rakshya considered her a mentor, a senior on whom she could lean. She described Sapan Shila as an intrepid guerrilla, who implored her not to depend on men and become a tough commander in her own right. Together, the two had garnered a reputation of being fearless fighters on par with men. This standing in the party would see her through a low phase which tested her courage in a different way.

After being severely wounded in the battle of Bhalubang, she stayed home in Korchabang for several months in late 2003 to recuperate, until the party decided that she needed advanced medical treatment in India. The Maoists had established a network of party cadres who helped wounded rebels travel secretly to hospitals in India. One late afternoon in April 2004, two Maoist cadres arrived at her shelter in Gugauli, a border village in Kapilvastu district in the southern plains. Kushal Rakshya rode pillion on a motorbike through a dense forest on the border, and on the Indian side of the border, she met a Maoist leader. After more nerve-racking rides by bus and train along the north Indian plains, she arrived at the hospital in Lucknow late that night. The state security forces patrolled the Nepal side of the border because they knew Maoists used it as a gateway for their cadres' safe passage to India. She shudders at the memory: 'I still feel scared when I remember the journey. I was more worried about my trip back'.

The two Maoist cadres who helped her safely across the border were killed in a raid upon their return to Nepal. 'The news was unbearable; their lives were lost trying to save me. They were assigned the riskiest of jobs', she said. At the hospital in Lucknow, Indian doctors advised against extracting the bullet lodged in her leg because it would damage a vein, which in turn could cause paralysis. She returned home much better, but with a bullet still in her leg. She was not keen on going back to the battlefront, but there was pressure to re-join the army, due to the shortage of experienced female fighters. At the battle of Beni on March 20, 2004, several thousand PLA soldiers overran the district headquarters and achieved yet another military victory.

Love in the time of war

In the autumn of 2005, Kushal Rakshya, having participated in the battle of Khara (Cowan 2008) in April that year, received orders to move eastward to the Gandak region in central Nepal. Leading a group of 110 PLA soldiers, Kushal Rakshya, now twenty-two years old and promoted to battalion commander, left Jhyam, a village of Rolpa and trekked through Baglung district, arriving in the village of Kharkakot in Gulmi district a month later.

The Maoists had signed a deal with pro-democracy political parties to protest against King Gyanendra Shah, who had usurped executive power in a bloodless coup earlier that year. While the parliamentary parties organised mass rallies and protests against the king, the Maoists launched a strategy called Dhadhma Tekera Taukoma Hanne (stepping on the back and striking on the head). For the rebels, the capital Kathmandu represented the head and the back referred to areas surrounding it.

This was when she met her future husband, Tuk Bahadur Thapa 'Arjun', a brigade commander of the PLA. He was escorting PLA's Deputy Commander Janardan Sharma 'Prabhakar' when they met. 'Her style was different from other women PLAs. I was impressed,' said Arjun, who now lives with Kushal Rakshya and their two-year-old son in Kawasoti, a small town of Nawalparasi district in south-central Nepal.

The PLA was preparing for an attack on Tansen, the headquarters of Palpa district and also considering a raid on Tanahu district. During the reconnaissance mission, Arjun helped Kushal Rakshya and her troops. It was the first time a woman was commanding a force in the region. 'Commanders were always men. Even if there was a woman company commander, she would be under a battalion commander, almost always a man,' he said. Unlike the PLA's Western Division where she had spent most of her war years and had intimate knowledge of the topography, the Gandak region was unfamiliar, but Arjun remembers Kushal Rakshya as being fearless.

As the PLA soldiers trekked through the central hills of Palpa, Tanahu and Kaski, they enjoyed relative respite, which allowed them to mingle with one another. Although Kushal Rakshya and Arjun had met in Rolpa during a training camp in April 2002, the two hadn't spoken to each other. She was with the PLA's First Brigade while he was in the Fourth Brigade. Kushal Rakshya and her women colleagues were considered experienced and smart. A quiet man with a prize fighter's body, Arjun, a village boy from a Thapa family in Gorkha district, kept to himself.

For several months in early 2006, Kushal Rakshya and Arjun travelled together, retreating when the army advanced and staying at shelters arranged by the local party committees. The Maoists encouraged inter-caste marriages, but both were required to make a request about the union to their commander. As their love blossomed, word reached their commander, Yam Bahadur Adhikari 'Pratikshya', who talked to each of them separately to ascertain that both were willing.

What brought them closer was their poignant personal history. In 2004, six months after Kushal Rakshya's first marriage, her husband, Mohan Roka 'Grishma', a commander whom she met during the battle of Dang, was killed in an attack in Dhankhola, Arghakhachi district. Arjun had gone through a similar experience of loss. In February 2004, he had married Dil Maya Gurung 'Pragya', a woman guerrilla from Tanahu district. On May 19, 2004, a group of seven Maoists was killed in an encounter with the state security forces in Chitwan. Pragya was one of them. Both Arjun and Kushal Rakshya cherished memories of their partners who had 'sacrificed their lives for the revolution'. In August 2006, on the last day of a military training in Bhujung Khola of Kaski district, seven couples including Kushal Rakshya and Arjun got married at a janabadi bibaha, a party-sanctioned group wedding popularised by the Maoists.

Men and women worked closely in the PLA. The combatants had to spend time away from home for several months, even years. As there were fewer women, they received multiple proposals from lonely fellow combatants. The party didn't allow unmarried couples to live together. 'Those who couldn't follow the strict policy left the PLA. Even senior commanders were punished for sanskritik bichalan [a euphemism for adultery],' Kushal Rakshya said.

Curious to know Arjun's views on women and their emancipation that the Maoists passionately championed, I was taken aback when the PLA commander said: 'I think women are weaker and we need to support them.' But over the course of our conversation that stretched for several days in mid-April 2015, he appeared to have changed his views. 'Our women fighters were trustworthy; they never revealed party secrets. As far as torture is concerned, women endured the severest form, that is rape, but men had only to bear beatings,' he told me as we sat at the couple's one-room apartment in a single-storey concrete home. 'Another trait that women possessed was sacrifice. Even our enemy underestimated women fighters, only to realise this mistake later,' he said.

About his wife, Arjun observed, 'She's a rebel who fights against injustice. Our elders teach women to tolerate everything, but she would not tolerate injustice,' he said. Kushal Rakshya is the only woman commander who took part in and led major military attacks. 'The reason she was frequently wounded was that she was always on the frontlines,' Arjun said.

After the war

On November 15, 2007, Kushal Rakshya was one of 19,602 PLA soldiers verified by the United Nations Mission in Nepal (UNMIN). The UNMIN, however, disqualified more than 10,000 Maoist fighters, deeming them under-aged or late recruits. The PLA force was sequestered in seven main and twenty-one satellite makeshift camps across the country. Kushal Rakshya was deployed to the PLA's Fourth Division in a cantonment in Jhyaltungdanda, not far from where she now lives.

For the first few years, the PLA soldiers were feted by the powers that be. Kushal Rakshya recalled that in early 2009, dignitaries from Kathmandu visited the cantonment in Hattikhor of Nawalparasi and attended a show of strength by the PLA. 'We were very happy because we were assured by our leaders that we would soon join the Nepal Army and would serve people and our nation,' she said.

Once the PLA soldiers were cantoned, their life took a new turn.

Their routine suddenly changed; guerrillas now began to socialise. The pressure of civilian life began to weigh on them. Hundreds of PLA soldiers married. The meagre monthly stipend of 6,000 Nepali rupees was never enough. 'Many began income-generating schemes such as raising chickens and pigs inside the camps,' Kushal Rakshya recalled. Women combatants with babies were allowed to stay outside the cantonments, but this only put an extra burden on their expenses because they had to rent rooms in towns and bazaars close to the camps. All along, she kept fighting for the rights of women combatants. 'When our party was in power, our leaders persuaded the Peace and Reconstruction Ministry to provide free school education for the children of PLA soldiers. They had even promised to set up a Montessori for our kids, but nothing happened,' she said.

When she was verified by the UNMIN, Kushal Rakshya was a battalion commander at the PLA's Salim Mandal Nishan Smriti Brigade, but was later promoted to brigade vice commander. In November 2011, the government offered three alternatives to the former PLA soldiers and regrouped them accordingly. They were to be rehabilitated and integrated into the ranks of the Nepal Army and offered a retirement package of 500,000 to 800,000 Nepali rupees for rehabilitation and vocational training. The PLA soldiers overwhelmingly chose to join the national army in numbers that clearly exceeded expectations. Their integration into the Nepal Army, was however, delayed due to differences between the Maoists and the Nepali Congress and the Communist Party of Nepal (Unified Marxist-Leninist). The enthusiasm to join their former enemy did not last long and the feeling of having been cheated slowly grew.

On April 10, 2012, the Maoist leaders decided to hand over control of the PLA cantonments to the Nepal Army, now stripped of its 'Royal' prefix after Nepal became a republic through a vote in the Constituent Assembly in 2008, fulfilling one of the tenets of the peace deal. The decision was hailed by the international community and Nepal's political parties as 'historic'; but it deepened the ongoing conflict within the Maoist party, with the vast majority of PLA soldiers viewing it as a betrayal of the revolution (Basnet 2015). The majority of them chose voluntary retirement and only about 1,400 opted for integration into the Nepal Army. Yam Bahadur Adhikari 'Pratikshya', the commander who approved Kushal Rakshya's marriage, is now a Lieutenant Colonel of the Nepal Army, the highest ranking Maoist to be integrated as part of the deal.

The disillusionment following the agreement to disband the PLA soldiers has now become a tragic yet familiar story of the 'people's war'. But PLA commanders such as Kushal Rakshya and Arjun genuinely thought that they were going to join the national army with a major's rank, as promised by Prachanda. Kushal Rakshya and Arjun chose the voluntary retirement package. 'We had never thought that our party would abandon us. We had hoped that as in the war when our party was our saviour, in peacetime too, it would support us. After dreams of ushering in a Communist era, we never thought we would end up like this,' said Kushal Rakshya.

The journey from military life in cantonments to settling down as civilians eking out a living proved long and agonising. In autumn 2012, after the cantonments were taken over by the Nepal Army[1] and the former rebels were forced out, she and Arjun took a break. Arjun headed east, crossed the border to India and visited Darjeeling. Kushal Rakshya headed west and travelled to the Bheri and Karnali regions. 'We were used to living in army quarters and in groups. It was difficult for us to settle down,' she said.

Displaying the fortitude earned after years in combat, the former rebel couple moved on, investing in a livestock farm in Nawalparasi: 'PLA Livestock.' They also work as insurance agents, persuading middle-class people to buy policies.

---

[1] On April 10, 2012, during a meeting of the Army Integration Special Committee, a cross-party committee headed by Prime Minister Baburam Bhattarai and Maoist chairman Prachanda proposed to hand over the control of the Maoist cantonments to the Nepal Army. By then, only 3,129 former combatants remained in the camps. Following government orders, Nepal Army soldiers entered the cantonments. Clashes broke out; angry PLA soldiers set vehicles on fire; their chain of command was broken. Hardline Maoists accused the leadership of 'surrender', but the Maoists had signed a deal with three political parties on November 1, 2011 to disband the PLA.

It wasn't easy for Kushal Rakshya to transition from being a soldier to a mother. 'While we were living in the cantonment, we were hoping to join the Nepal Army and so we had deferred parenthood. But things changed after we took the voluntary retirement package,' she said. Kushal Rakshya gave birth to a baby boy on August 12, 2013 at Maula Kalika Hospital in Bharatpur in Chitwan district. The couple named the boy Samin. As a civilian, it was not difficult to be a mother. She quickly learned to adapt to her new life of nurturing her baby. Now she finds motherhood a fulfilling experience. She wants to ensure that her son is given the best education. She wants him to be a medical doctor, but she accepts the fact that he may have different ideas.

Kushal Rakshya and Arjun divide their time between Kawasoti, where they have a cattle farm and Kathmandu, sharing a ground-floor apartment with Arjun's parents in the neighbourhood of Siddhartha Banasthali on the city's outskirts. 'Arjun's father is a former British Army soldier. It's a traditional household, but they know what military life is,' she said.

In the summer of 2014, Kushal Rakshya, Leela Sharma 'Asmita', a former PLA commander and dozens of former Maoist guerrillas established the Former Women PLA Academy to support erstwhile women fighters. In late 2014, she moved to Nawalparasi and set up a district branch of the Academy with the goal of preserving the history of women combatants. 'When our leaders travel to Germany, they want to learn about Rosa Luxemburg, the Marxist philosopher. In a similar manner, we want to showcase our history which we are proud of. We want to tell future generations how we fought alongside men and how we defied traditional notions about women,' she said. The group plans to visit battlefields, collect information and photographs and set up a museum.

Through the organisation, she and other former women guerrillas have organised awareness campaigns for religious minorities. The day I met her in Rajahar, a village in Nawalparasi district home to about fifty Muslim households, the group was engaged in one such campaign. Inside a building of a local forest users' group on that sweltering afternoon, she chaired a meeting of more than hundred Muslim people and party representatives voicing anger at the state's discrimination. They were demanding burial grounds for Muslims in the Hindu majority country.

More meetings were followed by a visit to a local mosque and meeting with Muslim community leaders. Dusk was falling as we staggered towards her home in Kawasoti. I wondered how she reconciled her seemingly anti-religious communist ideology with a campaign targeted for the benefit of a religious community. The question didn't bother her at all. For her, it was yet another way of helping people. She spoke of Nepal's diversity and added that her organisation was keen to help people of any religion. 'It's their choice, their faith. We wanted to support them because no one cares about them. They don't figure in the agenda of local political parties,' she said. 'They have faced discrimination from local leaders who refuse to recognise their faith. I thought we could do something to minimise their suffering.'

Later that day, Kushal Rakshya discussed plans to raise funds through the Academy to provide Muslim women income generating skills such as sewing. Projects like these give her a sense of purpose. 'When I think about my past, about the betrayal we felt years after the peace deal, I feel dissatisfied. Ever since I have spent my time and energy on the Academy, I have been occupied with the work we have been doing. It will definitely make a difference in the lives of these women,' she said.

Bibliography

Adhikari, Aditya. 2014. *The Bullet and the Ballot Box: The Story of Nepal's Maoist Revolution*. New Delhi: Aleph Book Company.

Basnet, Madhab. 2015. 'Biraktiyera Bideshtira (Headed Abroad After Frustration)', *Nepal Weekly*, 8 March, Kathmandu.

Chalaune, Uday Bahadur, 'Dipak'. 2009. *Janayuddha Ra Janamukti Sena: Saiddhantik Adhar Ra Karyaniti* (*The People's War and the People's Liberation Army: Theoretical Basis and Tactics*). Kathmandu: People's Liberation Army, Nepal, Sixth Division.

Cowan, Sam. 2008. 'The Lost Battles of Khara and Pili', *Himal Southasian,* September, Kathmandu.

Sales, Anne de. 2010. 'Biography of a Magar Communist', in David N. Gellner, ed., *Varieties of Activist Experience: Civil Society in South Asia,* New Delhi: Sage Publications.

United Nations Mission in Nepal. 'Arms Monitoring'. Available at http://un.org.np/unmin-archive/?d=activities&p=arms Accessed in July 2016.

Yami, Hisila, 'Parvati'. 2004. 'Women's Participation in People's Army', in *The Worker*: #9.

The Battle Within

SEWA BHATTARAI

'The thought of having a baby made me feel caged, like I was being punished,' says 'Anoopam', a battalion commander in the Maoist army. The twenty-three-year-old, at the height of her career, had seen how motherhood stripped women of position and prospects of advancement in the party. She was not going to take that risk. When she discovered that she was pregnant, she told no one except her husband. She quietly underwent an abortion and was soon back to business. Her business was to lead her troops to battle.

Thus it was that on a hot, sunny day, Anoopam was at the head of her battalion, marching towards Syangja. They had been walking for a month, and Anoopam was reeling because of her recent abortion. She had no appetite, her stomach ached constantly and even short walks tired her. However, the only thought in her consciousness was that as a battalion commander she had a job to do.

'I led my team to victory that day, despite everything,' says Anoopam. 'The fight was ten hours long.' Her visible pride in her fighting capability was a poignant contrast to her soft-spoken self, as she went about preparing dinner for her husband and daughter in a cramped one-room apartment.

Anoopam, whose given name is Bhagawati Thapa, is a former Maoist soldier, one of the 3,846 women certified as a combatant of the PLA (People's Liberation Army) in 2006. Many former soldiers like her now live all over the country, in all appearances indistinguishable from the woman next door. But Anoopam, with almost twenty years of close association with the Maoist party, is no ordinary housewife, though her life today may not appear otherwise.

During the decade-long conflict, the Maoist party claimed that the membership of women in the party ranged from 33 to 50 per cent. The oft-quoted figure was 40 per cent (Pettigrew and Shneiderman 2004). After the peace accord, when the Maoist combatants began registering with the United Nations Mission in Nepal (UNMIN), the percentage of female combatants was found to be much lower than the purported figure—only 3,846 women out of a total of 19,602 verified combatants or 20 per cent. However, this figure does not account for the women who were involved in the Maoist party as full-time political workers and dedicated sympathisers. Many women were 'whole timers' of the party not only as soldiers, but as political, medical, cultural or administrative workers and lived and travelled with their party colleagues for years. They imbibed the party's values and ideology and internalised them, emerging with a significantly different personality.

By the time Anoopam joined the Maoist party at the age of twelve, the party was at war. Coming from the remote district of Jajarkot in western Nepal, which was one of the bases of the Maoist party, Anoopam already had a strong motivation to defy the state, and a determination to be a part of the armed militia. Several people she knew, including her cousin, had been murdered for supporting the Maoist party; when she joined the party it was with the encouragement of her family.

What constitutes the 'strong' is usually defined against what is considered 'weak'. In the hyper-masculine environment of war, strong was everything masculine, and weak was its exact opposite, the feminine. Fighting was what Anoopam was supposed to excel in, and everything else was trivial. And from a very early age, Anoopam wanted to excel. The young girl was given a gun, an old model, too heavy for her small frame. When her party colleagues doubted that she would be able to wield it, she cut the gun's barrel at its tip, making it light enough to carry.

Anoopam rose quickly through the ranks. Her first marriage as a sixteen-year-old had ended when her husband died in combat a year later, and she had not wanted to remarry. Later, everyone in the party persuaded her to consider the proposal of a journalist friend of her late husband. She accepted, but what she had not bargained for was a child. Anoopam was in no mood to have a baby. 'I wanted to rise up in the ranks,' she says. 'I felt that I could fulfil any responsibility given to me.'

She decided to abort, but could not get the necessary medicine until she was three months pregnant. When she finally procured the pills, the pharmacist advised her to take them at an interval of two hours each. Anoopam swallowed all the medicines in a single gulp. 'I wanted to make sure it worked,' Anoopam recounts. The next day she bled and bled, her blood coming out alternately in clots and streams. It seemed never to stop. When she lay down to rest in the sun, the blood formed a puddle around her. She told her friends that the bleeding was a side-effect of medication for menstrual cramps. She went on to lead her battalion to battle with nary a complaint. 'If the man next to me was doing it, I had to as well,' says Anoopam, 'I could not display any weakness by bringing up personal problems.'

Anoopam's attitude represents the perspective on women's experiences in war prevailing at the time: to bypass the personal. There were a number of women who took risks and put their health rather than their careers in jeopardy. As Cynthia Enloe writes in *The Morning After: Sexual Politics at the End of the Cold War*, 'The well-known commentators who then occupied the center stage of almost any critical discussion of imperialism or foreign interventionism apparently believed that there was little to be gained by looking at women's lives,' because while men's lives were inherently 'serious' and political, women's are 'private' and 'trivial' (Enloe 1993). Women's stories are thus subsumed into the 'history of mankind,' more so in the case of war, which is a typically masculine affair. The experiences of women, which are often significantly different from those of men, are not considered important enough to be documented or even discussed, let alone respected.

Promise of equality

For many women in rural Nepal, with opportunities for education and careers hard to come by, the Maoist party offered the only way of escaping traditional restrictive gender roles. The Maoist party's promises of emancipation and equal opportunities for women were immensely attractive. 'Girls were told that if they got married, they would be subject to their husband and parents-in-law's authority and would have to work like slaves. They would not achieve anything in life by cutting grass for their husband and their parents-in-law. On the other hand, if they joined the Maoist Party, they would be allowed to choose their own husband. They would be free and be able to dance and sing whenever they wished, they would be able to travel around the country and they would be given soap to wash themselves. Women were also promised pocket money. But above all, they would be given a gun and would be able to eat anywhere free of charge,' writes Satya Shrestha-Schipper.

Women were thus grateful for the opportunities offered by the Maoist party, and attempted to follow every rule set by the party in order to garner benefits. However, adhering to the prescribed standards of behaviour was more difficult for women. When it came to uniquely female experiences, the party enforced the same standards for both men and women. Women were expected to fit into the default template set for men, requiring them to make changes to their lifestyle, behaviour or values—expectations which did not apply to men. The result was that the experiences of female Maoists differed significantly from those of their male counterparts.

From the very beginning, female soldiers in the Maoist party were expected to abide by the same standards, whether it was their performance in war or how they looked and dressed. Maoist literature during the decade-long conflict gives clues about the ideal 'revolutionary' woman: 'brave,' 'courageous,' 'tough,' and dedicated to the cause. Those who fell in war were given the highest honour, as exemplified by Lekhnath Nyaupane who wrote about his deceased wife in the newspaper *Jana Astha*: 'You fought for light and fell. You became a martyr. Though I am sad to lose you, my head is bowed in respect' (Nyaupane 2004).

Women had thoroughly internalised these revolutionary ideals themselves. 'You can kill me, but you cannot break my dedication towards the revolution,' says Comrade Namuna in the battle memoir of 'Shikhar', a combatant, then in charge of the district of Bara. 'Sacrifice is made by a revolutionary, not by a particular caste or sex' ('Shikhar' 2004).

Their value systems were shaped by the ideals of armed conflict. Maoist women, even today, resent the notion that women are 'soft' creatures. 'It is said that man is the sky, and woman is the earth,' said Dharamsheela Chapagain, 45, district head of the Maoist party in Jhapa and a former elected Member of Parliament. She cited an oft-quoted line among Maoist women of Nepal, 'Why is woman compared to the earth? Because she is tolerant. She endures pain, which makes her strong and patient.' Chapagain believes that a woman's capacity to be soft and caring is given to her by nature, and it is something to be proud of. But Chapagain is also quick to add that women's capacity to nurture is misused by society to limit women to their roles as caregivers.

As a political leader who mostly worked in creating political organisations and leading social movements, Chapagain had never fought in an armed battle. Yet, even a non-combatant like Chapagain was quick to point out cases of women's aggression and victory. A case cited by many women was that of Kalikot. Some women of Kalikot were routinely harassed by police officers—a case also recorded by Kailash Rai (2013) in her comprehensive documentation of Maoist women's experiences. One day in 1998, women chased a group of police officers into a tunnel, sealed them inside, and set it on fire. 'Sometimes, the one who is the most oppressed reacts with the most ferocity,' says Chapagain, explaining the Kalikot women's violent reactions. 'Women being a most suppressed group, have a lot of latent aggression in them. And they can be not only tough but cruel too, if the situation demands.' Similar explanations were provided by other Maoist women, who more often than not, took pride in female aggression, whether their own or that of others.

Stripped to essentials

Beginning from their performance in war, the valorising of aggressive masculinity trickled down to how women looked and acted. It also influenced the way they tackled problems in their personal lives. Women's unique experiences in most of these aspects were subsumed in the name of 'equality'. For example, they were expected to give up all kinds of feminine accoutrements; attention to grooming was thought to be, variously, a sign of the feudal value system, slavery and a waste of time. From their denouncement of traditional jewellery to their opposition of modern beauty contests, the Maoist women have opposed what they call the 'objectification of women'. Their ideal is women's emancipation from being an object of desire, hence, attire that exposes the body is unacceptable. Hisila Yami (2004) is critical of what she terms 'imperialist agents' who hold beauty pageants like 'Miss Gurung', 'Miss Newar', 'Miss Tharu' and 'Miss Kathmandu', to target the aspirations of young women in various ethnic groups.

In a radical departure from traditional wear like saris or sarongs, Maoist women wore trousers or shorts and shirts. Yami, along with her daughter, the youth leader Manushi Bhattarai, sports cropped hair. The attire is immediately linked to women's emancipation, as Yami analyses in her famous work *Janayuddha ra Mahila Mukti* (*The People's War and Women's Emancipation*) describing how women, from being vehicles of feudal culture, now represent progress.

This switch to utilitarian apparel was a two-pronged attack on traditional restrictions placed on women: it was thought to be efficient, especially in times of war, and also to liberate women from the oppression that came with traditional wear which restricted movement, especially of the legs. Chapagain cited the example of an abused woman whose husband stripped her of her jewellery, pointing out that the woman was but a vehicle to display the man's prosperity, to be disposed of when she stopped pleasing him.

Maoist women also tend to shun other traditional markers of feminine beauty like long hair and makeup. Focusing on appearance was seen as making a doll out of a woman and reducing her to an object of desire, which was considered a fate to be avoided by any woman who wanted to be her own person and achieve something in non-domestic arenas. 'Wasting time on things like this leads to erosion of intellectual capacities,' says Sarita Regmi, a political leader from Dang who later went on to become a Member of Parliament. She dresses simply, sans makeup. 'Men will go far ahead of us because they do not waste time on these petty things. Instead, if you use that time to read something, or even just talk to people, you learn a lot,' she says.

The unisex look was, thus, a marker of equality, though in reality it too was built on default male standards. Though accepted and encouraged within the party, this radical change in the way women looked would not find easy acceptance in the larger world. Women were often berated in both private and public life for failing to live up to 'normal' feminine standards. Lalita Thapa, 23, of Pokhara, is constantly reproached by her mother-in-law for presenting herself so plainly. The former Maoist soldier does not wear even the simplest makeup. 'She tells me she does not want to wear anything that says she belongs to a man,' says Bhagawati, her mother-in-law, in her sixties, 'But I tell her, accessories are not for a man. It is for yourself. Bangles on the hands, ribbons in the hair. Unmarried women wear them too, and look auspicious.' Silently Thapa turns away, accustomed as she is to this taunting day and night.

The struggle was harder for women in public life. Chapagain was humiliated in front of large audiences for her apparent lack of traditional values. She had been wearing trousers all her life, and continued to do so when she was campaigning for elections in Budhabare in 2008. Her opponent Devendra Dahal said in a speech that Chapagain did not know who she was, she went strutting around in trousers and did not even 'look like a woman'.

Indeed, though their new appearance was theoretically 'equal', it came with considerable struggle for women. It was the male standards that were taken as desirable, and women faced the consequences of this change in both private and public life. Such hurdles did not deter women, and most women who identify as

Maoist continue to be very simply adorned. Many Maoist women, soldiers and political workers alike, expressed relief at the fact that they are valued for their work and not only for their appearance, as women traditionally are.

Love and desire

For women, the respite from being assessed for their looks alone extended to their personal lives: they would be judged for their work and not for their value as romantic and sexual objects. 'Respect' was a word that often came up when women described how they were treated by their male colleagues. They were regarded as party colleagues, as 'comrades', and not as 'women'. In a society that easily accuses women of promiscuity, women were eager to claim that within the party, they were not objects of desire.

'When I started out as a political worker, there were no women like me', remembers Chapagain. 'I was always the lone woman among several men.' Chapagain, as a party whole-timer, dedicated full time to party work, did not live at home. She was still a teenager when she began travelling with party colleagues. She went wherever the party leadership assigned her, conducting political education classes. Accusations of being 'characterless' or having loose morals came from everywhere: contemporaries and villagers, as well as opponents from other parties. To counter these, Chapagain took the only path available to her: to prove her 'good' character by building a sexless persona. 'For me there was never a shadow of doubt', says Chapagain. 'I was treated with respect, we all called each other "comrade".'

Instances of women placing the 'cause' over their romantic or sexual life, are many, though no such examples are found for men. Sarala Regmi had decided to forego marriage, because everyone used to tell her that women tire of politics after marriage. Eventually, Regmi did get married, at the age of twenty-eight, to a fellow Maoist who went by the nom de guerre 'Ayam'. After Ayam was killed in 2001, she married another fellow Maoist, Gunaraj Lohani, in 2006. 'I must say this to those who think I married for sex or children:

I was twenty-eight years old when I first married,' she writes in an anthology of Maoist women's writings (Regmi 2007). 'And my remarriage makes me determined to fulfil the dreams of my first husband, Urmila [Gunaraj's deceased first wife], those of thousands of martyrs.

Anoopam's second marriage is another example of the drive to rise above women's concerns deemed 'personal' or 'trivial' in order to prove herself 'political' and 'serious'. Before any accusations of marrying for the 'wrong' reasons could be flung at her, she made a statement that marital bliss was not what she sought. At her wedding ceremony, typically held on a stage without traditional rituals, she raised her gun and thundered 'after this marriage we will work together for the party. Our union will have more to contribute to the party.'

Chains of purity

Yami (2004) writes that 'Hindu-Arya women are forced to break feudal chains and enter the Peoples' Liberation Army (PLA) to escape the restraints of purity set on them.' Ironically however, the restraints of purity did not break even within the Maoist party. Women idealised the strict regulations of the Maoist party where love came first, then marriage approved by the party, and lastly sexual relations. This was true even of women who belonged to communities known to have less rigorous sexual mores. For example, the labels of purity are rarely applied to Magar women. Molnar (1978) writes that in some Magar villages, 'marriageable girls are openly permitted to have sexual relations with potential marriage partners in community houses where teenagers gather to sing and dance in the evenings.' It would seem that women from these communities lost their rights and freedom when they accepted the more rigid sexual codes endorsed by the party.

And yet, Sapana Rana, 33, a Magar woman from Gorkha, found the Maoists' severe sexual discipline appealing. She calls members of her community 'less disciplined than they should be', and claims that there is no space more disciplined than the Maoist party. On one occasion, after she had settled into civilian life, Rana took the lead in beating up a woman and her lover engaged in an extra-marital affair. This kind of moral policing was commonly carried out by the Maoists during the insurgency, providing a form of vigilante 'justice' in a country where the formal justice system was notoriously slow. Rana, a former party whole-timer, still feels entitled to intervene in the lives of others in the community, with the conviction that she is 'morally right'.

Rana links sexual expression with social ills, mentioning polygamy or extra-marital affairs as the cause of many problems faced by women, including disinheritance and domestic violence. Any deviation from a strict sexual code, according to her, is responsible for breaking up the social fabric and inviting degeneration.

Thus, at a personal level, dissociation from sexuality was necessary for women to be considered of good character and for their dedication to the cause to be taken seriously. On a social level, regulation of sexuality was seen as favouring women and emancipating them from the domestic violence arising from unregulated sexual relations. Regulation of sexuality at both levels was ultimately thought to lead to gender equality in the Maoist framework.

Unequal mothers

Women had little complaint when they were asked to walk the extra mile to achieve equality, but this became problematic when it came to the uniquely female biological experience of motherhood. Typically, the Maoist party had pro-equality policies for motherhood. In fact, these policies went one step ahead by actually providing for extra facilities for women that would, theoretically, allow them to continue to work as well as fulfil their responsibilities of motherhood.

Baburam Bhattarai (2000), a major ideologue of the Maoist party, wrote in the newspaper *Jana Astha* that since reproduction is the woman's special responsibility, it should be respected, and women should be given special facilities. He goes on to elaborate the facilities by stating, 'If a woman is in any committee and becomes a mother, she should not be removed from it. Instead, she should be given leave for a fixed period (approximately one year) and later reinstated in her position with full respect. Else, women will always have to start from zero and their development will be arrested.'

Such statements from the party's policymakers led women to believe that motherhood would not come in the way of a career in the Maoist party, whether as political workers or as soldiers. However, the reality was different, and they were rudely awakened from their utopian dream once they became mothers. Specific mechanisms about how to care for mothers and how to handle their workflow were not developed.

Many women became disillusioned with the party after they became mothers. Renu Chand, central committee member of UCPN Maoist party, shares such an experience in her essay *Garbhawati Ladaku ko Bakpatra (Confessions of a Pregnant Fighter)*. When she became pregnant, she proposed to her husband (also a leader in the Maoist party) that they both share the tasks associated with childcare. In fact, the Maoist party had a policy of assigning one-third of childcare to the mother and two-thirds to the father (Rai 2013). Instead, Chand's husband almost ironically declared that he 'would not want to take her historical and biological responsibility away from her'. Her husband's refusal to shoulder the responsibilities of childcare would leave him free to work, while severely limiting the time she could give to political work.

Ultimately, quarrels about the responsibility of childcare led to her divorce. Her struggle to raise her child all alone was daunting enough; she had to borrow money to feed the infant cheap potatoes with salt. But it was her unceremonious dismissal from the party, with no future plans of continuity that proved most disheartening. She walked into a meeting with a ten-day-old baby, only to be told that due to her condition, she was dismissed from her post at the Women's Organisation. The dismissal sent her into deep depression.

Such struggles for mothers in the party were the norm rather than the exception, despite the avowedly inclusive policies. In practice women were left to fend for themselves, find personal ways to adjust to motherhood, and try to continue to be politically active. In her comprehensive essay on the experiences of female members of the PLA, Rai (2013) writes about the systematic exclusion of mothers, both in the militia and in the party leadership. She recounts Asha Mahatara's account of giving birth on a riverbank, running from the village after two days, and going back to work after nine days, carrying her child. Rai also recounts Jaypuri Gharti's experience of carrying her infant to work until the child was two years old, all the while leading a guerrilla life. Also included is Baraki Jwala Sah's terrible account of her one-and-a-half-month-old son fainting at the sound of bomb blasts while her friends were dying around her in a battlefield, and the subsequent struggle to revive her son as she watched colleagues prise out bullets from her wounded friends' bodies. None of these women felt that their party took any steps to make it easier for mothers to continue, let alone rise in the ranks.

The perception that motherhood would limit their role in the party led many Maoist women to go to drastic lengths to avoid pregnancy, like Anoopam. Sarala Regmi was another such woman. Having married at the age of twenty-eight, she was against having children, and even wanted to opt for permanent contraception. 'I asked my husband to support me, to help me continue my career as I did not want to be bound by anything. But he kept putting it off,' Regmi says. Two years after her marriage, everyone, including her husband, convinced her to have a child. At the time she and her husband Ayam occupied the same position in the party: both were in charge of their districts, Regmi of Surkhet and Ayam of Banke. But as soon as she had a child, she was removed from her position, and it was her husband who was deputed to take her place. Regmi's faith in the party that preached equality was shaken.

Years later, Regmi continues to struggle with motherhood. In her 2014 essay *Chhoro Harayeko Din* (*The Day My Son Disappeared*), Regmi recounts how her fourteen-year-old son ran away from her mother's home where she had left him and was found washing dishes at a hotel. After the demise of her first husband Ayam in combat, Regmi had married Gunaraj Lohani, also a Maoist leader. In the eyes of the public, her second marriage was to blame for her son's disappearance. It did not help that she was not with her son but with her husband in Kathmandu when her son ran away. Her son was eventually found, and she decided to stay close to him, giving up her position in the party's central committee. Again, her faith in the party was shaken, when the party leadership decided that it could not have two whole-timers from the same family within the party (she and her husband) and advised her to take time off for her child.

In the meantime, her first husband's family had claimed the relief amount for martyrs' families, prompting her to sue them and claim the money on her son's behalf. She compared her situation to her second husband's, who still has good relations with his first wife's family, and faces none of the hassles that she does. Mothers like Regmi were often blamed for giving priority to work over children, while career-oriented men did not face the same level of stigma for leaving their children in the care of relatives.

Women emerged from the Maoist experience with deeply conflicted views on motherhood, disillusioned by the party that promised to make careers easier for mothers. Some women, like Chand, believe motherhood does not limit women, but that men and women must share in childcare. Anoopam decided against having a baby at the height of her career, but later decided to have one after five years of marriage. By this time, the peace process was well underway and she knew her career was not going anywhere. Regmi concludes by saying that women fall behind due to child rearing, since men with equal skills and experience can devote more time to work and thus get much further ahead in their careers. The solution that Regmi envisions is social institutions, such as childcare centres, that take on the responsibility of childcare and leave women free to work.

The experiences of women who became mothers during the insurgency indicates that though the Maoist party had well-intentioned policies, childcare was mostly relegated to mothers.

Ironically, while women wanted to escape the shackles of traditional society where motherhood was seen as their primary and exclusive duty, the same ideas followed them inside the party, where they were expected to bear the major burden of parenting.

Many of these women have today gone back to live in mainstream society. Some, like Chapagain, still live active political lives, leading the party in Jhapa district, while other well-known leaders like Sarala Regmi are now focusing on family and motherhood. Anoopam and Sapana Rana have retreated into traditional roles as wives and mothers, where they face the constant struggle of balancing their family's expectations of a wife and mother with their ideas about women's emancipation internalised during their years with the Maoist party. What binds these women is their faith in the principles that they fought for, faith in the notion of equality and in women's capacity to achieve anything. These are changed women, who think, act and take decisions differently from women who have never received political coaching. The change in them may not be measurable, but the fabric of society has certainly changed because of who these women are. Only time can assess the extent of impact of these radically schooled personalities on Nepali society.

Bibliography

Bhattarai, Baburam. 2000. 'Mahila Chhapamarharuka Samasyabare (About the Problems of Female Guerrillas)' in *Jana Astha* 20 November.

Chand, Renu. 2014. *Garbhawati Ladaku ko Bakapatra (Confessions of a Pregnant Fighter)*. Published on 8th December 2014. Available at: http://np.recordnepal.com/art-letter/71. Accessed on 2 March 2015.

Enloe, Cynthia. 1993. *The Morning After: Sexual Politics at the End of the Cold War*. Berkeley: University of California Press.

Molnar, Augusta. 1978. 'Marital Patterns and Women's Economic Independence: A Study of Kham Magar Women' in *Contributions to Nepali Studies*. 6 (1). p. 15-30.

Nyaupane, Lekhnath 2004. 'Shahadat Prapta Sangini lai Chitthi' (Letter for a Martyred Wife) in *Jana Astha*, June 9.

Rai, Kailash. 2013. 'Sahasik Jeewangatha: Maovadi Mahila ka Sansmaran'(Courageous Life Stories: Memoirs of Maoist Women) in *Media Adhyayan 8*. Martin Chautari.

Regmi, Sarala. 2007. 'Ayam Marga Bata Pratibaddhata ko Dosro Patra' (Second Letter of Commitment from Ayam-road) in *Peeda Bhitra ko Aakash*. Pragatisheel Adhyayan Kendra.

——2014. *Chhoro Harayeko Din (The Day My Son was Lost)* in *Annapurna Post* Published on 27th September 2014. Available at http://annapurnapost. com/News.aspx/story/272. Accessed on 1 March 2015.

'Shikhar'. 2004. 'Ankhai Agadi Sangini ko Shahadat' in *Jana Astha* 01 September.

Shrestha-Schipper, Satya. 2008-2009. 'Women's Participation in the People's War in Jumla' in *European Bulletin of Himalayan Research* 33 (34). p 105-122.

Yami, Hisila. 2004. *Janayuddha ra Mahila Mukti*. Kathmandu: Janadhwani Prakashan.

An Incomplete Revolution

DARSHAN KARKI

At around 11 p.m. on a cold winter night in January 2005, a heavily pregnant Jwala Kumari Sah, member of the Bara District Secretariat and area secretary of the Communist Party of Nepal (Maoist), crossed the Nepal border riding pillion on a motorbike. No sooner had she entered India from somewhere between Raxaul and Ghorasahan in Bihar, men on five motorcycles began to follow her. Jwala's escort somehow managed to evade them and when they reached his wife's village past midnight, other villagers helped them chase their pursuers away.

Early the next morning, Jwala left for a private hospital in Chandimari Chowk in Motihari. The following day, by the time she gave birth to a baby boy, her husband Amrit Sharma Bajgain, a commissar of the outlawed Maoist People's Liberation Army (PLA), had also arrived. Given his distinct facial features and the inability to speak the local language, there was a risk that he would be easily identified as Nepali. To prevent being apprehended, he left for Nepal after a day. By this time, Jwala's mother had arrived.

Two days later, twenty-two-year-old Jwala and her mother went to a different hospital for a check-up because of suspected jaundice in the newborn. Keeping her face veiled with a ghunghat, Jwala faked her name and address in the out-patient card and joined the queue of ten people. At that very moment, two truck-loads of Indian security forces stormed into the hospital and headed straight into the doctor's room. They began interrogating the terrified doctor about a Nepali Maoist woman. Outside, in the waiting room, Jwala's legs began to shake uncontrollably. After a while, she pulled herself together, handed the newborn to her mother and summoned a rickshaw. Her mother followed and they quickly headed for the nearest bus station. They now had to get to Nepal as soon as possible.

By the time they reached Sripur, a village about 15 kilometres from Motihari, it was already dark. A local aide whom she called dai or older brother, suggested that they stay at his place. But Jwala was adamant about returning to Nepal. So the three of them headed towards the border on foot; Jwala walked ahead, followed by her mother who carried the child, and dai walked alongside a bicycle. After dragging herself for a few hours, Jwala, who was still bleeding after childbirth, simply could not take it anymore. She passed out near a temple; the priest who was drawing water from a well, insisted that they stay until both mother and child completed their medical treatment. But it was too risky to stay.

When they finally reached the border at 2 a.m., the Indian police suspected that the women had been trafficked, so kept up a barrage of questions. They finally managed to convince the police that they were just poor people who had gone to India for medical treatment. They had to walk for two more hours before they reached the village of Beldari in Bara district where Jwala's aunt, her thuliama, lived. As they neared the village, their approach was greeted by barking dogs who woke up the villagers. They had to continue walking so as not to arouse suspicion. At long last, they reached Piparpati, another village along the border in Bara, where Jwala's sister lived. Finally, Jwala was able to rest for four days. On the fifth day however, she was already attending the party's meeting, her newborn child in tow.

Reminiscing about that day, Jwala remembers thinking to herself that she would continue to walk until her last breath to avoid getting caught. It was this fearless resolve that drove her to constantly push her boundaries. Throughout her pregnancy and even after childbirth, Jwala refused to rest and would walk with her fellow comrades along with her baby. These days, she wonders how she managed to stay alive and out of jail despite close encounters with the state forces. On one occasion she had to crawl, and on another slid off a slippery trail in the hills during the monsoon, with her son tied to her back. Her fellow comrades would joke that Jwala should be declared a bhirpakhasahi or a 'martyr of the hills'. Somehow, she always managed to survive.

Currently, the thirty-two-year-old is in charge of Parsa district for the United Communist Party of Nepal (UCPN) Maoist. She suffers from severe backaches. Doctors have told her that she needs to undergo corrective surgery. She plans to do so, but only after her three sons—a ten-year-old and eight-year-old twins—have completed high school.

Even so, Jwala, the former State Minister for Land Reform and member of the Constituent Assembly, argues that it was a lot easier being a war-time Maoist cadre always on the run from state authorities than being a peace-time politician. The Maoists had clear goals then—to fight against the state, to capture a specific police station or win a certain battle. There was also a visible enemy: the monarchy and the state of Nepal. 'We had to focus on only one thing,' she says. 'After signing the peace agreement with the government in 2006, the party has had to fend off attacks from all directions. At times, it feels as though we are trapped from all sides. We have to constantly explain ourselves to the people and convince them that the party has not deviated from its goals by entering the peace process. It gets really tiring at times. More so when people pretend not to understand anything,' she laments.

To an activist born

Khedu Sah Kanu, Jwala's father, was an active member of the Communist Party of Nepal-United Marxist Leninist (CPN-UML). At the time of her birth, Jwala's parents had already lost two sons, one to poisoning and another to pneumonia. So Jwala's mother, Kalawati Devi Kanu, was not happy about giving birth to a girl. On the other hand, Khedu Sah, lodged in Parsa District Jail at the time, was elated on beholding the baby girl for the first time. He told his wife that the child would be their 'son' and fulfil his dreams. After holding a quick discussion with his fellow comrades in the prison, he named his daughter 'Jwala' or 'intense flame'.

When the war began in 1996, many of Khedu Sah's friends and colleagues quit the CPN-UML to join the Maoist party. When she was eleven, one of these frequent visitors presented her with two books titled *Sunaulo Bihani* (A Golden Morning) and *Krantikari Bidhyarthiko Kitab* (The Book of a Revolutionary Student). The books discussed social problems and the need to implement Janabadi Shiksha or people-oriented education, also called 'new democratic education'. The philosophical base of this education included an analysis of the Marxist principle of dialectical materialism by replacing the 'idealistic foundation of state driven education'. The primary focus of the new curriculum was on the development of the students' materialist understanding of nature, human society and culture, and history (Baral 2011).

Aware of her father's imprisonment for going against the establishment, Jwala initially refused the books. All that the young girl wanted in life was to complete her studies, get a good job and take care of her parents. Eventually, she relented and turned some of the pages of the book targeted at young students like her. Jwala was hooked. She would wake up at four in the morning, finish her homework and then read the books for an hour every day before leaving for tuitions at six. They were the best books she had ever come across; they dealt with the various forms of oppression which she had been hearing about from her father since she was a child. She could relate to the writings about children being kidnapped, parents being tortured and young girls being raped. Jwala was so influenced by the books that she began to recommend them to her friends.

In 1997, fourteen-year-old Jwala became the Bara District Committee treasurer of the Maoist student union. By then, she had been working informally for the student body for three years. A year after being a whole timer committing to full-time work for the Maoist party, she quit the student body and joined the All Nepalese Women's Association (Revolutionary) (ANWA-R), the women's wing of the Maoist party.

Invisible women

In the aftermath of the Maoist war (1996-2006), there has been no dearth of research on the participation of women in the Maoist movement. Stories contrasting the life of former PLA soldiers to the lives they currently lead frequently make it to the media. There is a comparative silence, however, about the participation of Madhesi women—whose first language could be Awadhi, Bengali, Bhojpuri, Hindi, Maithili, Marwari, Rajbanshi, Tharu, Urdu or other languages spoken by those living in the Gangetic plains (Gaige 2012). Literature on the role and participation of Madhesi women in the Maoist war is almost non-existent, barring the documented experiences of women from the Tharu community, one of the indigenous communities of the plains.

There are two possible reasons for this. First, the war which began in the mid-hills of midwestern Nepal, reached the Madhes plains much later. Second, it reached the Madhesi men first because of the deeply patriarchal nature of Madhesi society. Usha Pathak (2010) argues that Madhesi society encourages women to stay indoors, cook, bear and raise children. Indeed, the more a woman is confined to the home, the more respectable she is considered to be. Such a mindset dissuades women from joining politics. 'Furthermore, as society defames those who dare to step out of their houses, most women are scared to do so. As a result, the participation of Madhesi women in the Maoist war remained minimal,' she writes.

Jwala Sah is one among the few Madhesi women who took part in the Maoist war, which was predominantly fought in the hills. Even towards the end of the war years in 2003, only one of the twenty districts in the Tarai—Dang—was classified as 'Sensitive Class B' and none as 'Sensitive Class A', in terms of the priority of Maoist operations (South Asian Terrorism Portal as cited in Kantha 2010). Supporting this argument, Magnus Hatlebakk (2009) writes, '... Maoists have basically no control in the Tarai (plains) region of Nepal. By including a number of non-Maoist districts from a region where basically no district has been under Maoist control, one will get a biased representation of the determinants of

Maoist control, as the Tarai region is in many ways different from the hills.'

From a strategic point of view, it made sense to wage a war from the hills where guerrilla tactics were more effective. It was relatively easy for the state forces to conduct security operations in the plains. In addition, the Tarai, with a long history of participation in and support for democratic movements since the 1950s, did not provide a favourable environment for the communists (Kantha 2010; Shah 2011). The regions in the Madhes that have a history of left-leaning politics are around the Mahendra Highway; poor settlements near the Bagmati River in Rautahat and Siraha; settlements close to the Kamala River in Dhanusha and Siraha and those near the Kosi River in Saptari and Sunsari (Shah 2011). Settlements close to the river, according to Shah, were primarily inhabited by the poor, faced constant flooding and were far from the reach of the police and the local administration. This made it easier for the left-leaning parties to carry out their activities and expand their base. Likewise, the people from the hills who settled around the Mahendra Highway were largely supporters of the CPN-UML.

The primacy of caste in the politics of the Tarai also made it difficult to mobilise lower castes in large numbers for a radical left movement (International Crisis Group 2007). While the Maoist movement did acknowledge the prevalence of caste as well as class-based discrimination, it was unable to dismantle the feudal, rigid caste structure of Madhesi society. The Maoist agenda wishing to do away with all forms of discrimination appealed to many Dalits, but at the same time, they depended on the higher castes for their livelihoods and could not go against them.[1] Most of all, the anti-India rhetoric deployed to evoke nationalist sentiments in the hills could not resonate with people in the plains who share an open border with India (Kantha 2010). Of the forty-point demands submitted by the Maoists to the government of Nepal before they declared war against the state on February 13, 1996, four points

---

[1]Interview with Tula Narayan Shah, October 20, 2015.

under the heading 'demands for nationalism' were explicitly related to changing relations with India.[2]

In the initial years of the conflict, the Tarai used to be considered a Maoist-free zone. Four years into the war, in 2000, the CPN (Maoist) formed a Madhesi wing of the party, Madhesi Rashtriya Mukti Morcha[3] in Siliguri, India. To expand the party's base in the Tarai, the first strategy used by the Maoists was to recruit Madhesi government officials working in the hills, train them as Maoist workers and then assign them the task of spreading the message about the party upon their return home during the holidays (Shah 2011). Despite this, expanding the party in the plains remained a difficult task. The Maoists then came up with a new strategy. The party began to recruit labourers, particularly from eastern and central Madhes, working in different parts of India, mainly Delhi, Punjab and Haryana. The International Department of the CPN (Maoist) would train these Nepali labourers and send them back to Nepal. It is unclear how many women, if any, joined the party in this manner.

The Madhesi Rashtriya Mukti Morcha's list of demands, nonetheless, did include two women-related demands: putting an end to dowry and women's exploitation. Its other demands were: proportional inclusion of Madhesis in state institutions; full

---

[2]The first point called for removing all unequal provisions in the 1950 Treaty between Nepal and India, while the second demanded the nullification of the Mahakali Treaty relating to sharing of water of the Mahakali River which forms the international border in the west. The other two points called for regulation of the border: banning the entry of vehicles with Indian number plates; and putting an end to 'cultural pollution' from imperialists and expansionists by imposing a ban on 'vulgar' Hindi movies and magazines.

[3]The Madhesi National Liberation Front was formed under the leadership of Jaya Krishna Goit. But the party's stance of dividing the Madhes into two (Tharuwan in the west and Madhes in the east), angered Madhesi Maoists who were in support of a single autonomous Madhes. Goit also accused the party leadership of 'Pahade' (hill) domination. In 2004, Goit quit the party and formed Janatantrik Tarai Mukti Morcha. The party has since split multiple times giving rise to various armed groups in the Tarai.

distribution of citizenship certificates; use of Maithili, Bhojpuri and Awadhi as local official languages and protection of other cultural rights; revolutionary land reform; reinvestment of Madhes tax revenues in the region; and putting an end to untouchability and social discrimination (International Crisis Group 2007).

For the women

During the war, the women's wing of the Maoist party was actively engaged in ensuring that villages were free from domestic violence, the exploitation of women, child marriage, forced marriage and polygamy (Manchanda 2010). As the Bara district chairperson of ANWA-R, Jwala Sah also led the movement against gender-based violence. As part of the campaign, Maoists would demolish shops that sold alcohol and destroy the liquor. If a man who was alcoholic was found to be beating his wife, the Maoists, according to Jwala, would tie his hands and legs together and dip his head in water until he agreed to quit drinking. If this method did not work, the Maoists would make his wife beat him with a stick. If the man still did not change his ways, he would be tied to a pole and starved for a couple of days. Jwala claims that such measures controlled domestic violence to a large extent.

The Maoists also implemented programmes against dowry. For example, if a girl's parents were found to be tormented for dowry, the Maoists would marry the couple onstage and make the parents deposit any money they planned to spend on the wedding in the couple's joint bank account. Further, while expanding the Maoist organisation in Makwanpur, Jwala observed that women in this hilly district would sit, eat and talk frankly in the company of men. In the Tarai districts of Bara and Rautahat, however, the practice of seclusion and veiling or ghumtopratha was widely prevalent. Women in Rautahat, in particular, would not even come out of their houses. This made it relatively difficult to expand the party's base among women. Initially, the Maoists sought to attract and inform people through the usual routine of singing revolutionary songs and performing skits in local dialects. The most effective strategy, however, turned out to be helping the women with their household work. The Maoists would cut grass, till the land, milk buffaloes and also help the women in the kitchen. In this way, they were gradually able to win the trust of the women of the area.

Jwala claims that the men in their families were not opposed to the Maoists. Rather, they treated the Maoists as guests and even gave them new clothes as farewell gifts. 'Apart from expanding the base of the party, our presence in the villages also helped clear many misconceptions about the Maoist party in the Tarai,' she says. 'Fraudsters had spread rumours that the Maoists were scary beasts, as big as elephants with huge teeth, long nails and large frightening eyes that lived in the forest,' Jwala laughs. 'People were so scared of this creature called the Maoist that they would not step out their houses at night to take a leak.'

Not a cat

Kismati Devi Ram, a Dalit rights activist, who lived in Inaruwasira Ward No 7, in Bara, remembers hearing such rumours about the Maoists. Even though she was twenty-three when the war broke out in 1996, Kismati had no inkling whatsoever about the Maoist party. Villagers often spoke of the Maoists in hushed tones as the war progressed but because 'Mao' sounded similar to a cat's 'meow' she wondered if they were a species of cat!

It was only after she found bottles of beer and pieces of meat lying in a sugarcane field one morning that she knew that the Maoists were human beings. Soon, the Maoists began taking shelter in her village and would frequently come to her house demanding food. They wanted rice, pulses, maize, meat and, at times, money. As her husband's family was relatively better off, the demands kept increasing. And as soon as the Maoists had left her house in a mess, the police would barge in. The frequent visits of the Maoists and the interrogation of the police and local authorities added to the mental torture she was already suffering due to violence at the hands of her in-laws.

Married at eleven, Kismati came to live with her husband, a

sixth-grade student, when she was twelve. Since then, her life largely consisted of being beaten up by her in-laws for the tiniest of things. Sometimes, her illiteracy was a problem. Other times, she was too dark-skinned for their liking. Nothing seemed to reduce the violence, even though Kismati's parents had done everything they possibly could to ensure their daughter's happiness. They had given a dowry of 1,500 Nepali rupees in cash, clothes for thirty people, a bicycle, a watch and a vessel to cook rice. What remained was a brass gagri. And for not being able to provide that coveted brass water container, her in-laws demanded that Kismati's parents, along with her brother, come to work in their farm as labourers. They obliged. Though Kismati and her husband's family were both Chamar, a Dalit caste in the plains, the latter were better off, and that class difference seemed to validate all the maltreatment of her family.

'At that time, I led the life of a bonded labourer,' she says. She was always busy looking after her in-laws' buffaloes and oxen or collecting fodder for the cattle. The beatings, however, were a constant. Clearly, the Maoists' campaign of making villages free of domestic violence never reached Kismati.

In 2001, after the Nepal Army was mobilised against the Maoists, they would barge in anytime they liked, regardless of what she was doing: cooking food, out to fetch water or taking a bath. 'They [army and police] never beat or touched me, but it added to the psychological torture I was already facing,' she says.

With both the Maoists and the state forces interrogating them constantly for allegedly providing support to the other side, it became extremely difficult to live in the village. During the nights, Kismati worried about her house being burned to the ground or her children being kidnapped. Furthermore, as her husband was a teacher in a school near the India-Nepal border, he was constantly harassed by both the Maoists and the police about his movements and it became difficult for him to travel there every day. So in 2002, Kismati along with her three children, her husband and his sister left Inaruwasira for Kalaiya, the headquarters of Bara district, to escape the Maoists.

Recalling those days, Kismati concedes that perhaps the torment she faced at the hands of the Maoists was because her father-in-law was a staunch Nepali Congress supporter. 'It is easy to win Dalit support,' she says, 'because they largely function as somebody else's remote control. Most do not know the way politics works. And their loyalty can be bought easily.' Political party leaders, according to Kismati, visit the villages during elections, take a dirty child on their lap and wipe its snot for all the people to see. Innocent villagers mistake this display to secure votes for genuine concern. Besides, Kismati argues that any party which distributes free alcohol to young Dalit Madhesi men gains their support; their wives vote for whosoever their husbands tell them to.

The lack of agency of Madhesi women, including those in politics, is arguably the most recurring theme in writings about them. In an article about female Madhesi leaders, Prashant Jha (2008) writes, 'Women's participation in politics is passive at best: as a voter told by her father, husband or son which way to cast the ballot, and as fodder when street agitations are launched.' Manchala Jha (2011) further adds that even though there were fifty-seven Madhesi women among 197 women elected to the 2008 Constituent Assembly, most of them seem to have only acquired the post due to the backing and influence of men. She writes, 'The presence of women seems to be merely an attempt to meet the quorum and to support the party's agendas when it issues a whip.'

NGOs, according to Kismati, have played a greater role in raising awareness among the Dalits than political parties. She admits that many NGOs raise money from donors in the name of Dalits and do not spend it all on them, but at least they 'do something,' she says. Her own meteoric rise as a go-to-person in case of human rights' violations in the district is an example of NGO empowerment. Since 2006, Kismati has been working as the chairperson of the Bara Chapter of the Feminist Dalit Organisation (FEDO), an NGO based in Kathmandu with branch offices in fifty-six districts across Nepal.

Rhetoric and reality

'The Maoist War,' Jwala says, 'helped the Madhesi women find their voice. It enabled them to speak their minds and to speak for themselves.' At the same time, she acknowledges that much remains to be changed as society still suffers from a centuries-old patriarchal mindset, despite the Maoist war and the 2007 Madhes Movement—a struggle for the rights of the Madhesis, which firmly established the agenda of the Madhes in the political discourse of Nepal. These days, the Maoist leader, who once campaigned against dowry, often gets invited to rokka or engagement ceremonies where dowry amounts are fixed. Her presence, she says, helps the girl's family to reduce the dowry amount. Jwala laments the fact that women are bought and sold like cattle till date.

Anju Jha (2012), a social mobiliser in Rautahat, agrees with Jwala and argues that Madhesi women still do not have the opportunity to go beyond being good daughters, daughters-in-law and mothers. 'The identity of a Madhesi woman was in crisis in the yesteryears and is in crisis even today… In addition, the problems women face due to the prevalence of the dowry system, ghumtopratha, infanticide, accusations of being a witch and the murder of couples who marry outside their castes is heinous,' she writes.

'Madhesi men still do not want their wives to step out of their houses. And they pretend to lend a voice to the issues of the Madhesi women only when we are around,' Jwala claims. Other Madhesi women leaders and activists from across political parties agree. One of these women, Mina (name changed) currently with a Madhes-based political party, says that despite completing her undergraduate studies in political science, she had been a housewife all her life until the 2006 People's Movement. When invited for a discussion in Birgunj sometime in April 2015, she arrived with her husband, a doctor. He stayed at a table nearby and drank coffee as she spoke to me and they left together after thirty minutes. Three other women leaders from different Madhes-based parties were also present. When I wondered about the presence of her husband while meeting another leader separately, she replied, 'This is the Madhes.' Parvati (name changed), who has been in politics for the last 15 years, also admitted to repeatedly getting calls from her husband demanding to know her whereabouts when we met for the first time at five in the evening. Apparently, she is used to it by now and had retorted, 'At a hotel, sleeping around. Why do you care?' Later, I came to know that yet another leader, who has been divorced for the last five years, had also been getting frequent calls from her ex-husband during our discussions.

After meeting Sita Devi (name changed), it becomes even more difficult to establish any link whatsoever between the Maoist war and the long-term empowerment of Madhesi women. Sita Devi works as a tailor near Pratima Chowk in Birgunj where she earns a paltry ten Nepali rupees for sewing a nightgown. Each day, she manages to sew around five or six of them. A local journalist gave me her number, telling me that she is a member of the hardliner Maoist splinter party led by Mohan Baidya who broke away from the Unified CPN (Maoist). But when verifying this with her, she replied, 'Does the faction matter to a sahid pariwar?' reflecting the views of many families of martyrs.

Sita's husband was one of the early members of the Maoist party and also an Area Commander during the war. However, he would not allow her to step out of the house. After he was killed by the Armed Police Force, her in-laws began taunting her endlessly. She speaks of it as though it is a way of life, 'They did what they had to, and I suffered as I had to.' Her membership in the party does not seem to have encouraged her to be active in public life; she told me that she had never been invited to any meeting by the party.

The missing half

Most of the women interviewed for this essay had joined politics only after the 2006 People's Movement or the 2007 Madhes Movement. And all those who had joined the Maoist party during the war came from families with a political background. Given this reality, one would expect the post-Madhes Movement literature to go more deeply into the role of the Madhesi women. After all, it has been eight years since the uprising and a lot has been written about the Madhes since then. However, most writings on the Madhes Movement make only passing references to the fact that women were also part of the protests. In *The Battles of the New Republic* (2014), by Madhesi journalist Prashant Jha, whose cover reads 'generations of readers will turn to it to understand Nepal's transition to democracy', there is just one line which explicitly talks about the role of Madhesi women in the Madhes Movement: 'Women in Siraha took out "broomstick" processions.'

These processions finds mention in the book *Madhesi Bidrohako Nalibeli* (*Intricacies of the Madhes Revolt*) too. It was apparently the very first women's political march in the district (Yadav 2012). The next day, women and men rallied together with broomsticks and a few days later, they also protested carrying vegetables and fish. One frequently comes across images of women with broomsticks and batons in writings about the movement, but they lack much-needed nuance. The identities of these women, their caste and class affiliations, along with an analysis of their motivations and aspirations are difficult to find. More often than not, issues of Madhesi women are subsumed under the problems of the Madhes and, if not, the women are portrayed as victims of gender-based violence without any agency. While such depictions do indeed reflect one aspect of reality, they do not do justice to the complex lives the women lead.

Going back to the women I spoke to, none of them seemed to be very hopeful about their future prospects in politics. Not a single one among them thought that they would get decision-making posts within their party even if, hypothetically speaking, the state met the political demands of the Madhes-based parties.

Usha Srivastava, a leader of the Tarai Madhes Loktantrik Party, evocatively illustrated this reluctance to share power. Picking up a piece of roti lying in front of her, she said, 'Giving power to women implies a smaller share of the roti for the men. Furthermore, it will also invite more groups within the Madhes to claim their rightful share. The men will never agree to it.' Pinky Yadav, a thirty-year old who contested the 2013 elections from Bara from the Tarai Madhes

Loktantrik Party, is even less optimistic: 'Even if there were a rule to ensure fifty per cent women's participation in all the parties, the men would just drag their wives, daughters and other women members of the household into politics. These women would all be inactive participants. Men will still make decisions while women will merely fulfil the quota.'

Almost ten years after the war, the relevance of the UCPN (Maoist) party is being increasingly questioned. More often than not, it is compared to the CPN-UML, a party which was once considered revolutionary, but is now accused of being increasingly regressive in its agendas. Jwala, on her part, concedes that the party has indeed lost touch with the concerns of the people, and that this resulted in the party's extremely poor performance in the 2013 Constituent Assembly elections. She thinks that the party could regain its glory if it went back to the people's houses, as it did during the war years, and raised their concerns. 'The problem is, we keep saying political issues and in the process, forget what is important to the people. For instance, if there is a case of domestic violence then we must rush to the village to support the women. It is a people's issue. Doing so would instil hope in the women that there is at least someone in their support. This is the kind of politics we need.'

Bibliography

Baral, Roshan Raj. 2011. 'Pedagogy of Liberation: A Case of Nepal' in *Nepal Journal of Social Science and Public Policy.* Available at: http://www.nepalpolicynet.com/images/NewAngle/Vol1/5_Baral_Pedagogy%20of%20liberation.pdf. Accessed on 20 July 2015.

Gautam, Bhaskar. 2012. 'Madhesi Bidroha: "Nairasyako Rajneeti" (Madhesi Revolt: The Politics of Discontent)' in Gautam, B (ed) *Madhes Bidrohako Nalibeli (The Intricacies of Madhes Revolt)* 2nd edn. Kathmandu: Martin Chautari, pp 1-36.

Gaige, Frederick H. 2012. *Regionalism and National Unity in Nepal.* 2nd edn. Kathmandu: Himal Books.

Hatlebakk, Magnus. 2009. *Explaining Maoist Control and Level of Civil Conflict in Nepal.* Norway: Chr. Michelsen Institute.

International Crisis Group. 2007. *Nepal's Troubled Tarai Region.*

Jha, Anju. 2012. 'Madhesi Mahila Kina Pachadi? (*Why Do Madhesi Women Lag Behind?*),' Kantipur, July 10. Accessed on July 12, 2015. <www.ekantipur.com/np>.

Jha, Manchala. 2011. 'Madhesi Rajneeti Ma Mahila (Madhesi politics and women)'. *Lal Madhes*, Year 3, Issue 10, June-July 2011, pp 26-27.

Jha, Prashant. 2008. 'The new Madhesi woman' in *The Nepali Times,* Issue 401, May 23-May 30.

——. 2014. *The Battles of the New Republic.* New Delhi: Aleph Book Company.

Kantha, Pramod K. 2010. 'Maoist-Madhesi dynamics and Nepal's peace process in The Maoist Insurgency' in Lawoti and Pahari (eds), *The Maoist Insurgency in Nepal: Revolution in The Twenty-First Century.* London/New York: Routledge.

Manchanda, Rita. 2010. 'Women's Question In Nepal's Democratic Post Conflict Transition: Towards A Policy Research Agenda' in *Peace Prints: South Asian Journal of Peacebuilding,* Vol. 3, No. 1 Spring 2010.

Pathak, Usha. 2010. 'Awadh-Madheska Mahilako Awastha (The State of Women in Awadh-Madhes)' in *Lal Madhes,* Year 3, Issue 5, Dec 2010-Jan 2011, pp. 42-43.

Sah, Nisha. (date unknown). *Khalbaliyeko Madhesma Nidayeka Mahila (Women Asleep in a Disturbed Madhes).* Darshan Dainik.

Sah, Birendra Kumar. 2012. 'Bara-Parsa Rautahatma Madhesi Bidroha (Madhesi Revolt in Bara, Parsa and Rautahat)' in Gautam, B (ed) *Madhes Bidrohako Nalibeli* 2nd edn. Kathmandu: Martin Chautari. pp 119-145.

Shah, Tula Narayan. 2011. 'Janayuddha Ra Madhesi Samaj (The People's War and Madhesi Society)' in *Lal Madhes,* Year 3, Issue 7, Feb-March 2011, pp 18-21.

Yadav, Ramrijhan. 2012. 'Madhes Bidrohama Siraha-Saptari (Siraha-Saptari During the Madhes Revolt)' in Gautam, B (ed) *Madhes Bidrohako Nalibeli* 2nd edn. Kathmandu: Martin Chautari. pp 75-102.

KASHMIR

Introduction: A History and its Witnesses

SIDDIQ WAHID

The dispute over the erstwhile Jammu and Kashmir State (henceforth J&K State[1]) is among the world's most complex international problems. A leading analyst of South Asian political history has described it as a dilemma layered in several vertical strata that would require a political archaeologist to unearth, analyse and interpret (Cohen 1995). A comprehensive historical perspective on the dispute would lead us back to at least the year 1846, when the state was founded by Maharaja Gulab Singh (1792-1857). That history is yet to be written, and the need to understand the problem in the context of the human relationships, economic ties and political associations that have bound four of its five diverse regions for centuries remains unaddressed. Yet, it is possible to examine the dispute on the canvas of geopolitics, wherein the current argument is, at base, a territorial dispute over its sovereignty between three key claimants—the J&K State, India and Pakistan—following the British withdrawal from South Asia in 1947. A brief capitulation of the positions of each of these stakeholders illustrates why the clash in a highly militarised region that has been called 'the most dangerous place on earth' has become a wrangle of well-nigh intractable claims.

---

[1]The term J&K State refers to the state as it existed between March 1846 and October 1947 as a sovereign, independent territorial state of five constituent parts: Kashmir, Jammu, Gilgit, Baltistan and Ladakh.

The positions

India has argued, unrealistically, that there is no dispute to resolve. It claims all of the erstwhile princely state, bolstering its argument with a 1994 unilateral resolution to that effect in the Indian parliament. New Delhi's argument is based on the conditional Instrument of Accession to India that was signed on October 26, 1947, by Maharaja Hari Singh, the ruler of the J&K State at the time.

Pakistan argues, anachronistically, that its claim to the J&K State is based on the two-nation theory that gave birth to its own existence as a nation-state. It rejects the validity of the accession to India and augments its position by demanding a referendum, as was stipulated in the three resolutions passed by the United Nations on April 21 and August 13, 1948, and January 5, 1949. Islamabad too claims the entire state, declaring the portion of the state in its possession[2] 'Azad' (free) J&K.

The two countries have fought three wars over the state, the most recent being a short 'undeclared' war in Kargil in 1999. Meanwhile, unable to defend its territorial and political rights, the J&K State itself has gradually been excluded from international discourse about its own future. In part, this is because although it had been a geopolitically well-positioned independent sovereign state for more than a hundred years, by 1947 it had become an anachronism in governance, bereft of both home-grown institutional support and a strategic plan for its future. Unsurprisingly, the voice of the J&K State became an inchoate dynamic in the dispute over its own territory. As a result, the political rights and interests of its diverse peoples have faded into the background and the dispute has come to be redefined as a bilateral contest between the two status quo states, India and Pakistan, albeit without a result.

The effect of the non-resolution of the dispute *over* the state has led to the exacerbation of conflicts *within* it, ranging from issues of religious and regional identity to those of ethnic and vocational

---

[2]See footnote 3 for details about the shifting areas occupied by India and Pakistan.

(such as pastoralist nomad) rights which, coupled with the sheer march of history, have made it a complex of riddles. These riddles can be put into three categories: historical idiosyncrasies, legal ambiguities and political inequities, each with intertwined and fluid boundaries. Although this essay focuses on the first of these enigmas, a brief description of the latter two will help us to contextualize the discussion.

Scholarly and analytical accounts of the legal ambiguities surrounding the conundrum of the J&K State are readily found (See Anand 1980; Lamb 1966; Noorani 2011). These legal issues have to do with several questions including the legitimacy and authenticity of the Instrument of Accession (Jha 1996; Anderson 2012) and the contemporary relevance of the United Nations resolutions stipulating a referendum. To complicate matters, Indian and Pakistani positions over the years have tended to attenuate the dispute by limiting it to the valley of Kashmir. The tacit logic of this shift in position is that the preferences of the other constituent parts of the J&K State are self-evident and that the ethno-linguistic Kashmiri Muslim population is the only disaffected element. But this is an argument of convenience that, apart from contravening the stated official positions of the two states and arbitrarily excluding the other constituent parts of the erstwhile J&K State, merely adds to the complexity of the problem by redefining the historical origins and legal foundations of the dispute.

The political inequity for the citizens of the state in its entirety is aptly symbolised by what is called the Line of Control (LOC)[3], which divides the state. It is a control mechanism that has *de facto*

---

[3]The term 'Line of Control' was coined in 1972 during the Simla talks between India and Pakistan in the aftermath of the Liberation War that created Bangladesh. It was instituted to replace the term Cease Fire Line, a dynamic line that was defined and redefined several times during the four wars between the two countries in 1947-48, 1965, 1971 and 1999. The first two and the last were fought specifically over the J&K State's territory. The third, although focused on East Pakistan/Bangladesh, also saw battles and territory exchanged in J&K State.

resulted in a diminishing of the political rights of the citizens of the state who live on either side of it. On the Indian side of the Line of Control, or LOC East[4], these inequities, especially since the outbreak of armed rebellion there in the 1990s, have been recounted in many anthologies and individual studies (Thomas 1992; Bose 2003; Schofield 2004; Shaffer 2009). The literature on the opinions and conditions in LOC West is scanty, but two recent works (Puri 2010; Snedden 2013) on the history of that area since 1947 give us substantive insights into its working. There is also a growing body of literature, including journalistic reportage, on contemporary Gilgit-Baltistan, recording how sectarian strife has been increasingly used to further partisan ends in this part of the erstwhile state (See Hunzai 2013; Bansal 2013). These works will help the reader to better understand the political dimensions of the problems in the region.

The creation of the Dogra state

For a full historical understanding of the dispute, the founding of the J&K State between 1810 and 1846 must be understood against the backdrop of more than thirteen hundred years of interaction between Baltistan, Ladakh, Kashmir and Gilgit and in the context of the expansion of the Tibetan, Arab and Chinese empires through the centuries. This explains how these nations were incorporated as constituent parts of the Dogra state in the comity of mid-nineteenth-century Central Eurasian and South Asian states. However, neither context nor space allows for that discussion here, so we will have to content ourselves with a summary of the birth of the modern J&K State in the context of mid-nineteenth-century politics in Central Eurasia and South Asia.

---

[4]We use the terms LOC East and LOC West, respectively, for the Indian and Pakistani sides of the line. They are more neutral than the more common 'Pakistan Occupied Kashmir' and 'Indian Occupied Kashmir', which presents the conundrum as an exclusively bilateral dispute, ignoring the peoples of the State. The terms 'LOC West' and 'LOC East' accept the de facto involvement of Delhi and Islamabad, while maintaining the focus on the need to include the peoples of the J&K State in the discourse on resolution.

The J&K State came into being in the milieu of what came to be known as the 'Great Game', fuelled by the British Empire and the Sikh monarchy of Maharaja Ranjit Singh (See Cunningham 1849; K. Singh 1999). Among Ranjit Singh's allies was the vassalage of Jammu, annexed in 1808 and handled by an uncommonly astute soldier named Gulab Singh who had consolidated the principality of Jammu for his family. Kashmir had been a Sikh possession since 1819, and the substantive profits from its shawl trade with Europe brought it to the attention of Gulab Singh: first during his participation in the Sikh conquest of it and then again in 1841, when he participated in a campaign to quell a mutiny there against Lahore, the centre of Sikh power.

Gulab Singh had begun his military career as a foot-soldier in the Punjab army of Maharaja Ranjit Singh. He rapidly consolidated his power base under Sikh patronage in the scrub hill countryside of Jammu that was his home. In 1820, Maharaja Ranjit Singh conferred the title of Raja on Gulab Singh as a reward for his loyalty. Less than fifteen years after this impressive achievement, the Raja dispatched his troops under the formidable General Zorawar Singh through the uncharted and arduous terrain of the Tibetan plateau to conquer Baltistan and Ladakh. He accomplished this feat between 1834 and 1842, after quelling several insurrections, concluding with the incorporation of Baltistan and Ladakh as part of Gulab Singh's territories.

This accomplishment was not just a military feat undertaken in Jammu, but a diplomatic one that had to be addressed simultaneously in Lahore and Calcutta. By the time he was done, Gulab Singh had successfully allayed suspicions about his loyalty in Ranjit Singh's court and at the same time engaged in deft negotiations with the British to dispel any concerns they may have had about his ambitions in territories abutting its greatest rival, Russia. The British were wary of Russian interests in the Great Game being played out between British India, Tsarist Russia and Qing China in Central Eurasia (Meyer and Brysac 1999). In less than half a decade after the consolidation of Dogra rule in Baltistan and Ladakh, Gulab Singh negotiated the purchase of the valley of Kashmir from the British with the signing of the Treaty of Amritsar on March 19, 1846. The Dogra kingdom of the J&K State was born.

The results of the military conquests of Ladakh and Baltistan, and the diplomatic 'adjustment' over Kashmir were no mean feat. Gulab Singh had catapulted himself from foot-soldier to the ruler of an independent sovereign state in the British-dominated subcontinent. It also became the largest of the South Asian princely states and a significant player among them (See B. Singh 1974; Panikkar, 1953). To be sure, the creation of the new state was facilitated by growing Anglo-Sikh rivalry and Dogra access to the Lahore court of the Sikh Empire. Yet, there is little doubt that the rise and rule of the J&K State was the accomplishment of Gulab Singh (Charak 1977; Khan 1937).

The J&K State created a new paradigm for politics in South Asia. Though the Mughals had acquired Kashmir in the interests of imperial expansion, it had remained largely peripheral to the geopolitics of their empire. It was a place where the Mughal emperors went to escape the summer heat of the plains. Similarly, the occupation of Kashmir by the Afghans (1742-1819) and Sikhs (1819-1846) were exploitative ventures and short-lived, remaining peripheral to the centres of power in Afghanistan or Lahore. The Dogra innovation was that, for the first time, Gulab Singh made the valley of Kashmir the *centre* of a larger state. It had the effect of securing Kashmir as more than a summer resort and bringing Gilgit, Baltistan and Ladakh in closer proximity to, and the attention of, a new power centre.

The British were not unaware of the strategic value of the newly consolidated state for their South Asian possessions. But there were differences of opinion in London and Calcutta between those who advocated a 'forward policy' and others who argued for consolidation through what was referred to as 'masterly inactivity' in the approach to empire maintenance. Was the J&K State a strategic invention bequeathed to Gulab Singh? Did he identify the geopolitical significance of a potential state independently of the

British? Or was the idea of the J&K State an accident of history? Regardless of the answers to these questions, the birth of the J&K State was a unique feat. In its broadest effect, the new state had formalised ancient relationships in military competition, cultural exchange and commercial cooperation between five very disparate nations—Gilgit, Baltistan, Ladakh, Kashmir and Jammu—into a single unit and merged them into an independent, sovereign and territorial Himalayan state in the Westphalian model.

Genesis of the conundrum

Present-day partisan polemics apart, it would be fair to say that a definition of the conundrum of the J&K State as it stands today eludes a consensus even in theory. Is it the consequence of a nineteenth-century state that has become an anachronism? Is it a failure of the rule of law, of territorial acquisitiveness, among the comity of nation-states? Is it about dispensing justice for political inequity? Or a wrangle about religious identity? To answer these questions is akin to asking when the dispute began. Were the seeds of the dispute sown in 1846, when it was formed? Is its genesis located in the 1931 Muslim rebellion (Bazaz 1941; Abdullah 1993)? Or is it the 'unfinished business' of the British withdrawal from South Asia in 1947?

Historically speaking, the first 'layer' of the dispute over the J&K State may lie in the very reason for its creation—the containment of a wave of Islamic revivalism. South Asia, including Afghanistan, was witnessing just such a wave, along with an assertion of Muslim identity, in the first half of the nineteenth century. The British East India Company's empire, bordered as it was in the north by Muslim populations, felt threatened by any power vacuum in—or assertion by—entities that could exploit them against British rule. These included Maharaja Ranjit Singh's Punjab, a restless Afghanistan and, putatively in British eyes, Muslim Kashmir. These threats, internal to South Asia, were underlined and often exaggerated by an expanding Russian empire.

In response to these challenges, perceived or real, Lord Hardinge, the Governor General of India, first made over Kashmir to Gulab Singh and then, in rapid succession, allowed him to form the J&K State, with the argument that the latter would be a client state of British India. After Kashmir was sold to Gulab Singh for seven-and-a-half million rupees, Hardinge faced growing criticism, both official and private, for his action. His counter-argument was that the new state would help prevent a 'Muhammadan [sic] power to establish an independent State on this side of the Indus' and act as a 'counterpoise against the power of the Sikh' (Ghose 1975, p 2 footnote 3; See. also Rai 2004). In other words, the J&K State was created to allay British concerns about Muslim religious revivals and identity quarrels, which were manifesting themselves in the region. Afghanistan and Kashmir, with their Muslim majority populations, needed to be contained. Hardinge proposed to do so by absorbing Muslim majority Kashmir into a state headed by a Hindu kingdom and then control its Hindu ruler (Ghose 1975, p 3; Kapur 1970).

The dispute: 1930 to 1987

Ironically Maharaja Hari Singh, the fourth-generation Dogra ruler of the State, lost his kingdom because of the failure of the Hardinge plan. While the British were successful, although unevenly so, in controlling Gulab Singh's descendants, the latter were either unable or unwilling to understand that the three-hundred-year-long subjugation of the Kashmiris under Mughal, Afghan and Sikh rule needed mitigation by delivering social justice in the interests of the Dogra kingdom itself, if not political equity. Instead, an assertion of Kashmir's Hindu historical antecedents to legitimise Dogra rule further alienated its Muslim subjects (See Zutshi 2003; Rai 2004). Predictably, the reaction to this policy approach progressed from angry uprising to sustained rebellion to political movement.

The process began in 1931, when Hari Singh's Muslim subjects revolted, first in Jammu (Snedden 2013) and then in Kashmir, over issues of religious freedom and cultural identity. The leadership of this rebellion consisted of several prominent men, among them a school teacher named Sheikh Mohammed Abdullah. The latter's

role in the modern movement in Kashmir takes centre stage almost
immediately after the 1931 rebellion when, in 1932, he helped form
the Muslim Conference. Abdullah, who quickly emerged as one of
the rebellion's most prominent leaders, transformed the movement
into a struggle for a secular modern state and renamed it the
National Conference. This radical shift in strategy and direction
appears to have taken place between 1937 and 1939, when the
aims of the movement, or more accurately the faction of it led by
Abdullah, were debated and distilled into a document mandating,
among other things, a program of radical land reform, economic
fairness and equality of class. It was called the Naya (New) Kashmir
document. As a result, an uprising based on resentment against the
suppression of a sub-nationalist identity within a sovereign state
became part of the legal question surrounding the future of the
560-odd sovereign independent princely states of India. In broader
South Asian effect, the Kashmiri peoples' ethno-religious rebellion
against the Dogra monarchy and the movement against the British
Raj in the subcontinent were conflated.

At the time of the British withdrawal in 1947, the problem for
J&K State hinged on the then ruler, Maharaja Hari Singh, choosing
between independence and accession to either India or Pakistan.
Even as he was weighing his choices, an impatient Pakistan forced
the hand of the ruler with a raid from its soil into J&K State. The
Maharaja asked India for help; the latter refused until he agreed to
sign the Instrument of Accession, conditional to a referendum of its
peoples at a later date. It was under these circumstances that India
sent its first contingent of troops into Kashmir on October 27, 1947.
Meanwhile, relations between India and Pakistan deteriorated into
a full-blown war that lasted for a year, until the first day of 1949,
which yielded a Cease Fire Line that has territorially divided the
state since, with later adjustments.

The dispute was taken to the United Nations by India and debated
over several years, resulting in several resolutions. For a variety
of reasons, not least the partisan voting patterns of the Cold War
regime, the latter proved to be ineffectual. In 1952, Sheikh Abdullah,

the leader of the state on its Indian side, reached an accord with New Delhi, which came to be called the Delhi Agreement. The latter negotiated a maximised federal status for the portion of the J&K State on the Indian side of the Cease Fire Line, while providing 'reservations' in the state's Assembly and other institutions for those in LOC East, pending the resolution of the dispute. A similar arrangement was reached for the territory in LOC West.

There was another war between India and Pakistan over the territory in 1965, which resulted in a stalemate. The 1971 war that led to the creation of Bangladesh, resulted in an India–Pakistan concord known as the Simla Agreement in 1972. This was a compact between India and Pakistan on war reparations in which was included a discussion on the J&K State. Part of the 'agreement' was that the J&K dispute should be treated as a bilateral issue between them, the agreement being concluded without any representation from the J&K State.

The State became party to this agreement in 1975, when Sheikh Abdullah, by far still the most popular leader, agreed to a pact with the then Prime Minister Indira Gandhi, based largely on the Simla Agreement, albeit not without dissent. Sheikh Abdullah died in 1983 and four years later, the agreement had collapsed over allegations of rigged elections and continued latent opposition to the Indira-Abdullah accord. By the 1987 elections, the opposition to the accord was strong enough to result in an oppositional coalition called the Muslim United Front (MUF). The election results were robustly disputed by the opposition but they remained unheeded.

This denial of democratic dissent resulted in large segments of youth concluding that they were being systematically marginalised and denied democratic rights. As a result, they grouped around the Jammu & Kashmir Liberation Front (JKLF) and initiated an armed insurgency. Pakistan soon injected itself into this by inviting youth across the LOC and arming and training them. The Indian army was immediately called in to counter the uprising, resulting in twenty-five years of violent battle, the death of tens of thousands of Kashmiri youth, rancour over human rights violations and deepened uncertainty about the future of the state. Although there have been several attempts by New Delhi and Islamabad to engage on the future of J&K State since 1990, the dynamics of this three-cornered relationship have led to a stalemate. This impasse is occasionally interrupted with attempts at talks about talks, but the persistent deadlock continues.

Militarisation and the J&K dispute

The militarisation of the J&K State began when the armies of both the newly independent Pakistan and India poured into different parts of the state in October 1947. Subsequently, the wars between the two countries—three of which were specifically because of disputes over J&K State—resulted in a steady build up of troops, particularly in LOC East, earning the region the dubious distinction of being the most militarised zone in the world. Depending on the sources, there are today anywhere from half a million to seven hundred thousand military personnel in LOC East alone.

Numbers, however, are just the quantitative side of the story. Until 1989, the presence of the army was largely concentrated along the border with Pakistan as, in the context of the earlier 'bilateralisation' of the dispute, this provided legal legitimacy to India. However, soon after the armed resistance against the Indian state asserted itself at a popular level between 1987 and 1990, the involvement of the army, paramilitary and intelligence agencies has resulted in a qualitative shift so that, to quote a former Indian bureaucrat, 'not a chinar leaf stirs' in Kashmir without the administration's knowledge. In other words, coercion, including militarised coercion, was legally deployed against civil society. This was made instrumental by the application of 'an arsenal of national security laws' (Mathur 2016) including the Terrorism and Disruptive Activities [Prevention] Act (TADA), the Disturbed Areas Act and the Public Safety Act (PSA). The speed, precision and force of the application of these laws in Kashmir was more efficient because the central government in Delhi had practiced them in the Northeast since 1958 and in Punjab since 1983. Arguably the Armed Forces

(Jammu and Kashmir) Special Powers Act (AFSPA), promulgated in 1990, was the most democratically challenged of these laws. It is against this background of the assertion of raw power by the Indian state in Kashmir that we must understand the essays by Shazia Yousuf and Zahid Rafiq.

The human toll of the brutal laws that place the burden of proof of innocence not only on suspected militants but also civilians has been an alarmingly widespread feature of governance in Kashmir and an embarrassing yoke for the 'largest democracy in the world'. The law most invoked here is AFSPA, which empowers the military to make preventive arrests, search premises without a warrant and enable shoot-to-kill orders even when the suspects are civilians. AFSPA, notes Sanjib Baruah, 'also provides significant legal immunity to soldiers charged with misusing powers: court proceedings are made contingent on the Central Government's prior approval'. The qualitatively empowering element of AFSPA is contained in the clause that allows the 'use of armed forces in aid of the civil powers' (Baruah 2014).

This immunity, the pivot of the qualitative power of the agents of the state, started to come into force in Kashmir even before the promulgation of AFSPA in September 1990. The Delhi-based bureaucrat Jagmohan took charge as Governor on January 19, 1990. Two days later, the infamous Gawkadal massacre took place, killing fifty-two civilian protestors and injuring many more. The civilian governor justified his orders less than four months later thus: 'Every Muslim in Kashmir is a militant today. All of them are for secession from India…The bullet is the only solution for Kashmir' (Jamwal 2013). The history of Kashmir for just over the quarter century since then is a virtual catalogue of killings, both en masse and individual (See Mathur 2016).

There were other consequences to the militarisation in Kashmir, including forced disappearances, physical torture on the mere suspicion of involvement in militancy, the burning down of entire neighbourhoods on suspicion of harbouring militants, custodial killings and, even as late as the summer of 2010, shoot-to-kill orders of unarmed protestors. More than 110 youth, averaging about eighteen years in age, were gunned down that summer during multiple protests against, among other things, militarisation. But militarisation has also spawned hidden crimes such as rape and the plight of the victims of 'counter-insurgency' against civilian populations. Though known, these impacts are less talked about. Not entirely coincidentally, the most impacted by these crimes are women.

The two essays by Zahid Rafiq and Shazia Yousuf address rape—almost always prefixed by an 'alleged' because the laws do not require a trial, leaving the victims in limbo—and the social stigma against the widows of militant counter-insurgents (the Ikhwani or, ironically, 'brothers'). Yousuf relates how the widows are shunned by their own community because of a decision in which they had little or no role. Her essay is unique for two reasons: (a) it addresses an issue that has seldom, if at all, been formally written about and (b) it offers an insight into the damage that is done to an already ravaged community: its most vulnerable members are promised a job, convinced they are under state protection, made to turn against their own society and then, once exposed or killed, they or their families are left to fend for themselves. Not only does it further damage the society, it portends an aversion, even abhorrence, of the Indian state that will have deep consequences for the latter's efforts to win 'hearts and minds'. In other words, it prolongs the conflict.

The topic of Rafiq's essay on rape as an instrument of war has seen relatively more discussion. A recent example of this are the essays by five young Kashmiri women in their book *Do You Remember Kunan-Poshpora?* (Batool et al. 2016). But prominently accounted for in Rafiq's narrative is how the crime is premeditated and carried out without fear of legal reckoning of any kind for the officer in question. It also highlights, given the conservatism of Kashmiri society, how the crime is hidden from view, once again, for the stigma that the crime attaches to the victims themselves. It, too, prolongs the conflict.

We began this essay with a consideration of the genesis of the dispute as an acquisitive grab for territory in 1947 between India and Pakistan and, albeit in a marginalized frame, the J&K State itself. Very quickly, it transformed into a political argument about three nationalisms which in turn transmuted into conflicts of religious, regional and ethnic identities. Ultimately, and all too often, the parameters of disputes such as the one over J&K State involve state-to-state relations in the context of history, law and political theory. However, the two essays on Kashmir, and indeed the others in this volume, are intimate narratives of the impact of the dispute and the conflicts they nest on the ground. Inasmuch as they are anthropological accounts, they 'provide a means of witnessing, in both the legal and the moral sense of the word' a forum in which to record the 'lived reality of life under state terror' (Mathur 2016). It is this that gives value to the essays in this anthology, that of being witness to the deep and lasting impact of militarisation on society.

Bibliography

Abdullah, S. M. 1993. *Flames of the Chinar*. New Delhi: Viking.

Anand, A. S. 1980. *The Development of the Constitution of Jammu & Kashmir*. New Delhi: Light and Life Publishers.

Anderson, Perry. 2012. *Indian Ideology*. New Delhi: Three Essays Collective.

Batool, Essar et al. 2016. *Do you remember Kunan-Poshpora?* New Delhi: Zubaan Books.

Bazaz, Prem N. 1941. *Kashmir in Crucible*. New Delhi: Pamposh Publishers.

Bose, Sumantra. 2003. *Kashmir: Roots of Conflict, Paths to Peace*. Cambridge, MA: Harvard University Press.

Bansal, Alok. 2013. 'Gilgit-Baltistan: An Appraisal', Manekshaw Paper No. 37, New Delhi: Centre for Land Warfare Studies.

Baruah, S. 2014. 'Routine Emergencies: India's Armed Forces Special Powers Act' in Aparna Sundar and Nandini Sundar (eds.) *Civil War and Sovereignty in South Asia: Regional and Political Economy Perspectives*. New Delhi: Sage.

Charak, S.S. (Trnsl). 1977. *Gulabnama of Diwan Kirpa Ram*. New Delhi: Light and Life Publishers.

Cohen, Stephen. 1995. 'Kashmir: The Roads Ahead' in Marvin G. Weinbaum and Chetan Kumar, (eds.) *South Asia Approaches the Millennium: Reexamining National Security*. Boulder, CO: Westview Press.

Cunningham, J. D. 1849. *History of the Sikhs* (1910). New Delhi: Rupa.

Ghose, Dilip K. 1975. *Kashmir in Transition*. Calcutta: World Press Private Limited.

Hunzai, Izhar. 2013. 'Conflict Dynamics in Gilgit-Baltistan' in United States Institute of Peace, *Special Report 321*. Washington D.C.

Jamwal, A. Bhasin. 2013. 'A Moon of Many Shades', in *Economic & Political Weekly*, April 27. New Delhi.

Jha, Prem S. 1996. *Kashmir 1947: Rival Versions of History*. New Delhi: Oxford University Press.

Kapur, M.L. 1970. *History of Jammu and Kashmir*. Jammu.

Khan, Hashmatullah. 1937. *Tarikhi Jammu o Kashmir*. Lahore.

Lamb, Alistair. 1966. *Crisis in Kashmir 1947 to 1966*. London: Rutledge and Kegan Paul.

Mathur, Shubh. 2016. *The Human Toll of the Kashmir Conflict – Grief and Courage in a South Asian Borderland*. New York: Palgrave Macmillan.

Meyer, K. and Brysac S.B. 1999. *Tournament of Shadows: The Great Game and the Race for Empire in Central Asia*. Washington D.C: Counterpoint.

Noorani, A.G. 2011. *Article 370: A Constitutional History of J&K*. New Delhi: Oxford University Press.

Panikkar, K.M. 1950. *The Founding of the Kashmir State*. London: George Allen and Unwin.

Puri, Luv. 2010. *Across the LOC: Inside Pakistan Administrated J&K*. New Delhi: Viking.

Rai, Mridu. 2004. *Hindu Rulers, Muslim Subjects: Islam, Rights and the History of Kashmir*. New Delhi: Permanent Black.

Schofield, Victoria. 2004. *Kashmir in Conflict: India, Pakistan and the Unending War*. New Delhi: Viva Books Private Limited.

Shaffer, Howard B. 2009. *The Limits of Influence: America's Role in Kashmir*. New Delhi: Penguin Viking.

Singh, Bawa S. 1974. *The Jammu Fox: A Biography of Maharaja Gulab Singh of Kashmir* (1792–1857). Carbondale, IL: Southern Illinois University Press.

Singh, Khushwant. 1999. *A History of the Sikhs, Vol. 2.* New Delhi: Oxford University Press.

Snedden, C. 2013. *Kashmir: the Unwritten History.* New Delhi: Harper Collins Publishers.

Thomas, Raghu G.C. 1992.*Perspectives on Kashmir: The Roots of the Conflict in South Asia.* Boulder, CO: West View Press.

Zutshi, C. 2003. *Languages of Belonging: Islam, Regional Identity and the Making of Kashmir.* New Delhi: Permanent Black.

Widowhood of Shame

SHAZIA YOUSUF

The room is awkwardly clean. There is a walnut wood bed, a few embroidered curtains and deep silence. The sliding glass door of the almirah screeches a little, as Dilshada takes out the only adornment in the lifeless room. It is a neatly framed picture of a young couple, hand-in-hand, shyly posing in front of the Taj Mahal—the monument of eternal love. With the bright sun above and her husband's protective hand on her shoulder, Dilshada shines in her moon-white silk shalwar kameez. It is an old picture, taken more than a decade ago when Dilshada was cheerful and her husband, Mohammad Yousuf Dar, was an ordinary shopkeeper with an extraordinary passion for family outings and photography.

In the uncomfortable silence of the room, the picture speaks loudly about the happy times that have gone, never to return. Today Dilshada, 55, is a sick and sad woman. Every breath she takes reminds her of an ugly truth. The bullet lodged between two ribs for the last eight years doesn't sit quietly. Every gulp of air budges it a little, causing a piercing pain on the right side of her chest. The ache never lets her forget who she is. 'I am a widow of a renegade. It is a shameful widowhood,' Dilshada says.

Dilshada is one of the hundreds of widows of the Ikhwanis, ironically the Arabic word for brethren—a term used for renegades who were paid by Indian security agencies to counter militant operations in Indian-administered Kashmir. The Ikhwanis were mostly militants who had surrendered and switched sides, helping to break the backbone of militancy in Kashmir. Their widows feel dumped by the Indian agencies and are ostracised by the rest of society for the terror their dead husbands once unleashed.

Until the mid-'90s, Dilshada lived a peaceful life with her husband and their four children: two daughters and two sons. Dar ran a grocery store, close to their home in the main market of Pulwama, about 40 kilometres from the capital, Srinagar. The small house that Dilshada got as a gift from her father when she married had only a few rooms, and the family of six was held close. But one day everything changed. During an ordinary afternoon's conversation Dar broke the bad news: 'I have joined Ikhwan.'

Ikhwan-ul-Muslimeen, or Ikhwan in short, was a pro-government militia counter-insurgency group formed in the early '90s as part of a strategy to aid Indian forces fighting escalating militancy in the Valley. The group was formed by the infamous counter-insurgent Mohammad Yousuf Parray alias 'Kuka Parray', after he surrendered to the Indian government. Prior to joining hands with Indian government forces, Parray was an active militant who had received arms training from Pakistan.

Ikhwanis, under the supervision of Parray, acted as informers, leading soldiers to militant hideouts and revealing details of their activities and movements. They were also locally known as 'Nawabid', after Nawabadi Mohalla in the Sonawari belt of North Kashmir, which was the hub of the counter-insurgency movement in the '90s. Besides receiving a monthly stipend ranging from 3,000 to 10,000 Indian rupees, they were also allowed to keep the weapons that they had possessed as militants. This meant that several thousand armed men were let loose to unleash terror on unarmed civilians under the guise of crushing militancy, supported by the Indian Army, which never took responsibility for their misdeeds.

Licensed mayhem

Soon, Dar began spending most of his time away from home. Though physically away, he was ever-present in the hush-hush conversations of local people; present in the form of terror that he and other Ikhwanis unleashed.

'They ruled the state. It was the most dangerous group because they followed no rules and had no identified enemies or friends. Brutal men were let loose to kill and terrorise people, no matter who they were. Everybody was equally vulnerable,' says Khurram Parvez, Programme Coordinator of the Jammu and Kashmir Coalition of Civil Society (JKCCS).

With the sentiment of azadi (freedom) and resistance in the air, Ikhwanis were intensely hated. For the Kashmiri people, even for those who were not actively involved in the uprising, Ikhwanis were traitors who weakened the cause and broke the back of the resistance movement. Having operated as militants, the Ikhwanis knew all the strategies, secret hideouts and identities of militants operating in their areas. Thus, they were able to penetrate where Indian soldiers could not.

The Ikhwanis were vicious not only to militants but to unarmed civilians as well. It was during this counter-insurgency operation that some of the worst human rights violations occurred in Kashmir. The weapons they were allowed to keep were not only used on militants but also on locals to settle personal scores. Ikhwanis reportedly raped women, maimed children and killed men. Loot, extortion, kidnapping and killing were carried out in a grand exhibition of their power.

'There are no authentic statistics about Ikhwanis available. We are preparing a report but it is still in its infancy and most of the stories we learn from Ikhwanis and their victims cannot be disclosed due to the risk involved. Many of those who carried out brutalities are alive and holding powerful positions in the government. Revealing their stories of cruelty can bring more harm than good to their victims. Thus, very few victims dare to speak out against them,' adds Parvez.

Sajad Ahmad Wani is one such. On June 6, 1993, Sajad was standing hand-in-hand with his father in a passenger shikara that was quietly rowing them towards the mosque in their village in Bandipora. Sajad was a student in Class Ten and his father, Abdul Khaliq Wani, was the principal of a nearby high school. Khaliq, besides being known for his contribution towards the education of children in his village, was also known for being an ardent supporter of Jamaat-e-Islami.[1]

'My father was a happy man, respected in his village and loved by all. He wanted to give the best possible education to me and my younger sister who studied in Class Four at that time,' remembers Sajad.

When the boat was halfway across, a group of armed men shouted at the boatman: 'We have to kill this man. Either bring the boat back or get ready for your death. All of you.' There were some ten other people in the boat, so the boatman quietly obliged. 'The moment my father and I stepped ashore, they fired a bullet in his head. He died instantly,' recalls Sajad. 'When he fell, his body brushed against mine.'

On the insistence of his mother, Sajad spent most of his time in Srinagar—away from his sister and mother. Rumours about him being the next target made them live in constant fear. Relatives and friends maintained a distance, since helping a family which was close to the Jamaat-e-Islami would invite the wrath of the Ikhwanis. This isolation plunged them into unbearable loneliness. 'You have no idea how much we suffered after they killed my father. Everyone— relatives and friends—left us at the mercy of God. Nobody entered our house to check on us, even to see if we were dead or alive,' he says.

Sajad graduated, got a job in the Social Welfare department under a scheme for appointment on compassionate grounds known as SRO-43, and got his younger sister married. When it was the time for his marriage, he was bluntly refused any match in his village. One day when his mother angrily asked a matchmaker the reason for such continuous rejection, he replied: 'Death is certain; but some deaths are more certain than others.'

'I got a wife who empathised with me. She has witnessed the death of her own mother in a cross-firing. She is angry like me and inspires me to take up the fight. And I will fight. No matter who wins,' says Sajad, his eyes empty.

---

[1]Jamaat-e-Islami Jammu and Kashmir is a religio-political organisation that considers itself as the true representative of the people of the state and feels it should be part of any deliberations on its future.

Payment in blood

Whenever Dar visited home, Dilshada argued with him about his wrongdoings and how they caused suffering to his whole family. She told him about the loneliness that had engulfed his house and family. At social gatherings, she told him, his family sat alone in a corner and waited for people to notice and greet them. People passed by but there were no smiles.

Dar did not listen; he liked what his association with Ikhwan offered him—money, power and security. When Dilshada closed her doors to his associates and did not let them in for their anti-militancy meetings, Dar obliged. Arguments became fewer and more frequent became the news of Dar's activities. From a man who loved family outings and photography, Dar became a killer. He spilled blood and talked about death. Dilshada resisted and tried hard to keep her distance. But one day she became a part of it. Willy-nilly.

It was a sunny morning in the late '90s. The children were at school. Dilshada had a lot of time to kill. She climbed up a stool, brought all the utensils down and began to scrub the kitchen shelves. A small window above the shelves let in an unusual sound and Dilshada peeped to check.

A neighbour came running towards her. Militants, he gasped, had murdered a relative in revenge for Dar killing one of their associates. The relative was eighteen-year-old Bashir Ahmad Wani, Dilshada's youngest brother.

Dilshada ran barefoot to her father's house, no scarf covering her head, the scouring pad clutched tight in her hand. She had not thought of putting it down. She had not thought about anything.

At her father's house, Dilshada was not received as Bashir's sister but as the wife of his killer. Some cursed her, some spat and some held her by the arm and forced her to leave. Dilshada at first tried to explain and prove her innocence, but when she saw her elderly parents tightly hugging their son's dead body, she froze. 'I was too ashamed to explain anything.'

Dilshada was the eldest child of her parents. She was smart and dynamic and maintained the accounts for her businessman father who owned apple orchards and exported fruit. Her father never wanted her to go out of his sight. So when he started receiving marriage proposals, he accepted one from a man who was ready to move into their house.

Dar and Dilshada spent the first few years of their marriage at her father's house. Later, he gifted them a house not far from his home. Dilshada's younger sister was married and lived in a far away village. Her parents lived with their two sons; Bashir Ahmad was the youngest.

A few months after their son's killing, Dilshada's parents died of grief, one after the other. Her elder brother, too scared to live alone in the house, locked it up and fled to safety. Dilshada too wanted to run away from her husband, her father's empty house and the guilt about her brother's death that lay heavy on her chest. 'Everyone blames me for what happened to my father's house; and I blame him. I will not forgive him for this,' she said.

Dar was always apologetic for Dilshada's loss. Every time he witnessed hostile behaviour by any of her relatives towards her, he asked for forgiveness. Dilshada couldn't forgive, because she couldn't forget. 'Only my death can wash away that memory.'

After the birth of counter-insurgency operations, militancy showed a sharp decline. New Delhi was able to hold the Jammu and Kashmir Assembly elections in 1996. This was also when Kuka Parray formed his own political party, the Awami League, and contested the elections. He won and became a legislator in the state assembly. Dar too joined the Awami League after working for Ikhwan for eight years. He contested elections twice—in 2002 and 2005—only to lose both times. Dilshada did not cast her vote.

Fragments of life

An unofficial figure quoted by Kuka Parray's son, Imtiyaz Parray, puts the total number of Ikhwanis at 4,000, of which more than 1,500 were killed by militants in retaliatory attacks. But Khurram Parvez rejects these statistics: 'There have been no studies conducted on them. Even journalists have left this topic unreported. Counter-insurgency, we may argue, has died. But Ikhwanis have not. They are here and many of them are more powerful than before.'

Parvez refers to people like Abdul Rashid Parray alias Rashid Billa, a former government gunman and now a close aide of ex-minister Akbar Lone. On October 5, 1996, Billa, accompanied by some twenty government-supported gunmen and Indian soldiers, killed seven people in Sadrakoot Bala in Bandipora.

It was 7:30 p.m. and Billa knocked on the door of Ghulam Qadir Dar. Qadir was a worker with the National Conference party and often tortured and kidnapped by Ikhwanis in those days. 'They wanted me to work for them. First they tried to buy me with offers and when I turned them down, they resorted to violence,' Qadir remembers. He was offered money, power and the leadership of a forty-member Ikhwani group, but he wanted to remain loyal to National Conference, for which he had worked for many years.

As Qadir went out to open the door, his family members came running after him—first his wife, then son, then daughter and then nephew—only to be killed one by one by Rashid Billa and his group. 'I was made to stand against the wall and watch as Billa carried out the massacre in my house. It took him less than five minutes to turn my world upside down,' Qadir says. The gunmen entered three adjacent houses, killing the family heads of each house.

For Qadir, the rest of his life has been filled with nothing but guilt, shame and responsibilities. His son Abdul Salam Dar was a carpet weaver and father of four daughters. Five months after his killing, his wife Shakeela Bano gave birth to a son. Qadir's nephew, Abdul Rashid Dar, was also the father of four small children. 'It was because of me they died: my wife who had no idea what I was doing, my daughter who was too young to be sent to her grave, my son who couldn't see a glimpse of his son and my nephew who paid a huge price for visiting his uncle.' Qadir breaks down. 'It is a terrible feeling. I have a huge rock on my chest.'''

Qadir could hardly think of taking up the fight. He had many mouths to feed: his daughter-in-law, five grandchildren and two unmarried children—a son and a daughter—who had escaped the

massacre. 'The enemies were powerful and I was weak. I thought the
National Conference would support and back my struggle, but they
too abandoned me. I feel ditched and disgusted. In the next world
how will I face my family for their killers still roam around freely?'

Of the twenty or so men who barged into Qadir's house that
fateful night, he recognised nine. Six are already dead, while three
are alive to remind him of the horrors of the past.

Although Qadir has learned to keep himself busy raising and
educating his orphaned grandchildren, once in a while, when Rashid
Billa's vehicle passes by his house and he sees a dozen policemen
guarding it from the front and the back, Qadir says he 'breaks into
pieces.'

Home alone

On a sunny morning in the summer of 2006, Dilshada's husband
left home for Baramulla town for an official meeting with his party
members. Since she too had to meet a relative in the same town, they
decided to go together. Dar drove the car with Dilshada sitting by
his side. The two security guards sat in the back. Barely a kilometre
away from their house, a group of boys waved for help. Dar ignored
them but Dilshada asked him to stop. 'They have notebooks in their
hands,' she told him, 'and it is exam time. They seem to be getting
late for exams.'

The vehicle reversed and stopped right in front of the boys. The
youngest of them showered a rain of bullets. Dar received countless
shots in his chest, fell on to Dilshada's lap and died on the spot. The
two security guards survived. So did Dilshada. Of the four bullets
that hit her, three were successfully extracted. The fourth one wasn't.
The bullet was embedded between her ribs and if removed surgically
might have paralysed or even killed her. 'I tell my children to let it
stay in my chest. There is no balm for the wound. Bullet or no bullet,
the discomfort in my chest will not go,' Dilshada says.

More than the wedged bullet, what pains Dilshada is her strained
relationship with relatives and friends and the bad name that Dar has
left for the family. Sometimes, when she is alone, Dilshada imagines

being a militant's widow. She imagines people coming over to her house on festivals and other occasions and she busily going up and down, serving and seeing them off. She imagines someone talking enviously about her martyr husband, his bravery and her patience, and how the two would walk hand-in-hand in heaven. 'And when my dream ends and I come face to face with reality, I want to dig my own grave and hide in shame,' Dilshada says.

Dilshada was left vulnerable and alone, in a hauntingly silent house in Bahrabad Hajin in Bandipora district. Once in a while when she tried to go out and socialise, she was greeted by hateful stares and whispers. Like Dilshada, hundreds of widows of slain Ikhwanis were ostracised and became victims of social boycott. The rest of their lives offer nothing but loneliness and the life-long taint of being a renegade's widow. 'As soon as dusk falls, I ask my children to draw the curtains and sit quiet. I think I don't want to see anyone. I don't want anyone to see us.'

Dilshada's story of loneliness and melancholy, shared by hundreds of widows of slain Ikhwanis, is a harsh but hidden social reality in Kashmir.

False promises

The public response to the deaths of Ikhwanis at the hands of militants was not unexpected. However, the response of the Indian state for which the counter-insurgents worked took everyone—especially their families—by surprise. The worth of Ikhwanis for Indian forces proved to be no more than that of disposable cutlery, to be trashed once the grand feast is over.

'Indian forces lured them with promises of jobs, money and security for their families after their death. Leave aside these monetary promises, none of them even came to see us. They knew how society looked down upon us. It was their responsibility to help us morally and financially,' says Sajad Ahmad Dar, Dilshada's elder son.

Twenty-six-year-old Sajad is angry. All his father's claims have been proved painfully wrong. None of the people for whom his father worked visited his home. When his father was killed and his mother battled for her life, Sajad felt isolated and helpless. His two siblings were not in the state and his elder sister was inconsolable and fainted every now and then. Sajad found himself all alone with his father's dead body. 'Those days, dozens of Ikhwanis would be killed on a daily basis. I was scared to lose my father. One day I asked him what would happen to us if militants killed him, and he replied that the Indian government was there to take care of us,' recalls Sajad. 'How wrong he was!' he sighs.

For years after his father's death, Sajad lived in a state of perplexity and confusion. He dreaded the Indian state, hated its soldiers and regretted being on the 'wrong' side. Militants haunted his dreams and he foresaw only death and a dark future. Sajad was insecure. One morning he woke up and decided to join the Indian National Congress and contest elections from his constituency. Two weeks later, he resigned. 'I didn't know what I was doing or what I should do,' he says. 'I was lost.'

When the counterinsurgency operations began, the Indian state promised jobs to the surrendered militants who joined Ikhwan and contributed to the decline of militancy. However, only 250 Ikhwanis were accommodated in the Territorial Army and a few more in the paramilitary Central Reserve Police Force (CRPF). A small number work as SPOs (Special Police Officers) in the Jammu and Kashmir Police.

Sajad too works as an SPO posted in Jammu. He earns a monthly salary of 5,000 Indian rupees. 'This job was secured by my father when he was alive. I was not even eligible for it at that time. Thankfully, had he not done that, I wouldn't have even this little security.'

While the sons of renegades struggle with perpetual anger and frustration, daughters face difficulties in finding proper marriage partners. Dilshada's two daughters are 'thankfully' married now. It was extremely difficult to find a match for her elder daughter. Nobody was ready to initiate a relationship with a traitor's family. Then, one day a cousin came to Dilshada with a marriage proposal for her son. Dilshada thanked God and went ahead with the wedding. Her second daughter is married to Imtiyaz Parray, Kuka Parray's son. 'It is not only us, many renegade families have married into other such families to avoid taunts and torture. My daughters have suffered a lot in this house. I wanted their new lives to remain untouched by their past.'

Where dreams die

Sixteen-year-old Mudasir, Dilshada's youngest son, has just styled his hair. He is very conscious about it. While talking, his hands involuntarily reach for the gelled spikes to pat them into order. While the rest of the family dresses almost alike, Mudasir stands out. An over-sized green T-shirt and multiple-pocketed trousers overwhelm his frail frame. Besides, he talks only in English: 'I wanted to become a pop star,' he says.

A dark, narrow corridor leads to Mudasir's room. A guitar hangs on a wall alongside posters of Western pop singers. Mudasir stops near his glass cupboard. This is where the remains of his unrealised dreams hide. There are dozens of merit certificates bunched to each other, almost screaming for attention. Medals dangle in the middle of the cupboard, alone, like nooses around the neck of a just-hanged hope. 'At one point, this seemed the beginning of a journey; now it reminds me of the abrupt end,' Mudasir says, with his eyes fixed on the glass cupboard. 'I am sad but have accepted defeat. I will never become a pop star now.'

As an award for Dar's 'excellent' services, the Indian Army had sponsored Mudasir's education. Barely five years old then, Mudasir was sent to Allahabad and enrolled in the prestigious St. John's Academy. 'My parents accompanied me and I was crying. I was too scared to live without them. But when they took me around the campus, I stopped crying. It was like home.' It was at St. John's Academy that Mudasir discovered his love for music. He took part in music competitions and brought laurels to his school. The school administration and his music teachers assured Mudasir all possible help in realising his dream. But then Dar was killed; the Indian Army withdrew its sponsorship of his son's education.

'All of a sudden, I was thrown out. I was brought to this place which I had left as a little kid. It felt like someone killed me too.'

Mudasir now studies in Class Eleven in a Srinagar school. He wants to forget his past and move on but sometimes when he thinks of his childhood and how it became victim of a dirty game, he gets angry. 'That time, I was a kid and believed that fathers could never be wrong. But now, when I have grown up, I can tell you that he shouldn't have done what he did,' he says. 'My perception about Kashmiri people and their demand for freedom has also changed. One day when I saw Indian soldiers ruthlessly beating stone throwers almost my age, I suddenly felt like going out and throwing stones at them with all my energy.'

Dilshada and Mudasir love to watch India-Pakistan cricket matches together. They shout, hug and cook special food when Pakistan defeats India, something that Dar would not have allowed. 'His father would make me pray for the Pakistan team's defeat. I would lie to him and pray for their success.'

Cursed legacy

Zareefa Akhter had just finished high school when her parents chose a husband for her. Noor-ud-din was a handsome college boy, soon going to be the first commerce graduate in his extended family. Until their marriage in 1992, the couple had not seen each other face to face. Zareefa, however, had heard that Noor-ud-din looked like the Bollywood actor, Aamir Khan. This helped her to visualise him and their lives together.

Noor-ud-din was a loving and hardworking husband who ran a grocery store just outside his home in Watpora Payeen village of Bandipora.

The couple had three years of blissful married life. Zareefa couldn't ask for more. Although her in-laws treated her badly, Zareefa didn't mind. After all, it was just few steps away from the house that Noor-ud-din sat in his shop. She could always find an excuse to go outside and get a glimpse of the person in whom she had found the love of her life.

One day a friend told Zareefa that she had seen Noor-ud-din entering an army camp. When she questioned him, he told her that he had started working as an informer. Zareefa's first reaction was to walk out of the marriage but the child she had just learnt she was carrying did not let her. Things were never the same. Zareefa always found herself on edge, thinking about possible reprisals that her husband's activities could invite.

A few months later, she gave birth to her son, Azhar-ud-din. The boy had barely turned one when Zareefa gave birth to another son, Naseer-ud-din. 'Life was giving me one gift after the other. My only complaint was Noor-ud-din's association with the Army. I knew he was doing wrong,' Zareefa remembers.

On the night of March 19, 1997, two young men knocked on the door and asked for Noor-ud-din. They wanted a few minutes of his time to discuss some important issue, they said. The next day his body was found in a nearby field. 'It had to happen one day. He had jumped into the well of fire,' says Zareefa. Noor-ud-din had not only jumped into the fire but also left behind burning embers for Zareefa and their two little sons.

Speaking of the fate of Ikhwanis, Khurram Parvez says, 'Many of them were later killed by the Indian soldiers for whom they worked. We are following a case where more than fifteen Ikhwanis got disappeared at the hands of the Indian Army who used them for an anti-militant operation and disposed them off once their job was done".

Zareefa wanted to leave her marital home and make a new life for herself and her children. But her in-laws wanted to raise her children and retain their property. When she refused, a new condition was put before her: marry Ali Mohammad, her brother-in-law.

She remembered seeing Ali Mohammad as a little boy too shy to meet his brother's wife. As she sat in her bridal attire with her husband in their decorated room, his younger brother stood hesitatingly at the door, making one unsuccessful attempt after the other to come inside and meet the new member of his family. 'My husband stood up and dragged him in by his ear. Here is my son, he told me. And from today, he is your son too.'

It took Zareefa a while to see him as her new husband. But he seemed a perfect father for her orphan children who needed love. 'It was a marriage of compromise. My heart was still with my dead husband,' Zareefa remembers. The day of her second wedding was her most uncomfortable ever. The man she had married was still the younger brother of her dead husband.

Today Zareefa lives in a new house. Ali Mohammad is an employee at the Education Department. 'My children are still orphans; you can read it from their faces,' Zareefa breaks down. 'Their uncle could never become their father.' Ali Mohammad's son, six-year-old Samiullah born from his marriage with Zareefa, goes to one of the best private schools in town. It is not the same for Azhar and Naseer. They have to earn their school fees if they want to continue their studies. While Naseer has already given up his studies, Azhar wants to continue. During the apple harvesting season, Azhar helps make wooden fruit boxes for packing. This fetches him enough for his school fees and some savings for other study-related expenses. While Azhar has to resort to menial jobs to earn his school fees, Samiullah's school bus honks outside his house every morning.

'They don't talk about the discrimination, but I know it is eating my children up from inside,' Zareefa glances at Azhar and bursts into tears. 'Some needs are to be felt by parents. A child cannot always ask for everything,' Azhar says. 'When we have exams, I see the fathers of my classmates waiting for them outside the examination centre. When I come out, I know there is no one. I am sure if I tell my stepfather, he would come. But had my real father been alive, he would have just been there, like other fathers.' Azhar's mature conversation does not match his lean young body. He is frail and has a bony face, overburdened with a thick pair of spectacles.

While children in the neighbourhood maintain a distance, Azhar and his younger brother call their father shaheed, a martyr. 'I am proud of my father. He is my hero. When someone sacrifices his life for a cause, people call him martyr, then why is my father not one?' asks Azhar confusedly.

Azhar is a sensitive boy. Every now and then he returns home crying about being called a renegade's son. Being an orphan, he says, is different from being the fatherless son of a renegade. 'You are cursed. People do not sympathize with you. Your needs do not mean anything to anyone.'

Silent in grief

Sixty-five-year-old Zooni Begum is bitter. She barely listens to anyone. If you ask her about her life, she responds with ironical Kashmiri proverbs. '*Yim zakhm chi khalaan, ballan ni kenh*' (these wounds only swell with time, they do not heal).

Zooni was married as a child to her cousin Abdul Ahad Koul. The couple lived with their four daughters and two sons in a small village on the banks of Wullar Lake in Bandipora. The family of eight survived on the sale of chestnuts picked from the lake. Sometime in the mid-'90s, Zooni's brother-in-law, Ghulam Ahmad Koul, a Pakistan-trained militant joined Ikhwan and began anti-militant operations in his village. Seeing his brother enjoying wealth and power, Zooni's husband joined too. Zooni learnt about it a few days later. The first thing that came to her mind was his death, their roofless house, the four unmarried daughters and two little sons they so wanted to educate. Zooni resisted. She fought with Ahad for his life, for her life and the life of their children. There were tears, pleas and warnings but Ahad listened to no one. His involvement with Ikhwan went on for years until one night when he did not return home. Zooni sniffed a tragedy.

'I had told him when he drowns, he will not drown alone; we too will go under,' Zooni remembers.

The family waited till dawn and when Ahad did not return, their search began. The three elder daughters left early in the morning in their boat, paddling through the waters of the Wullar Lake. Almost an hour later, when the sun had just begun to shine, the youngest, teenaged Saleema, screamed and pointed at Ahad's body on the bank, his throat slit.

More than the loss, that day reminds Zooni of the unending

loneliness. She cried and cried harder, but no relatives, neighbours or friends visited the house. The hours of crying and wailing were followed by a long silence. She was tired.

'I thought people would not punish me for something that my husband had done. But they did. They watched from a distance and reminded us that we were different people and that they could not become like us,' she says.

It was only many hours later that a group of elderly neighbours came and hastily completed the last rites. From the graveyard where they buried Ahad, the neighbours straightaway headed for their respective homes.

'Renegades are not respected. Had he been a militant, people would have poured in with their condolences. My daughters wouldn't have had to search for their father's dead body by themselves,' says Zooni. Ahad's killing and the subsequent reaction gave Zooni some idea of politics, of militants and renegades, and of the different lives their widows live. 'I have lived all my life in this village. I know nothing about who is fighting whom and what they are fighting for,' she says. 'My husband did something I don't even know about and a storm came and took over my life.'

In her own battle for survival, Zooni has almost forgotten her husband. She doesn't have a photograph of him and his image in her memory is clouded with bitterness and anger, 'Short. Plump. What else?' Ahad had assured Zooni that in case he was killed, the family would be taken care of by his brother, his party members and the Indian agencies he was working for. No one came.

Zooni and her daughter together make 50 to 100 Indian rupees per day by selling chestnuts. She has managed to get three daughters married and also renovated her house. Now 65, she lives with Saleema and two sons, who work as manual labourers.

Saleema watches and listens from the edge of a curtain, and runs back to the kitchen where she spends most of her time. When she brings in tea and biscuits, she looks at no one. As her mother narrates her story, the curtain edge begins to flutter. Behind it, Saleema pays attention to minute details, perhaps in an attempt to understand what has happened to her and why.

'Since that scream, we hardly hear anything from her. She is always like that. Like a corpse,' says her mother. Saleema was the first to spot her father's body on the banks of the Wullar. Ahad's throat was slit, his lips dark and face like mud. Saleema screamed and then fell silent.

'She had no idea what was happening around her. She remained stiff like a stone and did not shed a single tear. For some time I thought she would go mad,' her mother says. Saleema took a month to utter another word. Even though her doctors say she is normal, she is not what she used to be.'

On the way back, a young boatman rows this writer to the other side of the lake. He is curious to know what the visit was about. I explain and express sadness over the ill-treatment the family had received at the hands of the villagers.

The boatman points to a rosy-cheeked young girl in a floral cherry-red scarf: 'You see that little girl? She is my sister. She was barely a year old when our mother was killed by the husband of the woman you just met. She turned down his sexual advances and he beheaded her with an axe,' he says, with his eyes fixed on his sister. The girl calls her brother for supper and disappears into the slum-like colony.

The boat reaches the shore and stops with a thud. The boatman extends a hand to climb the slippery bank. 'Madam, do you think we can still be sympathetic to them?'

Shadows of a Dark Night

ZAHID RAFIQ

Every other month, for a day or two, something takes over a young woman whom we shall call Nasreen. She suddenly ceases to be her usual soft and calm self. She withdraws from everything and everyone, even from her two daughters, four and six years old.

Since her marriage seven years ago, Nasreen, 32, has lived with her husband and his family in a small village in the southern part of Indian-administered Kashmir. Her in-laws own some land and apple orchards. Her husband makes a decent living and their two daughters go to a private school.

But her in-laws complain to her mother and sister that on some days, Nasreen desperately beats the floors and claws at the earth with her nails. On the days of the 'sickness', Nasreen froths at the mouth, wails like a little girl and then faints.

Her family fears that someday her in-laws, the more powerful in the marriage as the 'boy's side,' will send Nasreen and her daughters back to her natal family. 'They [Nasreen's in-laws] are well off, and things are, thank God! thank God! good for Nasreen,' her older sister, whom we shall refer to as Farida, says. 'And I hope nothing bad happens now!'

Her in-laws took Nasreen to a doctor; he couldn't find anything wrong. They were then sure that she was possessed, but even faith healers have not been able to rid her of her demons.

'Only the afflicted can know pain,' Farida says. 'I was older and somehow I could deal with what happened to us, but my sister was just a child then. No one else can understand her pain. I only hope that she forgets it or else they [Nasreen's in-laws] might not tolerate her for long.'

'After all, with two daughters and no son and these bouts of pain,' Khadija (the name we shall use for Nasreen's old and ailing mother) says, 'my daughter's position in her in-laws home is a knot of weak threads.' With Farida already divorced, Khadija cannot bear to contemplate a similar fate for her youngest daughter.

Farida describes how they explained to Nasreen's husband and mother-in-law that the disappearance of their father eighteen years ago wreaked havoc on the then fourteen-year-old Nasreen. She has never gotten over the loss of her father. 'They knew what happened to our father and they understood,' she says. 'But God forbid, God forbid, if the secret ever comes out. If her husband and her in-laws ever come to hear of it,' Farida says, 'my sister will be back here in no time.'

'So please don't write her name, and please don't write our names. Please don't identify us. Please just have lunch with us and then go. We have lost everything and we don't want any justice now. Please don't bring another calamity into our home,' Farida says, tears welling up in her eyes.

Farida, her thirty-year-old son Ahmad, her twenty-seven-year-old daughter Zeenat, and their grandmother, Khadija all look appealingly at me: leave us alone.

They had just returned from their paddy fields where they had been working in the sun since morning. All they wanted to do was eat the meal they had cooked before leaving for the fields. But a tiny bit of them wanted to speak out and I conversed with that part.

Reluctant to draw memories from the dark well of the past, they talked about the present—their fields, their family, Ahmad's job in a candle factory.

Khadija, the grandmother, is getting more deaf and blind by the day; she walks slowly around the house, her aching back doubled up. The family is looking for a match for Zeenat and if everything goes well, they say, she will be married soon. Ahmad, her elder brother, after a silent and lonely adolescence of seeking an escape and some solace in sleeping pills, is finally becoming the man of the house. Their mother, Farida, is slowly growing older and more numb, while her mind wanders often to the scars on the soul of her youth and the brutality and betrayal that she witnessed. Her feet go cold, Farida says, and her legs begin to shiver whenever anyone from the Indian Army passes by or comes into their house.

'Don't bring the Indian Army to my house again,' she says. I promise that I will do nothing and write nothing that will bring the Indian Army to their home again.

Curfews and clampdowns

In the 1990s, the soldiers of the Indian Army came too often to their house in Anantnag district in the southern part of Indian-administered Kashmir. They would leave only after threatening and taunting them, turning sacks of grain upside down and rifling through the rice and their clothes. Amid all this, they would also beat up their father, Mohammad Abdullah, a carpenter in his late fifties with a weak heart.

'They would pull him by his white beard and ask him to hand over his son-in-law,' Farida says. 'In front of us, they slapped him, kicked him, dragged him around by his hair and threatened to kill him if he didn't bring in my husband.'

'We would beg the soldiers to spare our father. I asked them to go and kill my husband who was a militant with a gun who had left home to fight the Indian forces,' Farida says. 'But they would go on thrashing my old father.'

The eldest of Mohammad Abdullah's three daughters, Farida was married in 1984 to a government employee in an adjacent village. A year later, their son Ahmad was born and three years later, their daughter Zeenat.

In 1990, when thousands of Kashmiri youth picked up arms as the Valley erupted in a popular armed uprising against New Delhi's rule in the disputed territory, Farida's husband too picked up the gun.

Soon after her husband went to fight, Farida returned with her two children to her father's home. Her father worked as a carpenter while the women looked after the domestic front and tended the cattle, sheep and hens.

By 1997, Farida's husband had grown to be a well-known militant commander of the Hizbul Mujahideen, whom we shall call 'Abu Usman'. What irked the army, Farida says, was that the camp of the 5 Rashtriya Rifles (RR) battalion was just next to her in-laws house. 'That house consistently reminded them that my husband was a militant. They would have killed my in-laws had they not fled to Jammu after the first few raids on their house,' Farida says.

After her younger sister Nargis was married in 1994 into a neighbouring village, Farida, her two children, and her youngest sister, Nasreen, lived with their parents.

As in the rest of Kashmir, there were crackdowns and search operations and civilians were driven out of their homes and beaten, tortured and killed. Mornings would often begin with recounting the stories of the previous night's horror, and each day was as dreadful as the previous one. Farida and her family continued to live with hopes of a better future, until that one winter night.

Night without end

It was the afternoon of January 3, 1997, when soldiers from the 5 Rashtriya Rifles camp in the village came to the house.

'I was standing in the yard feeding the animals when the soldiers came. There were almost a hundred of them,' Farida recounts. 'There was a new major. Major Arora, he was called. He asked me about my husband and I said that he was a militant and that I had not seen him for many years.'

In fact, by then, her husband who had been on the run for seven years, had found another woman in one of his several hideouts. She was almost half his age and much younger than his first wife. He had since stopped contacting Farida or his children.

But the Indian Army wanted 'Abu Usman', and when they could not lay their hands on him, they went for his family instead—a routine practice followed by the Indian armed forces operating in Kashmir. And with 'Abu Usman's' father and brothers having already

fled to Srinagar and Jammu to save themselves from the wrath of
the army, Farida and her family became the targets.

Fourteen-year-old Nasreen was standing on the porch while
Farida answered Major Arora's questions. When the army arrives on
the doorstep in Kashmir, no one can run away or hide; that would
amount to a tacit admission of guilt. So when Major Arora walked
toward Nasreen, she just stood there, looking down. Ahmad and
Zeenat, Farida's children, were also sitting on the porch.

"'What are these things in her ears," he turned around and asked
me,' Farida says. "'She had her ears pierced yesterday and it is a piece
of thread tied in her ear", I told him,' Farida says. 'And he looked at
her and then left without asking any more questions.'

At around 8 p.m. that evening, when the family was about to have
dinner, all four rooms in their house were suddenly full of soldiers
from the 5 RR camp, led by Major Arora. They pushed Abdullah
against the wall and then started dragging him out. Khadija and
Farida begged them not to take him away but Major Arora said,
'He has met with Usman in the afternoon today and we need to
know some details.'

'We told him that it was not true and that none of us had seen
my son-in-law for three years,' Khadija says.

'I went up to the Major and told them that they should use all
their force to fight my husband. Why were they going after my old
father,' Farida says. 'The Major did not listen. He was drunk and
smelled of alcohol. He slapped me and then someone hit the light
bulb. There was a shattering noise and then darkness,' she says.

Reluctantly Farida whispers what happened next.

While Major Arora took fourteen-year-old Nasreen to another
room, other soldiers held Farida.

It was a night of darkness and terror. Their cries filled the silent
night, but it was as if no one heard them. The villagers shut their
windows and doused their lights and in darkness, the two sisters
kept shouting for help.

'It was 1997. The Indian Army was brutal and we knew that if
we went out, they would kill us and do the same to our daughters.

We were afraid,' says Mohammad Yaqoob, a neighbour who lives a few houses away. 'Sometimes one becomes weak, and trust me, it is the worst memory of my life. Sometimes I wish I had gotten killed saving them, but the reality is that I hid with my family in my house like everyone else,' he says.

Farida says that she somehow managed to hide in the darkness with blood dripping from her lips, cheeks and breasts where she had been bitten. 'When the soldiers left, my sister was lying in the room and she was bleeding and semi-conscious. She was all torn and smeared with blood,' Farida recalls. She gathered her wits, roused her sister and they fled, fearing that the soldiers would return.

'When we stepped out, it was silent. I still remember that silence,' she says. 'I was crying and I asked a neighbour who was peeking from the window for a shalwar for my sister, who was completely naked.'

Khadija had hidden in a mosque that night and says she was crying and praying for her husband and daughters. The two children had been whisked to safety by a neighbour. Bleeding and wounded, Farida and Nasreen hid themselves in a public lavatory by the banks of a stream near the village. 'We sat there bleeding and crying, hugging each other. At first I thought she was dead because she wouldn't speak, she was in complete shock,' Farida says.

While the two sisters were in hiding, as expected, the soldiers came again looking for them. 'They went to our house to look for us but when they did not find us there, they burnt it down completely and took our sheep from the barn,' Farida says. 'Had they found us, they would have killed us.'

Occupied land

Kashmir has for centuries been called a 'Paradise on Earth' by those who set eyes upon this idyllic valley nestled in the Himalayas, but for its people, Kashmir's beauty has been its curse. It has lived through more than four centuries of foreign rule, beginning with the Mughals in 1586. Each of the regimes—Afghan, Sikh, Dogra and the present rule by New Delhi—is largely remembered as a regime of tyranny.

For centuries, the Kashmiri people have resisted foreign rule. During the 1930s and '40s, Kashmiri leaders, in their struggle against the Dogra reign, forged friendships with Indian leaders who were fighting British rule in their country. In the mid-twentieth century, at the twilight of the Raj and the beginning of decolonisation, when power seemed to flow to oppressed peoples, Kashmiris believed that they too finally were going to be free.

But in the post-colonial period, both India and the newly-created Pakistan, modern nation-states which replaced empires and princely states, have administered Kashmir in part and claimed it in full. When, in 1989-1990, the Kashmir Valley rose en masse in an armed rebellion against the unpopular Indian rule, the possibility of freedom came into being. Azadi.

The conflict escalated and Pakistan jumped into the fray by supporting the uprising. India sent in more soldiers—now numbering more than half a million—to crush the rebellion. Newspapers and human rights organisations like the Jammu and Kashmir Coalition of Civil Society (JKCCS) say that a whole generation of Kashmiris fell to the operations of the Indian Army. The army also raised a counter-insurgency militia from among the local population to fight the insurgents, and the several dozen militant groups that had emerged by the mid-1990s began fighting each other.

Today, according to international news organisations like Associated Press and local human rights organisations like the JKCCS, more than 70,000 Kashmiri people have died violent deaths and thousands have been subjected to enforced disappearances mostly by the Indian Army. Rape, torture and destruction of property have also been systematically used by the Indian state in its political and military campaign in Kashmir (IPTK-APDP 2012).

Women's bodies, linked to ideas of honour and shame in patriarchal societies, most often become the arena for psychological warfare in conflicts. While sexual violence traumatises victims and survivors, it also crushes their families under shame and guilt.

Armed with guns, shielded by impunity and with almost absolute control over life and death in the Kashmir Valley, Indian soldiers were accused of sexual violence and rapes soon after the armed rebellion started. In a 1993 report by the Human Rights Watch (HRW), the researchers came across fifteen cases of rape, twelve of which occurred during the week they were in Kashmir, giving an idea about the magnitude of rape as a weapon of war used by Indian soldiers.

'Despite evidence that army and paramilitary forces were engaging in widespread rape, few of the incidents were ever investigated by the authorities. Those that were reported did not result in criminal prosecutions of the security forces involved,' the HRW report says.

The report documents several cases of rape including the well-publicised case of May 1990 in which a young bride, Mubeena Gani, was detained and raped by Border Security Force (BSF) soldiers while she was travelling from the wedding to her husband's home. Her aunt was also raped. 'The security forces had also fired on the party, killing one man and wounding several others. The government claimed that the party had been caught in "cross-fire". After the incident was publicized in the local and international press, Indian authorities ordered the police to conduct an inquiry. Although the inquiry concluded that the women had been raped, the security forces were never prosecuted,' the report says.

The report also examined the use of violence by the Indian forces against doctors attempting to document evidence of rape, and cites the example of a doctor in Anantnag who was tortured after he called in a gynaecologist when seven women approached him saying they were raped by Indian paramilitary personnel.

The 1993 report—which only deals with three years of human right abuses by Indian soldiers in Kashmir—mentions scores of cases where women alleged rape but were left without any recourse to justice by a state that seemed to allow the use of rape as a weapon of war.

One of the most publicised cases of sexual violence reported against the Indian Army was the mass-rape in Kunan and Poshpora villages where more than thirty women alleged rape against the soldiers of the 4 Rajputana Rifles in February 1991. The women, from a thirteen-year-old girl to an eighty-year-old grandmother, from the two adjoining villages, repeatedly said over the years that while their men were taken away for an all-night interrogation, they were gang-raped by Indian soldiers.

When they registered the complaint a few days after the rapes, the then Deputy Commissioner of the district, S.M. Yasin, was the first to visit the spot. What he saw there was enough to convince him of the brutality that had been unleashed on the women of the village. Yasin wrote to his higher ups that the army 'had behaved like violent beasts'. 'I feel ashamed to put in black and white what kind of atrocities and their magnitude was brought to my notice on the spot,' he wrote in a confidential letter, parts of which were later made public (Batool et al. 2016).

Yasin had copied his letter to then Divisional Commissioner Kashmir Wajahat Habibullah, to the Director General of Police, two other senior police officers and the Superintendent of Police in his district. While Habibullah received the letter on March 7, 1991, he did not act for another eleven days. And finally, when he made a move, it was not to seek the truth in pursuit of justice but to counter the bad publicity the allegations of mass rape had brought on the Indian Army.

'The news of the alleged offence had attracted strong adverse comment from the local and national press and denials issued had failed to carry conviction,' he wrote in his confidential report to the government, which became public a few years ago. The investigation by the civilian administration headed by Habibullah seemed to be mostly an attempt to whitewash the crimes of the security forces.

When even the government report failed to clear the blot on the Indian Army, the report of the Press Council of India (PCI)'s investigation of the incident shows the army and the media to be varied but coordinated instruments of the state. The PCI committee, headed by veteran journalist B.G. Verghese, visited the village more than three months after the incident. After interviewing a number of the alleged victims, the committee concluded that contradictions in the women's testimony, and the fact that the number of alleged victims kept changing, rendered the charge of rape 'baseless'.

The committee concluded that the medical evidence was 'worthless', that 'such a delayed medical examination proves nothing' and that such abrasions are 'common among the village folk in Kashmir'.

The women fought not only a system stacked against them but the stigma attached to them and their villages. They tell stories of how their children were called 'bastards' and how it became difficult for young girls in Kunan and Poshpora to find partners. So much so, that the two villages were left to marry amongst themselves.

Giving voice

In 2013, fifty young women, most of them from Srinagar, filed a Public Interest Litigation (PIL) about the Kunan Poshpora rapes and reached out to the women. 'They were surprised to see us and said that no one had come to them like that before, wanting to help, wanting to lend a voice to their ageing voices,' says Ifrah Butt, a twenty-four-year-old student and a volunteer at JKCCS which is spearheading the legal case.

Over the next two years, the fifty women made regular visits to the two villages and wrote a longer narrative about the lives of the women, which has been published as a book (Batool et al. 2016). The process also brought the women of Kunan and Poshpora to the capital city, Srinagar, where they spoke for the first time in front of a full gathering about their ordeals and their struggle.

'When someone was killed by the soldiers, we all called them martyrs and their family was respected as the families of the martyrs. Wasn't it?' one of the survivors said in the gathering in Srinagar. 'Why then were we not seen as martyrs? We too suffered because we believed in the cause and that is why the soldiers raped us. We were martyrs too.'

Though the women came out and spoke freely, emboldened by the support of the younger generation, nothing really changed.

'More and more, with every step, we began to realise that the system was more against providing justice than for facilitating it. But our PIL was important, nonetheless, in the sense of breaking the idols for ourselves,' says Essar Batool, one of the petitioners.

Allegations of sexual violence against the army have been made for two-and-a-half decades, but since they have been rarely proven in courts under the same system that perpetrates them, they become rumours.

According to the JKCCS, while thousands of people have been tortured and over 8,000 subjected to enforced disappearances, the use of sexual violence against women is a reality that has largely remained unspoken. 'Only five percent of the sexual violence cases are known, the rest are buried in silence,' says Parvez Imroz of JKCCS. The senior human rights lawyer in Kashmir says that he is privy to information about several cases of sexual violence by security forces where the women and their families confided in him as a lawyer and activist but urged him to not talk about it publicly. 'Only those cases where the survivors could not hide the reality of their rape were reported, whether it be the Kunan Poshpora rapes by the Army in 1990 or the rape of the bride [Mubeena Gani],' Imroz says.

A 2006 report by Médecins Sans Frontières (Doctors Without Borders) in which 510 women in two rural districts had been interviewed, also said that sexual violence was an issue not openly discussed in Kashmir. 'Nevertheless, 11.6 per cent of interviewees said they had been victims of sexual violence since 1989. Almost two-thirds of the people interviewed (63.9 per cent) had heard over a similar period about cases of rape, while one in seven had witnessed rape,' the report said.

Sanctioned violence

In fact, the sexual violence against Farida and Nasreen might most probably have gone unreported too if their father had not been 'picked up' by the army that same night, never to return. With a missing father, Farida had to come out.

In a single night, many tragedies befell Abdullah's house. While he himself disappeared forever after the soldiers of the 5 Rashtriya Rifles dragged him to their camp, his two daughters, thirty and fourteen years old, were raped. His house was razed to the ground and his wife remained destitute for years. It was also the night when Nasreen had her first bout of unconsciousness.

I ask the family if I can just see Nasreen sometime without speaking to her at all and they unanimously refuse. 'None of this can be spoken about in front of Nasreen,' Khadija says. 'My husband cannot be mentioned, the Indian Army cannot be spoken about and nothing about what happened to us can be broached. She will go hysterical right there.'

The morning after they were raped, the two sisters walked to the Anantnag police station. 'It was like two dead bodies walking. I don't remember anything about that morning, just that we went on walking and walking and inside me I was still trapped in the darkness of the previous night and I felt that nothing was the same anymore,' Farida says.

'We told the police officer there to find our father. We wanted our father back. I broke down there and I told him [the police officer] about the rape,' she says. A First Information Report (FIR) was registered at the Anantnag Police station on the charge of rape. The police officer, Farida says, along with some other policemen accompanied them back to the village to get her children.

'The village was desolate, and what was even more desolate was where our house had been. My mother, I came to know, was sitting inside the mosque, and the streets were full of soldiers,' Farida says.

Both Khadija and the neighbours say that Major Arora had announced that anyone who gave shelter to Khadija or helped the family in any way would be killed and the women in their house would be treated the same way.

'When I saw the major, I walked up to him and told him that he had committed a sin. I asked him about my father and I was so angry that I told him that I would kill him,' Farida says. 'He looked at me and asked if I was in my senses and knew who I was speaking to. He said he would cut me up into pieces right there in the middle of the village in front of everyone.'

For three years after that day, Farida, her two children and Nasreen lived at an aunt's home in Srinagar. Nasreen was sick and Farida says that most of her time in Srinagar was taken up by visits to the hospital.

'Even after she healed physically, she would faint all the time and she had nightmares. She would faint more than five times a day. I took her to a neurosurgeon, who said that I should send her to school. With my world so shattered, it was not possible,' Farida says.

'Did you tell the doctor what had happened to her?' I asked.

'No, I didn't,' Farida says. 'I just wanted to bury it and not bring it up. She had her life ahead of her.'

But none of them could bury anything, neither the memories of that night nor their disappeared father's body, who like thousands of Kashmiris, continues to be missing.

'On Eid that year, I went with the elders from our village to the army camp to seek the release of my husband. Many of them were arrested and beaten up and told that if they ever came again, they would be killed,' says Khadija, who had remained in their village during those three years, living mostly in the mosque just outside their home.

There is no photo of their father left. Maybe there was one, they say, but that was gutted in the fire that night. The only thing forthcoming was a compensation of 100,000 Indian rupees as ex-gratia government relief and the promise of a job under the government scheme, SRO-43.

Like thousands of victims of state violence in Kashmir, Abdullah's family, living in penury, accepted the ex-gratia relief that the state government hands out to the family of any civilian who was killed or harmed at their hands. They also hoped for the promised government job, which, however, never came.

'It is an admission of crime on part of the state government but the army and defence ministry continue to deny it. While one arm of the state accepts that they killed an innocent man, the rest keep denying it. Such contradictions of the Indian state abound in Kashmir and it is not a coincidence, but a strategy,' says Khurram Parvez, a human rights activist who works with the JKCCS.

In the documents they show me, there is a news clipping of the State Human Rights Commission calling the rape a 'brutal human rights violation' and recommending punishment for Major Arora and compensation of 500,000 Indian rupees to the family. Not only did punishment to Major Arora not come, but even the compensation never came, as the army accused Farida of lodging a fabricated case against it.

The Jammu and Kashmir Police revealed in a communication to the state government in 2012 that though the case was charge-sheeted, sanction for prosecution under the Armed Forces (Jammu and Kashmir) Special Powers Act, 1990 [AFSPA][1] was declined by the central government.

The Ministry of Defence also declined sanction for prosecution under AFSPA for Major Arora of 5 Rashtriya Rifles. The letter, from the Ministry of Defence to the Jammu and Kashmir Home Department, stated that there was no prima facie evidence of the involvement of any 5 RR personnel in the case.

The letter said that Farida's husband was a 'dreadful Hizbul Mujahideen militant' and that she was forced to lodge a false allegation against Major Arora and his unit by 'anti-national elements/vested interests to malign the image of the security forces'.

The army's use of AFSPA to shield its officer and soldiers against accusations of rape was not confined to this case alone, but according to Imroz, it is the standard operating procedure. 'The

---

[1]According to the AFSPA, the armed forces may shoot to kill or destroy a building on mere suspicion. A non-commissioned officer or anyone of equivalent rank and above is allowed to use force based on opinion and suspicion, to arrest without warrant, or to kill. He can fire at anyone carrying anything that may be used as a weapon, with 'such due warning as he may consider necessary'. The AFSPA lays down that once it is implemented, 'no prosecution... shall be instituted except with the previous sanction of the central government, in respect of anything done or purported to be done' under this Act.

Indian state allows its soldiers to rape Kashmiri women in the line of duty... Sexual violence has been the highest in border areas like Uri, Kupwara and many others which are completely dominated by the Army. Since they [the victims] understand that there can be no justice, almost everyone stays silent. There are hardly any complaints,' says Imroz.

The past catches up

For years, Farida's son, Ahmad, says that he harboured a dream of picking up a gun to fight the Indian soldiers. He said he would always imagine finding Major Arora somewhere in his nice home, and shooting him dead. He says he wanted to avenge his mother, his aunt and his grandfather. 'And I want to avenge myself,' he says.

'I stayed because my mother is alone and my grandmother, sister and aunt all need me,' he says. 'But I have not stopped imagining.'

Ahmad was twelve years old when his mother and aunt were raped. For four years he knew nothing about it; he only knew of his grandfather's disappearance. 'I knew something had happened but I did not know what and when we went to Srinagar, I almost forgot about it, hoping only for my grandfather's return,' he says. 'We had a thick sheaf of documents that over the years thinned as journalists and activists took them. It was from those documents that I found out what had happened.'

Ahmad was sixteen years old when he found out, a student in Class Eight. They had just returned to their village to live in a single room they had constructed where their house earlier used to stand. For days afterwards, he says, he could not sleep and he kept away from everyone. He stopped playing with his friends and that was when he took to smoking and consuming sleeping tablets.

'There was nothing to talk to the neighbours about after I learnt that they had not come to our help,' he says. His mother Farida had said the same thing earlier, 'If they didn't help us on the night which shattered our world and lives, what is there to talk about now.' For years, Ahmad lived as a child in a house full of women and all of them, he says, were damaged and broken. He missed his grandfather. His father, he didn't really know.

Two years after his wife and sister-in-law were raped, Abu Usman surrendered to the police in 1999. Sources in the J&K Police say that he got off with a light imprisonment after he cooperated with the police and the army with details and logistical information. As soon as he was released in 2003, he went to Jammu with the same young woman he had been seeing and never came to visit Farida.

Farida does not know whether or not she is still married to him; he is said to have pronounced talaq (divorce) three times, but she is not sure. In a sense, for her, he died when he did not reach out to her after what happened to her and her family. 'He knew that I and my family had paid a price for his decision to become a militant, and we were part of that struggle too,' Farida says. 'But he went on to marry his young new woman and left me and my children to our fate.'

Farida's life is marked by absence: of her husband, of her father, and of justice. As for Nasreen, Farida says, it is the overbearing presence of the past that hurts. She is trapped in that night and the night is trapped within her.

But Ahmad, like so many people in Kashmir, lives with phantoms not merely of the past but of the future, where he faces them and slays them, hoping to free himself from the shame and servitude.

And Major Arora of the Indian Army, responsible for their marred lives, is merely a name, not even complete at that, just a last name: untraceable in the files. He has no first name, no face, no address, and all attempts to trace him stop at the impermeable wall of the Indian Army, which refuses to share any information about him or anything about the 5 RR Company posted in that village.

While his actions concretely damaged beyond recognition the lives of Farida and her family, Major Arora himself is a shadow. He is untraceable and untouchable, like more than a million Indian soldiers who have controlled life and death in Indian-administered Kashmir over the last twenty-five years.

Bibliography

Asia Watch, a division of Human Rights Watch and Physicians for Human Rights. 1993. *Rape in Kashmir: A Crime of War*. New York.

Batool Essar, Ifrah Butt et al. 2016. *Do you Remember Kunan Poshpora?* New Delhi: Zubaan.

International Peoples' Tribunal on Human Rights and Justice in Indian-administered Kashmir (IPTK) and Association of Parents of Disappeared Persons (APDP). 2012. *Alleged Perpetrators — Stories of Impunity in Jammu and Kashmir.* Srinagar: IPTK-APDP.

Kaz, Jong de, Saskia van der Kam et al. 2006. *Kashmir: Violence and Health: A quantitative assessment on violence, the psychosocial and general health status of the Indian Kashmiri population.* Amsterdam: Médecins Sans Frontières.

NORTHEAST INDIA

Introduction: Remembrance, Recounting and Resistance

SANJAY BARBORA

It might be useful to begin with a personal misgiving about conflicts in Northeast India and the binaries that they invoke for social scientists and commentators. For someone who has engaged with conflicts in the region for well over two decades, it is frustrating to annotate every piece of writing. There is a sense of the extraordinary about the place and its conflicts that is at once bewildering and annoying. If wilful ignorance forms one end of the spectrum, dealing with the other end saturated with stories and opinions about conflicts, is equally exasperating. It is almost as if there is nothing else happening in Northeast India and its citizens are only good for conspiring to find new reasons and ways to fight one another. Someone completely new to the area would be forgiven for the view that the region fluctuates between two polar extremes of legibility.

Hence, to be writing an introduction about one of the most important silences that exist along the two ends of the spectrum requires a short detour into the background of the conflicts. The following table is an effort to categorise the political conflicts and their causes:

ARUNACHAL PRADESH	
Conditions under which the state was created	• Earlier known as North Eastern Frontier Agency (NEFA), with certain parts like Tawang which were culturally linked to Tibet, while eastern areas like Pangsau were linked to upper Burma • Became a state of the Indian union in 1987
Major conflicts (broad causes)	• 1962, Sino-Indian war over border demarcations between the two countries • Conflicts with Assam on demarcation of borders between the two federal units • Conflicts arising because of the construction of hundreds of hydroelectric dams on the rivers that run through the state
Significant political groups (Constitutional and extra-constitutional)	• Constitutional parties (Indian National Congress, Bharatiya Janata Party) • Student bodies (All Arunachal Pradesh Students Union and other student bodies affiliated to different tribal groups) • Armed opposition groups active in neighbouring states [Different factions of National Socialist Council of Nagalim (NSCN), United Liberation Front of Assam (ULFA)]
ASSAM	
Conditions under which the state was created	• One of the eight provinces during colonial times, which comprised much of the present landmass of Northeast India (barring the princely states of Manipur, Tripura and NEFA) • After the Muslim-majority district of Sylhet merged with East Pakistan, the rest of the province was incorporated within India
Major conflicts (broad causes)	• 1950s Autonomy movement among the plains tribes (Udayachal)

	• 1960s Language conflicts (Assamese versus Bengali; Non-Assamese indigenous languages versus Assamese) • 1979 to 1984 Anti-foreigner agitation (that in turn is linked to a longer anti-immigration political movement in the 1930s); the Assam Agitation also raised the issue of the asymmetrical relationship between India and Assam • 1979 onwards, a separatist movement for sovereign Assam led by the ULFA; Separatist movement among the hill and plains tribe communities that variously articulated demands for greater autonomy and separate statehood within the Indian Union • Since 1983, the state has witnessed clashes between different communities at regular intervals. The clashes between Assamese speaking communities and Bengali Muslims in 1983 ended with the massacre of the latter at Nellie. Thereafter, similar conflicts have erupted between armed militia claiming to represent Bodos and Muslims (1993, 2008, 2012, 2013), Bodos and Adivasis (1993, 1996, 2014), Garo and Rabha (2010), Dimasa and Hmar (2003), Dimasa and Karbi (2005), Karbi and Kuki (2004), Dimasa and Zeme (2009), Karbi and Rengma (2014) among others • 1985 onwards, Autonomy movement in the hill districts of Karbi Anglong and Dima Hasao; the Udayachal movement that slowly morphed into the Bodoland movement
Significant political groups (Constitutional and extra-constitutional)	• National Constitutional Parliamentary parties (Indian National Congress, Bharatiya Janata Party, Communist Party of India and others)

	• Regional Constitutional Parliamentary Parties (Asom Gana Parishad, All India United Democratic Front, Bodo Peoples Front, Bodo Peoples Progressive Front, Autonomous State Demand Committee and others) • Student organisations (All Assam Students Union, All Bodo Students Union, different factions of the Karbi Students Union, other student unions representing ethnic communities and unions affiliated to national parliamentary parties) • Extra constitutional groups (ULFA, three different factions of the National Democratic Front of Bodoland, United Peoples Democratic Solidarity, Dima Halam Daoga and smaller groups supposedly representing Adivasi and Muslim interests)
MANIPUR	
Conditions under which the state was created	• Was a British Protectorate until 1947 • Annexed and incorporated within the Indian union in 1949 (as a union territory) • Granted statehood in 1972
Major conflicts (broad causes)	• 1950s onward, struggle for a unified Naga homeland • 1960s-1980s struggle of the Mizo-Kuki-Chin people that dissolved into various separate ethnic constituencies and armed groups • 1960s onward, struggle of Manipuri groups seeking to restore the sovereignty they had lost in 1949 • 1992, inter-community clashes between Kuki and Naga armed groups • 1993, inter-community clashes between Meiteis and Pangals

	• 1997-98, inter-community clashes between Paite and Kuki armed groups • 2001 onwards, a simultaneous movement to preserve the territorial integrity of Manipur and the demand for a special status for the hills
Significant political groups (Constitutional and extra-constitutional)	• Constitutional parties (Indian National Congress, Bharatiya Janata Party, Manipur People's Party, Communist Party of India, Naga People's Front and others) • Extra constitutional armed groups (People's Liberation Army, United National Liberation Front, factions of Kangleipak Communist Party, Kanglei Yawol Kanna Lup, different factions of National Socialist Council of Nagalim, different factions of Kuki National Army, different factions comprising the United Revolutionary Front and others) • Student groups (Manipur Students Federation, Democratic Students Association of Manipur, Kuki Students Organisation, Tangkhul Katamnao Long and others), • Women's groups (Naga Women's Union Manipur, different valley-based Meira Paibi groups and others) • Community-based pressure groups like Apunba Lup, United Naga Council, Kuki Inpi and others
MEGHALAYA	
Conditions under which the state was created	• Was part of the colonial province of Assam • Became a state under the Indian union in 1973
Major conflicts (broad causes)	• 1987 and 2010, Khasi-Nepali clashes • 1990s, separatist armed group

	Hynneiwtrep A'chik Liberation Council starts a movement for independence of the major tribal groups (Khasi-Jaintia and Garo); splits into Garo (A'chik National Volunteer Council) and Khasi (Hynniewtrep National Liberation Council) groups • 2005 Khasi-Karbi clashes
Significant political groups (Constitutional and extra-constitutional)	• Constitutional parliamentary parties (Indian National Congress, Bharatiya Janata Party, Nationalist Congress Party, Hills State People's Democratic Party, Khun Hynniewtrep National Awakening Movement and others) • Extra constitutional armed groups (Hynniewtrep National Liberation Council, A'chik National Volunteer Council, Garo National Liberation Army and others • Student unions (Khasi Students Union) • Traditional bodies (Dorbar Shnongs)
MIZORAM	
Conditions under which the state was created	• Was initially known as the Lushai hills district in the colonial province of Assam • Became a union territory in 1972 • Became a state in 1987
Major conflicts (broad causes)	• 1961 to 1986, movement spearheaded by the Mizo National Front
Significant political groups (Constitutional and extra-constitutional)	• Constitutional parliamentary parties (Indian National Congress, Mizo National Front, Mizo People's Convention and others) • Student bodies (Mizo Zirlai Pawl, Hmar Students Association, Mara Students Organisations and others) • Church-based bodies (Young Mizo Association) • Women's groups (Mizo Hmeichhe Insuihkhawm Pawl and others)

NAGALAND	
Conditions under which the state was created	• Called the Naga hills district (part of the colonial province of Assam) • Became a state in the Indian union by incorporating Naga hills, Tuensang and Mon in 1963
Major conflicts (broad causes)	• August 14, 1947: Naga declaration of independence • 1951 Plebiscite for Naga independence; Indian army deployed in Naga territories • 1975 Shillong Accord and internal rifts within the armed movement • 1980, formation of the National Socialist Council of Nagalim (NSCN) • 1988 vertical split within NSCN and emergence of two factions—one led by S.S. Khaplang and the other by Isak Chishi Swu and Th. Muivah • 1997 Ceasefire agreement between government of India (GoI) and NSCN-IM • 2001 Ceasefire agreement between GoI and NSCN-K • 2015 Abrogation of ceasefire between NSCN-K and GoI; Declaration of Framework Agreement between NSCN-IM and GoI
Significant political groups (Constitutional and extra-constitutional)	• Constitutional parties (Naga Peoples Front, Indian National Congress, Bharatiya Janata Party and others) • Naga National Workers (Naga National Council, different factions of NSCN) • Tribal bodies (Tribal Hohos, Zeliangrong Baudi) • Student groups (Naga Students Federation and different tribal student organisations that constitute NSF)

	• Human rights and organisations for gender justice and peace (Naga People's Movement for Human Rights, Naga Mothers Association, Forum for Naga Reconciliation and others) • Church groups (Nagaland Baptist Church Council)
TRIPURA	
Conditions under which the state was created	• Was a princely state and British Protectorate between 1809 and 1947 • Regent queen signed a merger agreement with India in 1949
Major conflicts (broad causes)	• Became a full-fledged state in 1972 • 1978 Tripura National Volunteers formed in order to combat Left parties and form an alliance of indigenous Tripuri groups against Bengali settlers • 1990s radical armed groups like the All Tripura Tiger Force (ATTF) and National Liberation Front of Tripura (NLFT) initiate armed campaign against the state, while the government undertook counter-insurgency campaigns in the tribal areas autonomous districts
Significant political groups (Constitutional and extra-constitutional)	• Constitutional parties (Communist Party of India—Marxist, Indian National Congress and its affiliate, Indigenous Peoples Front of Tripura and others) • Armed opposition groups (NLFT and ATTF)

This somewhat reductionist view of the political conflicts in Northeast India would present a confusing mix of acronyms to those who wish to understand the region. The similarities between the region's contentious political landscape and the kind of violent, fissured trajectories of conflicts in Burma (Myanmar) are stark and deserve more attention. The postcolonial reorganisation of spaces along the contiguous space between Burma and Northeast India has recently seen a renewal of interest among social scientists. Since the early 2000s, social historians and political scientists have challenged the received state-centric views of the region as a peripheral, conflict-ridden frontier of South and Southeast Asia (Baruah 2003, Scott 2009, van Schendel 2002). In 2002, Dutch scholar Willem van Schendel published a compelling essay that made a case for seeing certain upland fringes of South Asia, South East Asia and East Asia as zones that did not account for any academic concern in mainstream area studies. He called this space of no concern zomia by using a creative play of the Mizo-Chin-Kuki words 'zo' (highland) and 'mi' (persons), thereby evoking a persuasive world of valleys and hills that stretched from the eastern Himalayas to the uplands of Vietnam, inhabited by communities that felt marginalised by centralising modern states (van Schendel, 2002).

Adding a textured account to van Schendel's proposition, Sanjib Baruah (2003, 2005) analysed how Northeast India had become a contentious and coercive project of nationalising space in India. Tracing the trajectory of the developmentalist state that evolved from welfare to a corporate model, Baruah stresses the importance of the military option in the pacification and governance of Northeast India. It is one of the few places in the country where former military and intelligence functionaries are appointed to gubernatorial positions. Moreover, it is also a region where governors are not mere figureheads, but wield real power in deciding the allocation of resources (to autonomous districts) and defining due political process. Baruah's contention regarding the routineness of the exceptional in Northeast India resonates with the theoretical concerns raised in James Scott's work on the structural and historical conditions of governance in the wide swathe of upland space called zomia.

The region's pre-colonial political and social landscape was a reflection of the multi-dimensional migrations into its hills and valleys. It comprised old kingdoms and chiefdoms as well as wide swathes of land where the authority of the kings and chiefs was negligible. Commercial interests, coupled with a keen eye on the geopolitical balance of power, led the British to 'draw lines between hills and plains, to put barriers on trade between Bhutan and Assam and to treat Myanmar as a strategic frontier—British India's buffer against French Indochina and China' (Baruah 2004, p.5). During the course of the anti-colonial struggle in the twentieth century, notions about the region being a frontier were not challenged. In the emerging historiography of the region there was an attempt to restructure the relationship between the region and the national hinterland with an overriding emphasis on establishing a place in the national space for the emerging idea of India (Kar 2004, p.55).

The development of social and political structures in Northeast India has been characterised by extreme levels of violence for the last two decades. This violence has articulated itself in myriad forms. It has appeared as an outright conflict of interests between ethnic groups and the state, within ethnic groups and, at times, for or against notions of development. Natural resources and identity remain the first, and often last, explanatory comment on the expressions of violence. On the one hand, armed groups professing allegiance to certain ethnic groups in the state have been involved in militant political activities, directed mainly towards the preservation of their resources and identity. In some cases, this struggle has involved alliances across ethnic boundaries, subverting officially sanctioned definitions of the problems as one of migrants versus locals. On the other hand, the response of the state apparatus has been to restrain, regulate and repress these demands at various points of time. This has led to the institutionalisation of authoritarian practices that, though localised, are rather jarring (Baruah 2005, p.3).

A conception of civil society, in the liberal western construct, is inconsistent with realities in less-developed capitalist societies. If one takes civil society in its characteristically modern meaning—as a way of interfering in the terrain of voluntary associations that exist between economy and state—there are two reasons why politics in frontiers like Northeast India contradict this. For one, societies in the frontiers are typically shaped by a legal order that is autocratic and militarised (Baruah 2005). Secondly, such societies are less individually oriented than dominant societies as, being part of peripheries where the lure of the nation-state and citizenship had been relatively weak, they relied more on people-hood[1] constituted by genealogical and kinship ties (Murray 1997, p.11). It is apparent therefore that societies in peripheral, militarised regions had to be judged by different criteria from Habermas' original separation and opposition between the modern, public-civil-world and the modern, private or conjugal and familial sphere: that is, in the new social world created through contract, everything that lies beyond the domestic (private) sphere is public, or 'civil', society. The fact that one needed different criteria at all is a reflection of the failure of state-driven political processes in India. It is also a testimony to the myriad ways in which people of the region resisted assaults on their sense of dignity and managed to preserve a semblance of civic sensibilities in the face of adversity.

Impact of militarisation in Northeast India

Over the last few decades, issues of power, territory and distribution of resources have transformed into serious conflicts in Northeast India. Added to this are efforts by the government of India to formulate and implement policies that (for the most part) aggravate these conflicts. In such a process, there is greater exclusion of peoples within the state-building efforts. The liberal notion of democratic societies creating moral and minimal consensus around basic institutions in ambitious nation-building projects such as the Indian

---

[1]The notion of people-hood runs against the idea of modern citizenship. The latter is based on shared ideals and beliefs of collectives who are members of a state and its institutions. People-hood is a concept that has been used to define other—smaller—collectives who feel that their participation in state-building projects and institutions is limited because they are politically, culturally and geographically marginalised from the mainstream national communities and institutions and, therefore, assert their identities in opposition to that of citizens (Murray 1997).

one, is often confronted with the problem of dealing with a plurality of incompatible yet reasonable doctrines. These contestations are particularly apparent in the problem of citizenship vis-à-vis inclusion-exclusion of peoples marginalised in the vision of a nation. In many parts of the peripheries of state centres, clan, kin, ethnic and regional identities tend to precede personal commitment to a citizenship discourse that places the individual on an equal footing with other members of a national political community.

Militarisation of Northeast India has had peculiar consequences. After the Sino-Indian war in 1961, the region joined its immediate neighbour, Myanmar, in becoming a closed area that needed constant surveillance by the army. Civilian authority was constantly undermined and overruled in areas where the Armed Forces (Special Powers) Act (AFSPA) of 1958 was promulgated. Instead of engaging politically with the single insurgency (i.e. the Naga one) that existed in the region at the time, AFSPA and the Disturbed Areas Act were instrumental in the proliferation of armed rebellions against the rule of the Indian state. Commentators are often quick to point out the irony of this situation (Misra 2000, Barbora 2006). If the proliferation of armed rebellion was one side of the peculiar consequences of militarisation, the slow but sure erosion of civic values and sensibilities was another. There is hardly a state in the region, or a district within the various states that has not seen violence perpetrated by armed groups claiming to represent a particular ethnic community.

The garrison, which is a military institution that keeps armed men and their families safe within a physical space that reproduces their homes, has become a permanent fixture of everyday life in Northeast India. Since 1962, the government of India has used the external and internal threat perception to acquire and build more defence installations and garrisons around the region. Such places are found all over the world, especially in places where an army has been brought in to (re)construct the facade of a state that provides welfare and security to people. Garrisons therefore, are also symbols of power that cloak colossal lies. Within their confines, soldiers and their families live in colonies that seek to provide them a semblance of the homes that they have left behind in order to serve in counter-insurgency operations in the region. There are schools, cinema halls, canteens and clubs for servicemen that provide all the grocery and liquor available in other parts of India. Many have their families with them and the self-contained, secure perimeters of the garrison do not require the families to ever leave. The ability to reproduce a quality of life that is denied to those outside it is a remarkable achievement of the garrison. However, there is more than just a physical space that is associated with such institutions. They also become material symbols of closed ideas and minds.

Unfortunately, the garrison has become a regular feature of militarised societies the world over, and Northeast India is no different. Ideas of power, coexistence and governance are created within the confines of such institutions. They do not require any nuanced knowledge or experience of the world that lies just outside the confines of the high, barbed-wire walls that constitute the garrison. For instance, there is little need for soldiers to leave the security of their mess and kitchen to engage with the communities who live nearby. They are *civilians*—a term that is slightly pejorative in army talk—hence, not so important in the larger matter of life that involves the garrison. The only time that there is any non-military engagement with the world outside these antediluvian institutions, is when the officer in command (or his socially conscious spouse) wish to visit local women's collectives, or a self-help group that has been in the news locally.

This imperious military worldview has become a convenient political template for political entrepreneurs in the region. They employ a convoluted military lens to create a vocabulary of violence, wherein the need to secure one's own ethnic group, often at the expense of the other, is seen as the only way out of a vicious cycle of powerlessness, poverty and discrimination. This also points to the delicate and enduring entanglements that exist between the garrison (as a mentality) and a world outside. It creates the need to secure pure spaces for one group, while ensuring that others are excised from it altogether. It is no coincidence that despite the increasing presence of more armed personnel on the ground, the number of incidents of violence between different ethnic communities has only increased over the past three decades. In almost all cases, it has been the economically weak and marginalised sections that have been killed or displaced.

In such a situation, one can justifiably surmise that militarisation has created conditions where people are unable to live together. Reflecting on such conditions of human life, the philosopher Hannah Arendt writes: '…the only alternative to power is not strength—which is helpless against power—but force, which indeed one man alone can exert against his fellow men and of which one or a few can possess a monopoly by acquiring the means for violence' (1958, p.202). So too, in Northeast India, militarisation has created a world that inverts the ability of human beings to come together. It destroys the ability of people to negotiate and create spaces of coexistence, employing instead memories of personal cruelty and anger.

Women's voices—adding new dimensions to the conflict narrative

The two essays in this volume that reflect the experiences of women in the Northeast add much-needed shades to the existing monochromatic views that dominate accounts of conflict in the region. Thingnam Anjulika Samom and Yirmiyan Arthur Yhome join a small but extremely articulate group of women writers, whose descriptions of violence and its effects on everyday life have added a textured quality to the discourse on conflicts. In the last decade, women's writing from the region has taken on a completely different quality altogether. Women from every state of the region are writing absorbing accounts of what has happened in the last four or five decades in Northeast India. Women writers like Temsula Ao, Easterine Kire, Moza Zote, the late Indira Goswami, Arupa Patangia Kalita and Uddipana Goswami (to name a few) have added a completely different dimension to the otherwise jaded and fatigue-inducing conflict narrative in Northeast India. Through their powerful poems, fiction and non-fiction essays and books, women writers from the region have managed to allude to different languages and experiences of violence. Many have eschewed the traditional, two-dimensional accounts of the conflicts and have made it possible to think of new ways to tell old stories. The two essays in this volume will add to this growing list.

Samom focuses on individual accounts of violence and in doing so, she mines through an engaging area of inquiry that involves memory and resistance. She leads the reader through certain events that have been central in the narrative of violence against women in Manipur. She annotates well-known accounts of violence against women and in so doing, draws on her years of experience as a working journalist in Imphal. Samom's invocation of a political landscape of hills and valleys is central to her attempt to draw the reader into the layered political world of Manipur.

Samom is also mindful of the need to escape a problematic narrative that sees the Northeast as an exceptional space within the Indian polity. Important journalistic accounts of the region underline a curious strangeness about the place, one that (perhaps unwillingly) lends itself to using differences in culture and history in order to explain militarisation (Gupta 2015). Instead, Samom draws in examples from places that have had similar experiences. If society was able to address and engage with sexual violence in the former Yugoslavia and Rwanda—two countries that are as different and apart as geography would dictate—then the experiences of women in Northeast India too ought to have a universal quality, she suggests. She draws on stories of violence against women that are already in the public domain and in popular memory in order to show how they have become part of a culture of resistance. She focuses, for instance, on the tragic story of a Tangkhul woman, Luingamla, whose experiences are woven into the shawls that members of her community weave today.

Samom also describes the manner in which the memories and experiences of women survivors (and victims) of violence circulate in Manipur today. Names are chanted during night vigils, but this does not help in cementing solidarity among the people of the hills and the valley. Instead, Samom notes the growing divide between struggles of the different communities in the state. She notes how impunity for sexual violence is no longer limited to members of the Indian armed forces. Instead, she shows how such ideas permeate civic and political spaces where armed opposition groups have also gone on to commit horrible acts of sexual violence against women of communities other than the ones that they seek to represent.

Yirmiyan Arthur's essay deploys a personal narrative in order to tell the seemingly inchoate story of militarisation in the place that she calls home. She inserts herself into the narrative and tells a compelling story of negotiation and assertions of identity. Beginning with a seemingly simple childhood memory of travelling by road to Kohima, she follows the traces of conflicts that remain as markers for people along the highway. The road, therefore, becomes a metaphor that is both liberating and exhausting for those who live along the route. In the first instance, it is liberating because it is testimony to several personal and political journeys that individuals and communities have undertaken. Despite her interviewees' testimonies that inspire a belief in the genius and generosity of the human spirit, there is a melancholic subtext. It asserts itself in the repetitiveness of violence that occurs between various communities along the road.

The road has long been a potent symbol of change and progress. Yet, in Arthur's rendition of the story of the road, progress and change are ethereal. While the taste of pineapples remains the same, the conditions of the vendors have changed beyond recognition. She follows the lives and longings of activists and ordinary people, coming up with a narrative that forces one to reflect on the persistence of violence and the manner in which it morphs and mutates over time. Yirmiyan Arthur leaves the reader with many questions, as any serious reflection of violence ought to do. Eschewing easy, predictable solutions, she lets the reader savour the contradictions and pathos of the lives of those who live along the road. The choices that they make, the fears that they secretly harbour and the anxieties triggered by the sight of uniforms and other ethnicities are a poignant reminder of the passage of time and the devastation that the brutal exercise of power set off in Manipur and Nagaland.

The essays are different in their tone, but both emerge from a careful and nuanced engagement with conflict. Arthur and Samom reiterate a notion that needs to be nurtured: in amplifying the experiences of women in conflict in Northeast India, one is able to find a better understanding of the shortcomings of modern state-making and nation-building in the geographical margins of the country. However, far from remaining in the margins, these stories and experiences illuminate certain universal conditions of human existence. Indeed, there is no escaping the demand for the restoration of dignity that both essays call for. In the absence of a political will to address such issues, long form, non-fiction writing of the kind included in this volume will remain a crucial site of alternate visions for a just, more democratic future for regions that have been subjected to armed conflict in South Asia. Places like Northeast India, therefore, have a powerful mirror to show to the so-called urban, mainstream centre.

Bibliography

Arendt, Hannah. 1958. *The Human Condition.* Chicago: University of Chicago Press.

Barbora, Sanjay. 2006. 'Rethinking India's Counter-insurgency Campaign in North-East' in *Economic and Political Weekly.* XLI (35); pp. 3805-3812, New Delhi.

Baruah, Sanjib. 2005. *Durable Disorder: Understanding the Politics of Northeast India.* New Delhi: Oxford University Press.

——2003. 'Citizens and Denizens: Ethnicity, Homelands and the Crisis of Displacement in Northeast India' in *Journal of Refugee Studies,* Vol. 16 No.1, pp. 44-66. Oxford: Oxford University Press.

Gupta, Shekhar. 2015. 'Northeast's India Problem', in *India Today.* June 29. New Delhi.

Kar, Boddhisatva. 2004. *What is in a Name? Politics of Spatial Imagination in Colonial Assam.* CENISEAS Papers 5; Guwahati: Centre for Northeast India, South and Southeast Asia.

Misra, Udayon. 2000. *The Periphery Strikes Back: Challenges to the Nation-State in Assam and Nagaland.* Shimla: Indian Institute of Advanced Studies.

Murray, Stuart (ed). 1997. *Not On Any Map: Essays on Postcoloniality and Cultural Nationalism.* Exeter: University of Exeter Press.

Scott, James. 2009. *The Art of Not Being Governed: An Anarchist History of Upland Burma.* New Haven: Yale University Press.

van Schendel, Willem. 2002. 'Geographies of knowing, geographies of ignorance: jumping scale in Southeast Asia' in *Environment and Planning D: Society and Space* 20, pp. 647-668, New Delhi: Sage.

The Art of Defiance

THINGNAM ANJULIKA SAMOM

Seated in her sparse living room, eyes closed in an effort to recall every detail, her small hands move agitatedly in the air as though searching for the right words. Fifty-three-year-old Zamthingla Ruivah-Shimray narrates a story that is nearly three decades old. On January 24, 1986, Zamthingla, then twenty-four, had just graduated from Maharaja Bodhachandra College in Imphal. She had come home to Ngainga village, about 10 kilometres from the district headquarters in Manipur's Ukhrul hills. Her neighbour, eighteen year old Luingamla Muinao, was weaving inside her home situated a little away from the other buildings surrounding the Chief's house. Most of the villagers were in neighbouring Halang (now known as Huining), where the Tangkhul Katamnao Long (TKL), the apex students' body of the Tangkhul community, was holding its general body meeting.

'Luingamla did not go to the students' meeting. She was leaving for Imphal in a few days to enrol in Class Nine. The village school had classes only up to Class Eight. She needed new shoes. Her mother said, "Let's weave together to earn enough money for your shoes." So, she didn't go to the meeting,' recalls Zamthingla.

Zamthingla works in a government department in Imphal and stays in Lamphel area of the valley. 'I usually come home very late from work,' she explains apologetically over the phone when asked for an appointment. A few hours later, the Langol hills are already wrapped in darkness. Barely a kilometre away, the commercial area of Imphal city, dominated by high-rise buildings, glows orange under rows and rows of glaring street lights. Here in Lamphel, the rows of non-functioning street lamps stand in silent testimony to government apathy. Only the odd bulb at private gates and the yellowed light peeping out of someone's curtained window or doorway illumine the heavily potholed road.

The small side-lane to Zamthingla's house runs opposite the local ground where young boys play football or just sit around to watch the comings and goings. At one end of the ground is the Imphal Meitei Church, one of the many churches of all denominations. Zamthingla continues her tale in her soft, hesitant voice. Luingamla's parents had gone to help a friend construct a house. Her younger sister Tharawon was outside, working in the kitchen garden. Suddenly, there was a shout, a cry for help, followed by two gunshots. When the neighbours rushed into the house, they found Luingamla, her mouth stuffed with cloth, lying in a pool of blood. Capt Mandhir Singh of the 25 Madras Regiment was standing nearby, trying to wash the blood off his trousers. With him was 2nd Lt Sanjeev Dubey of the Mahar Regiment.

Seeing the villagers, the two army men ran out, shouting that the underground people had killed Luingamla. They called their colleagues from the army camp situated near the village school campus and announced a curfew. All the villagers were herded into the village ground to 'hunt for the killers.'

Zamthingla gives a half-smile, 'They killed her because she did not allow them to do their dirty deed. She died protecting her chastity. Yet the siphai [soldiers] were again torturing the villagers.'

The 25 Mahar Regiment and Madras Regiment were among the numerous army battalions posted in Manipur as part of counter-insurgency measures against multiple armed nationalist movements by the Naga, Meitei and Kuki communities. In 1980 Manipur was declared 'disturbed' and the Armed Forces (Special Powers) Act (AFSPA), an emergency law first enacted in 1958 to provide extraordinary powers to the Indian armed forces to quell the Naga insurgency, was imposed on the whole state.

'Those days, there used to be a lot of harassment from the army.

The army soldiers would come and beat up the men. Luingamla used to come often, carrying a child on her back, perhaps a nephew or niece, and say to me, "They are back. I don't like the sight of them. They frighten me. They will beat up my father again and throw our things around. Let me stay here for a while until they are gone", Zamthingla recalls, describing the army patrols and frequent operations.

The silencing

Luingamla's fear was not unfounded. No doubt she had witnessed the brutality of the Indian army against the men in her village. Perhaps she had also heard stories of the way these 'outsider' men in uniform had harassed the women of the region in unspeakable ways. Perhaps she had heard about how many women were sexually assaulted in Mao Songsong town and Shajaoba village in July 1971, and in Huining and Nungbi Khullen in 1981-82. More likely, she had heard about nineteen-year-old Rose Machui Ningshen of Ngaprum (now Kumram) village whose rape by two Border Security Force (BSF) officers and subsequent suicide in March 1974 had galvanised the formation of a collective of Tangkhul women.

Sexual violence including rape, forced prostitution, stripping, genital mutilation and forced marriage during wartime or armed conflict is not new. Evolving definitions and understandings of rape and other sexual crimes over the years have opened up the notion of sexual violence as a war crime in the International Criminal Tribunal for the former Yugoslavia and Rwanda in the wake of the 1992-95 ethnic cleansing in Yugoslavia and the 1994 genocide in Rwanda.

Feminist scholars from the region (Saigol 2008) have pointed out that viewing women and their sexuality as symbols of culture, tradition and the nation has meant that in times of conflict, women are violated in a sexually-specific way. 'It is clear that wherever identity and self are threatened by an "Other", an outsider defined as an enemy, women's bodies become the arena of the most violent forms of conflict,' she writes.

In both the hills and valley of Manipur, the instances of sexual assault, including rape, on indigenous women by the 'outsider' army were most likely to be silenced by existing patriarchal notions of honour and morality. While a few instances came to light, it is quite probable that many remained silent due to fear of the army and the disrepute that such a revelation might bring. Cutting across communities, women in Manipur are caught in the twin image of the model woman within the bounds of a patriarchal set-up and the defiant saviour of society. This is best explained by anthropologist MC Arunkumar and journalist Irengbam Arun as 'a dichotomy of two traditional Meitei female deities—the aging "patri-oriented model of an ideal womanhood" Imoinu and the youthful Panthoib… juxtaposed models of female blisshood (domesticity) on the one hand; and of the forthcoming and independent feminism breaking down the shackles of the rigid patriarchal Manipuri society' (Arunkumar and Arun 2009).

This contradiction also exists in Naga society. Tangkhul women for instance enjoyed a high degree of freedom to participate in socio-cultural activities; however they were considered subordinate to men and confined to domestic work. This image of the ever-toiling woman in the jhum[1] fields and domestic sphere, deprived of a place in the traditional village administration, is juxtaposed with the strong peacemaker, the Pukreila capable of stopping bloody battles mid-fight. Among the Tangkhuls, a Pukreila is a woman who marries into another village. When there is war between her natal village and her marital village, she has the right to step in and say that the war must end. Her decision in this matter becomes the final authority and the war has to cease at any cost. A Pukreila woman thus becomes 'a mediator, negotiator and security in times of war' (Shimray 2000).

Back in 1974, Rose Machui Ningshen was to be married but she committed suicide after she was raped. 'Traditionally and culturally, rape was taboo in Naga society, inviting capital punishment. But Naga society too has a patriarchal structure and a lot of emphasis

---

[1]Shifting cultivation

is placed on the moral standards of women. She (Rose) could not bear the stigma, that she was raped, says Grace Shatshang, advisor of the Naga Women Union, Manipur (NWUM).

'There were rapes in many of the army operations—be it at Patsoi or at Oinam. But the problem was that these women refused to speak up, or be identified as they feared the stigma, says senior journalist and former chairperson of the Manipur Human Rights Commission, Yambem Laba.[2]

Rise of the phoenix warriors

The emergence of the 'agitator-woman' can be traced to the first 'women's war' or Nupi Lan of 1904 when women vendors of Imphal's Khwairamband market rose against the forced labour of their men and the banishment of six Manipuri princes by the British government in Manipur. Scholars analyse this uprising not as a women's movement seeking liberation from patriarchal chains, but rather as an awakening of an anti-colonial national consciousness representing women's empowerment in the political domain. The Second Nupi Lan of 1939 demanding closure of rice mills and export of rice 'posed deeper questions on the colonial interests' and showed greater leadership and women's mobilising power (Arunkumar and Arun, 2009).

During the 1970s and 1980s women emerged as important socio-political actors in Manipur. Tired of rampant alcoholism and widespread abuse of cannabis by the males, women in the valley initiated the 'Nishabandh' or Prohibition movement. This gradually transformed into the Meira Paibi movement—female torch bearers grappling with army personnel to save their children and youth from arbitrary arrests, torture and 'fake encounters' or extra-judicial killings.

In the hills, collective action among Naga women became stronger

---

[2]A 1997 report by the Joint Forum of Indigenous Women-North East India states that in April 1980 around hundred women were stripped and assaulted in public during an army counter-insurgency operation at Patsoi area in Imphal West District, about 15 minutes from Imphal.

than before. In response to the rape of Rose and the rape and torture of Angai of Grihang village, Tangkhul women had already come together as the East District Women Association (EDWA) in 1974. Tying up with various other organisations, including many from the valley, the EDWA spearheaded the formation of the 'All Manipur Women Action Committee' (AMWAC) during a meeting held at CC Higher Secondary School in Imphal in August 1974 (Ningshen 2013). In 1981, EDWA became the Tangkhul Shanao Long (TSL), the main Tangkhul women's organisation working for the protection and promotion of human rights of the Tangkhul community, not only in Ukhrul, but even outside the district and the state.

The TSL-organised protest rallies against the attempted rape and murder of Luingamla in Ukhrul, and later in 1986 in Imphal, were attended by thousands, including members of valley-based organisations like Macha Leima, All Manipur Students Union and Nupilal Marup, besides the hills-based All Tribal Student Union Manipur (ATSUM), Tangkhul Naga Long (TNL), Naga Student Federation (NSF) and the Naga People Movement for Human Rights (NPMHR). During a meeting held after the rally, it was resolved to observe March 11 as the 'Unity Day' of the hill and valley people of Manipur (Ningshen 2013).

While a case was filed by the EDWA on the rape of Rose, the perpetrators went scot-free due to lack of evidence. The TSL also filed a case against Luingamla's killers, resulting in Lt Mandhir Singh's termination from service. Yet, this did not bring closure. The urge to speak out about the horrific incident, and valorise the young girl's courage prompted various forms of memorialisation.

Weaving resistance

'We wanted to tell Luingamla's story through a calendar with her picture on it. Even if we stop talking about her or forget the incident, we will surely remember every time we look at it,' Zamthingla said, showing a torn copy of the calendar. The calendar became an act of defiance and recovery. Inscribed in red are the words: 'An innocent 18-year-old, Miss Luingamla Muinao, was shot dead by

Capt. Mandhir Singh of the 25 Madras on the 24th of January, 1986 at Ngainga Village.'

The women of Ngainga village raised the required sum of around 15,000 Indian rupees for the printing by donating one day's pay of khutlang (wages for agricultural labour) and by selling poultry. Zamthingla recalls, 'the army said that the NSCN was funding us. We were called to the camp and asked to give proof of our source of money for printing the calendar. We gave our accounts and they were silenced.'

Zamthingla took a step further and came up with the idea of a new design on the traditional Tangkhul sarong known as kashan. Utilising the expertise of a few other weavers, she then set to work 'to tell the story of Luingamla and show the unity of the various people, the organisations, the groups who worked together through this design.'

The imagery starts at the front panel of the sarong itself, the bigger white-and-green twin comb patterns, the rikshi-phor and phorei-phor. Crossing her hands in front of her bosom in a protective gesture, her fingers spread wide, Zamthingla explains, 'This is the first fencing for a woman. To protect oneself we do this, we cross our hands across ourselves. Luingamla too must have done this when she came to know the intentions of the army men.'

A string of motifs run at regular intervals across the breadth of the kashan. Zamthingla points to each aspect as she explains the significance, a story that she must have told a hundred times over. 'We ran about from one place to another, searching for the path to justice, back and forth, just as this white line, the shongwui shili, runs zig-zag across the motif,' she narrates. Then come the konghar angacham and khaifa akashan—wings of butterflies and waists of frogs—which signify the places of judgements, the courts of justice. Framing these motifs on both sides, twin strings of beads-like patterns in white and light green threads—the malum-mik or termite's eyes—run through the sarong, representing the never-ending support of organisations like the Tangkhul Shanao Long. 'We moved together united and relentless till the end in our fight for justice,' she explains.

Broken threads

The newly designed Luingamla kashan was placed before the TSL for approval in 1991-92. By then, the National Socialist Council of Nagalim (NSCN) had already split vertically and in addition, tension was brewing between the Nagas and the Kukis over the demand for separate homelands. Mass exodus and disappearances preceded the death of the first recorded victim of the Naga-Kuki violent clash, Holkhojang Haokip, in May 1992. Neighbours were now fighting each other.

'We were happy when the sun rose. Our smiles became wider and wider as it rose higher and higher in the sky. But when it sank lower and lower in the west, the smiles would vanish for we did not know whether we would survive to see the next day. We huddled in the darkness, hiding, listening…and then we go out the next morning, we see our Naga friends, and we have a cup of tea together, happy that both of us made it through the night,' recalls Lalam Mate of Molnoi village in Chandel district. Lalam is a former president of the Kuki Women's Union for Human Rights (KWUHR) of Tengnoupal area. The Naga-Kuki killings, which were to last till 1997, seared through the hill districts of Chandel, Churachandpur, Ukhrul, Tamenglong and Senapati, killing hundreds and displacing thousands.

Meanwhile in the valley areas, the People's Liberation Army (PLA) of Manipur emerged as a strong guerrilla force, carrying out attacks on security forces while the primary focus of the United National Liberation Front (UNLF) was on earning public support through 'action' against social crimes. The first targets were crimes against women, especially instances of sexual violence (Phanjoubam 1996).

The trend of reporting cases of sexual violence and domestic discord to the UNLF (and other underground groups) for 'action' instead of going to the police is reflected in the 'Wakatchaba' (complaint) ads in the newspapers. Phanjoubam (1996) reports, 'At least ten persons were gunned down by the ultras between June 1990 and March 1991 for sex-related crimes. The extremists also warned that they would not hesitate to eliminate anyone involved in such crimes "without warning".

Indeed, the notions within militant groups about propriety and women's 'honour' mirrored those in conservative mainstream society. In 2001, a faction of the Kanglei Yawol Kanna Lup (KYKL) imposed a dress code banning women from wearing trousers and saris in public. Stating threats to the centuries-old traditions of the community from increasing 'Western and Indian influence', the KYKL had asked women to wear only the traditional phanek or sarong and warned of a 'death penalty' for women violating the new dress code. Though the move was resisted successfully by women rights activists under the banner of the All Manipur Democratic Women's Association (AMDWA), the dress code is a pointer to the social stereotyping, rigidifying of hierarchy, social taboos and exclusion which now marks a society in conflict (Nepram 2002).

Vigilante justice slowly gave way to reporting crimes to the newly-set up Manipur Human Rights Commission, says senior journalist Yambem Laba who served on the Commission from its inception in 1998 to 2006 as member, and later as chairperson.

Silence to voice

Zamthingla received endorsement for her Luingamla kashan in 1995-96. Around the same time, the shroud of silence on rape and sexual assault by the army began to lift. In 1996, Tohring, an Anal Naga woman from Chandel, came out publicly and narrated how an army man (a jawan of JK Light Infantry posted in Mahamani) had entered her room in the darkness of the night, tried to rape her and assaulted her husband.

The disclosure opened a Pandora's box on a subject which hitherto had been cloaked by a culture of silence based on the fear of social stigma and retaliation from a powerful state agency. The matter was taken up by the Anal women's group, the Anal Sinu Ruwl (ASR). 'The ASR women were enraged and came out in huge numbers demanding that this person be handed over. The Meira Paibi women from Imphal also came,' says Tohring.

Another housewife, Elangbam Ahanjaobi, who was raped in 1996 by two soldiers of the 2nd Mahar Regiment of the Indian army, spoke up against the incident and with the help of civil society organisations filed a case against the rapists.

In both cases the disclosure, more than outrage about gender-based violence, was in part guided by the social stigma surrounding rape and the fear of reprisal and accusations from the men.

'I came to know later that this person had raped another girl in the past, but the matter was hushed up. So, he had the audacity to commit the same crime again. That is why I spoke out. If I had kept silent he would continue doing the same thing to others. I do not want money. I want to live with dignity, and let people know that I was not at fault,' says Tohring.

Ahanjaobi adds, 'After that incident, I felt that even if I myself have lost, I should at least talk about it so that my fate does not befall others, so that these people should not go unpunished. My sons and husband should know that I was not at fault.'

Ahanjaobi's case was a turning point in the narrative of people's response to sexual violence in Manipur, especially in the valley. Her disclosure led to widespread and intense public protests, forcing the army authorities to court martial the accused Havildar Apparao Wariba Waghmare and Havildar Vithal Domaji Kalane of the 2nd Mahar Regiment. A year later, the Summary General Court Martial at Kangla found them guilty and convicted and sentenced the accused for a period of ten years. Twelve years later, in 2008, Ahanjaobi was awarded a compensation of 200,000 Indian rupees. In this regard, Ahanjaobi stands alone. Justice eluded most wartime rape survivors in Manipur. Tohring was told that her would-be rapist had died in an ambush.

The Naga-Kuki clashes, the signing of the ceasefire agreement between the NSCN-IM (Isak-Muivah) and the Government of India in 1997, and the resultant concerns about identity and territoriality fuelled enough tension to make the role of women's organisations crucial. The Naga women under the TSL and the Naga Women's Union Manipur (NWUM) assumed new roles as peacemakers, reaching out to rival factions and underground groups and urging them to give peace a chance. The Meira Paibi women in the valley became protectors, not only against killings and rapes by the army, but also of the land itself. Prompted by fears that Naga areas of Manipur would be handed over to a greater Nagalim as demanded by the NSCN, the All Manipur Kanba Ima Lup (AMKIL) joined hands with the civil society organisation National Identity Protection Committee (NIPCO) to organise the second integrity rally in September 2000, to assert that the territory of Manipur must not be divided.

Downslide

Stories of women facing the brunt of army atrocities are now spread across the hills and the valley. After Ahanjaobi, the list kept growing—Pramodini of Kairenphabi and Thoinu of Kakching in 1998, Mercy Kabui of Lamdan in 2000, Bina of Luwangshangbam in 2001, Sanjita of Jiribam in 2003 and Nengneikim of Kotlein in 2007. After a brief struggle to get justice, each of these women lost her voice; Sanjita committed suicide.

Perched on the edge of her mora, a little stool, huddling herself into a tight ball, Nengneikim said, 'I have spoken about it over and over again, but there have been no results. Now I am tired of speaking; I just want him in jail for life.' The wish for closure is echoed by other women who were raped by security forces in Manipur. 'My children are all grown up now. We want to forget such a thing happened, I don't want to talk about it again', was the standard answer when contacted for an interview.

The frequency with which army atrocities and other such issues of public concern began to occur in Manipur meant that reactions were short-lived and public movements for a particular cause could not be sustained for a long time. After the initial spontaneous process of organising public meetings, sit-in protests and rallies, these cases faded from public memory as fresh instances surfaced. Between 1992 to 2000 as many as 2,750 persons—including 1,411 civilians, 661 security force personnel and 934 'terrorists'—were killed in insurgency-related incidents, according to reports of the South Asia Terrorism Portal[3].

Meanwhile, the gulf between the Meitei, Naga and Kuki communities widened. The July 18 protest of 2001 in which eighteen protesters were killed in police action on the issue of extension of the ceasefire between the NSCN-IM and Government of India 'without territorial limits' into the Naga-inhabited areas of Manipur, Assam and Arunachal Pradesh, left a huge scar on both the Naga and Meitei psyche.

Recollections of the 2001 incident appealed to the masses, both in the hills and the valley.

With ethnicity becoming the centre point, the ethnic divisions of 'non-tribal' and 'tribal' categories, each comprising a range of sub-group identities at clan or village level, became almost sacrosanct and the antagonism between the two groups (especially between ''tribal' Naga claims to autonomy and 'non-tribal' Meitei groups' focus on the territorial integrity of Manipur) became sharper. This antagonism found expression not only among different underground groups but also in allied social movements, including the women's movements. A dichotomy of 'us' and 'them' now arose between the various ethnic communities living in Manipur.

Naked anger

On July 11, 2004, news desks hummed with details of a young woman found shot dead in the foothills of the Ngariyan hills in Imphal East district. Was she raped, was the question on everybody's mind. An elderly male journalist replied wearily, 'It was a sight that should not be seen. The clothes which should be inside were out.'

By the next day the stories were rampant—about how Thangjam Manorama Devi, 24, was picked up from her house by the paramilitary Assam Rifles, how she was tortured in front of her own mother and brothers, and how she was raped before being shot dead. How her body became a toy for the army and a message

---

[3]http://www.satp.org/satporgtp/countries/india/states/manipur/data_sheets/insurgency_related_killings.htm , accessed on October 2, 2015.

for the people of Manipur. How her own brother's clothes were stuffed into her mutilated genitals. How the bullets fell out and rang as they hit the cold floor of the post-mortem room. How in destroying Manorama, the army sought to destroy the spirit of the people of Manipur.

Four days later, on July 15, another legend was created and reinforced—that of the mothers. Twelve elderly Meira Paibi leaders took matters into their own hands, gathered at the southern gates of Kangla where the Assam Rifles was stationed, and stripped, shouting at the army to come and rape them. 'We sat behind closed doors. We didn't want words of our deliberations going out, even to our own men and sons. This was the honour of all the women of Manipur that the Assam Rifles had trampled upon so mercilessly, with such audacity. What was the use of clothing ourselves?' says sixty-three-year-old Laishram Gyaneshori of Apunba Manipur Kanba Ima Lup (AMKIL), one of the protestors.

Deepti Priya Mehrotra (2010) calls the incident a 'ritual of inversion' wherein the women (and Manipuri society) had transformed themselves 'from total victims to determined survivors.' This inversion from a state of patriarchal definition and appropriation of women's bodies to a revolutionary statement insisting on a woman's right to control her body marks the pinnacle of the women-led movements in Manipur, particularly the Meira Paibi movement.

Dhanabir Laishram, adviser of the All Manipur United Clubs Organisation (AMUCO), reads the peoples' agitation and protests after Manorama's suspected rape and murder, including the 'nude protest', as 'a political movement centred around the removal of AFSPA and the withdrawal of the army from Kangla. For the people, the belief is that if we control Kangla, we are not controlled by anyone else.' The intensity of the agitations and public sentiment also gave a chance for a collective movement hitherto unparalleled in the valley areas. Various civil society organisations came together to form the Apunba Lup, an apex body to spearhead the anti-AFSPA movement. However, culpability was never assigned, and Manorama's family still awaits justice.

The evolution of the Meira Paibi women during the 2004 protest to a gendered questioning of their place in the conflict was short-lived. In February 2006, two incidents shook the very foundations of the legacy of women power in the state, highlighted the deepening of impunity that had struck roots in Manipur and questioned the paradigm of armed struggle by the various underground groups. The incidents also marked a shift in the narrative of sexual violence during the armed conflict in Manipur: 'insiders' or local men as perpetrators.

The first case was the rape of twenty-five women in the Hmar villages of Lunthulien and Parbung in Tipaimukh sub-division of Churachandpur district by 'valley-based militants' later claimed to be the UNLF and the Kangleipak Communist Party (KCP). The stories which broke in a New Delhi-based magazine, the *North East Sun*, raised a hornet's nest in Imphal, with the issue rocking the state assembly sessions in March 2006.

The second case was the arrest, torture and suspected sexual assault of Maibam Naobi Chanu. Apparently her boyfriend Bikash, a cadre of the People's Liberation Army (PLA), was involved in an attack on a team of Thoubal police commandos, killing four personnel including its officer-in-charge N. Lokhon, before he himself was killed. Ironically in a press statement claiming responsibility for the attack, the Revolutionary People's Front (RPF), the political wing of the PLA, said that the attack was launched due to Lokhon's record of atrocities, including killing of innocent persons and disregarding the chastity of Manipuri womenfolk.

Following widespread protests, a lockdown and burning of effigies, Naobi was released from police custody after around ten days by the Judicial Magistrate of Thoubal on the ground that the police had not been able to substantiate the charges levelled against her. As soon as she was released, Naobi sought shelter with Meira Paibi groups and narrated her story to the media.

Pictures of a wild-eyed, dishevelled and weeping Naobi were plastered on the front pages of local newspapers, while stories of the Lungthulien-Parbung rapes hit the national media. Reactions became increasingly hostile and ethnicised as the divide between the hills 'tribals' and valley 'non-tribals' was reinforced by the Lungthulien-Parbung incident. While the UNLF and KCP denied the allegations, the Hmar's People's Convention (HPC-D) rejected the denial, charging that it was the atrocities of the UNLF and KCP that forced the people to flee to relief camps in Mizoram. A fact-finding team comprising rights-based and women's organisations such as Hmar Students' Union, Rongmei Lu Phuam, Human Rights Law Network, Human Rights Alert and Naga Peoples' Movement for Human Rights failed to come up with a concrete finding and has not yet published its report.

The silence of the Meira Paibi, celebrated as one of the strongest women's movements in the country on the issue, came in for severe criticism (Chhakchhuak 2006). The state government ordered a judicial inquiry headed by retired Calcutta High Court Judge Justice SP Rajkhowa to look into both the Lungthulien-Parbung rapes as well as the Naobi case. The Rajkhowa Commission report is yet to be made public.

Though instances of rape and sexual assault by members of armed underground groups were on the rise, there were few voices raised in protest. Among such cases are the rape of a twenty-year-old housewife, Lamneilhing of T Phaijol village in Churachandpur district in July 2012, by a member of a valley-based underground group; the rape of four school-going girls by members of the Zeliangrong United Front (ZUF) at Tamenglong in 2013 and the rape of a six-year-old girl by a cadre of the NSCN-IM in Chandel district in 2014. While the whisperings are endless, in most cases, there is only silence in public.

Yambem Laba comments, 'there were many instances of rape. But social upheaval from non-army rapes was minimal. There is more voice in army rapes. Probably because the army is seen as an occupation force and rape by them was interpreted as use of rape as a weapon of subjugation.'

Meanwhile, Manipuri society as a whole was witnessing an increase in rape and other sexual crimes, and while the Meira Paibi organisations directly intervened in some of the cases, their response was muted as compared to the response during the Ahanjaobi, Manorama and Naobi agitations. The statistics are telling. According to National Crimes Research Bureau (NCRB) data, there were thirty-one reported rape cases in Manipur in 2004, which rose to forty in 2006. By 2011, this figure reached fifty-three, including rapes by both army and non-army perpetrators. There were sixty-three cases of rape reported in the state in 2012 as per the NCRB, and most of them were ignored by the government.

However, one case served to galvanise action once again. In December 2012 Momoko, a Meitei actor, was molested by a cadre of the NSCN-IM at a concert venue in Chandel district. As the film fraternity took to the streets, the agitation was soon joined by various civil society organisations, many of them predominantly Meitei and quick to interpret the incident as yet another instance of the support given to the NSCN-IM by both the state and central governments.

Apex bodies like the All Manipur United Club Organisations (AMUCO), United Committee Manipur (UCM) and Meira Paibi organisations joined the agitation. Within two days, the issue was brought up in the ongoing session of the State Assembly and duly highlighted in the media—perhaps receiving the most media attention after the Manorama incident eight years earlier. Swift orders were relayed to arrest the assailant, and the government even went to the extent of declaring him a 'wanted' person. There were messages of solidarity by the apex Naga bodies such as NWUM, the All Naga Students Association, Manipur (ANSAM) and the TSL. However, the divide between the communities was sharp, and the polarisation only deepened with the mishandling of the case.

Seated crossed-legged on the wooden bench in her tiny living room in Imphal, the reason for the agitations, film actress Momoko gives a half-smile and asks, 'How would I know where the case is headed now? What was the conclusion? On the road, during shooting and public events, people always ask me the same question: "Momoko, what happened to your case? Has Livingstone been arrested?" My reply is the same—I don't have a clue. For my sake people have come to the road, a brother of the media had died, so many were injured, yet I have no answer for them. I had given everything including all related papers to those spearheading the movement, and I still have no answer, no closure.'

No answers

The armed conflict in Manipur—a standoff between the state and many armed underground outfits representing different goals and ethnic groups—is an intricate tapestry, an interweaving and parting of various seemingly parallel threads which makes an understanding of the overall design a complex task. The multiplicity and overlapping of conflicts, ideals and goals within a small geopolitical arena has made Manipur a cauldron brewing constantly over a fire, the ingredients sometimes gelling and sometimes separating.

Zamthingla feels that location plays an important part. 'When the Manorama incident happened, there was such a big response from all sides. For Luingamla, there weren't many,' she says. For Zamthingla, the traditional Tangkhul women's attire, the red and black kashan, becomes her storyboard to tell the story of hardships they faced at the hands of the army intent on suppressing the Naga national movement at any cost. She tells of the struggle of the people against the atrocities and the killing of a young girl which emboldened them to fight for justice.

Zamthingla absent-mindedly shoos away the grey cat trying to steal potato chips off the plate before her. 'I felt I had to do something so that Luingamla is not forgotten. Even if I might not be able to shout her name always, this kashan is her memory,' she repeats. In 2013 she further received endorsement for a set of bead necklaces which she had designed as accessories for the Luingamla kashan.

'Sometimes when I go home to my village, I visit her aged mother and I tell her, "Mother your daughter has left after completing her duties in this world. You might die, I will die, but your daughter Luingamla will live forever. She lives on in this kashan, our sarong, and in this string of beads. You see, Mother, she has been travelling a lot, to foreign lands and to many places nearer home. She has travelled into books as well."'

Like Luingamla, women's movements have travelled far since their inception. Organisations like the TSL and NWUM evolved into well-planned units working according to written constitutions. On the other hand, the Meira Paibi organisations continue to be an informal network. They have been able to assert their unique personality in the complex and conflicting political dimensions in the state and have continued to take lead roles in the social and political spheres, speaking out against repressive state actions and human rights violations by the army. However, they have not been able to holistically address the gender issue.

Notions of nation in the Meitei, Naga and/or Kuki communities are essentially feminine in construction. However as writer Shreema Ningombam (2011) remarks, '... the language of rights is predominantly masculine, focusing only on rights relating to security.' She calls this 'a double patriarchy'—that of a patriarchal society and a patriarchal nationalism. And when rapes—of both women and men—occur in wartime, they are aimed at feminisation of the masculinity of the patriarchal males and reiteration of the femininity of the women. This felt threat to the masculinity of the nation has led to a 'nationalist anxiety' stemming from increased 'notions of women's bodies as signifiers of nation, home, and honour.'

As journalist and rights activist Grace Jajo (2015) points out, '... selective silences are explained as a cautious political position to underplay the political tones when cases involve rival communities. But such selective silences are questionable if we emerge sporadically to bark for our political conveniences only.'

Selective silences will not bring about change; the need is for a collective response which should come not only from women's groups, but also all civil society organisations engaged in nationalistic movements.

Bibliography

Arunkumar, M.C and Irengbam Arun. 2009. 'The Transcendental Role of Women in Manipuri History' in *New Insights into the Glorious Heritage of Manipur* by H. Dwijasekhar Sharma (ed.). New Delhi: Akansha Publishing House.

Chhakchhuak, Linda. 2006. 'Women in the Line of Fire' at http://indiatogether.org/manirape-human-rights Accessed August 13, 2015.

Jajo, Grace. 2015. 'When Rape Outrage is Determined by Communal Colours' at http://ifp.co.in/page/items/25991/when-rape-outrage-is-determined-by-communal-colours Accessed August 13, 2015.

Joint Forum of Indigenous Women – North East India, 1997. 'Addendum III: Some leaves from our Diary' in *Statement of the Joint Forum of Indigenous Women – North East India: Sixth National Conference of Women's Movements, 28-30 December 1997, Ranchi, Bihar, India,* Manipur.

Mehrotra, Deepti Priya. 2010. 'Irom Sharmila's Protest Fast: "Women's Wars", Gandhian Non-Violence and Anti-Militarisation Struggles' in *Peace Prints: South Asian Journal of Peacebuilding,* Vol 3, No. 1: Spring 2010. New Delhi: Women in Security, Conflict management and Peace.

Nepram, Binalakshmi. 2002. 'Images of Defiance: Women, armed conflict and peace-making in Manipur' in *MRFD Bulletin,* Vol. 2, Issue 3. Delhi: Manipur Research Forum.

Ningombam, Shreema. 2011. 'Manipur: Women's rights in a traditional and militarized society' in *Ethics in Action,* Vol. 5, No. 6: December. Hong Kong: Asian Human Rights Commission.

Ningshen, Maireiwon. 2013. 'Contextualising Socio-Cultural and Political Life of Tangkhul Women in Tradition and Modern' in *State of Democracy in Manipur and Other Essays.* Aheibam Koireng Singh & Dr. Ruolkhumzo (eds). New Delhi: Sunmarg Publishers & Distributors.

Phanjoubam, Tarapot. 1996. *Insurgency Movement in North Eastern India.* New Delhi: Vikas Publishing House Pvt. Ltd.

Saigol, Rubina, 2008. 'Militarisation, Nation and Gender: Women's Bodies as Arenas of Violent Conflict' in *Deconstructing Sexuality in the Middle East: Challenges and Discourses.* Pinar Ilkkaracan (ed). Farnham, UK: Ashgate Publishing Limited.

Shimray, Sothing W.A., 2000. *History of the Tangkhul Nagas.* New Delhi: Akansha Publishing House.

This Road I Know

How many individual stories need be told to tell the story of a people or a place?

This is my lived narrative vis-à-vis a road I've travelled on much, the road that links people and states and works as the main lifeline with the body called India.

My first memory of this road: sitting on my father's lap and waiting to spot the headlights of the car bringing home my siblings as it turned the corner of the road. Home was in Kohima, on a hilltop about 100 meters above National Highway 39 (NH39), a British-style bungalow where we spoke the language of a Naga tribe called Tangkhul and communicated with our immediate neighbours in Nagamese, a creole based on Assamese.

My second vivid memory is that of the journey back to Kohima from Dimapur, the commercial capital of Nagaland, or from Imphal, the capital of Manipur state. My siblings and I would wait, as Kohima approached, to be the first to spot the city lights—no less grand than the stars in the sky—and burst into a song that celebrates its beauty. It goes 'Kohima will shine tonight, when the sun goes down and the moon comes up, Kohima will shine... There's no place in this world half as fair as Kohima.' I am told the song was written by the missionary G.W. Supplee who worked in the Angami Naga areas prior to the Second World War.

This road connects me to people and places that are important to me. Running between Numaligarh Oil Refinery in Assam and Moreh, Manipur, the most busy border trade centre with Myanmar, the 436-kilometre-long NH39 cuts through Nagaland. These three north-eastern Indian states have witnessed volatile conflicts, then and even now: with the Indian State, between states and between communities. Like the fractured polity, the Highway is no longer one entity. Since 2010, the stretch between Kohima and Imphal is called NH2 and the stretch between Dimapur and Kohima is NH29.

This region has consistently contested the political idea of the Indian nation, starting with the Nagas, immediately after independence. Until today, the diverse population of a myriad tribes, communities and ethnic groups has been independently engaged in a civil and armed strife with New Delhi, some struggling for secession and some for greater autonomy.

I am an ethnic Naga, born in Kohima in Nagaland, but my ancestral village is located in the hills of adjoining Manipur. This meant frequent travels between the two states. A little later we moved to Imphal, but with friends and relatives still in Nagaland, the road journeys only increased. I have felt an equal belonging to both Nagaland and Manipur, two strife-torn states with many similarities and as many differences.

A story of home

Home in Kohima, the capital of Nagaland, was where a bitter battle was fought during the Second World War to stop the advance of Japanese soldiers. Termed as the 'greatest battle in history', ahead of even D-Day and Waterloo, it was fought in this small town, where residents had little idea about the war they had been dragged into. Also known as the 'Battle of the Tennis Court', little remains of the battlefield except the white lines that demarcated the court. The Kohima War Cemetery became the final resting place of more than 1,400 Commonwealth servicemen. Growing up, one would definitely have a photograph taken by the cemetery in the heart of the town or walk past the defunct battle tank, intrigued by stories it held within its metal walls.

Road journeys in the early years were mostly joyful; they meant reunions and holidays; they meant picnics beside little streams or visits to relatives who'd shower us with their own kind of love. Road journeys also meant halts near open fields and the thrill of balancing ourselves as we walked on tiny raised pathways along paddy farms. Driving along this road, as I have known over the years, is a sort of balancing act.

Travelling meant sweetened milk at tiny hotels by the highway, hotels always run by migrants from the Indian states of Bihar or Uttar Pradesh. This hasn't changed much. 'Tea hotels' are still run by migrants who speak the local dialect fluently.

Travelling also meant stopping to buy fresh produce from wayside vendors. One would not cross Medziphema without buying pineapples. Or fresh bamboo shoot, a must for your Naga pork dish or the Manipuri eromba (a popular chutney made with potatoes, fermented fish and bamboo shoot). Other delicacies you might spot on the road: high-protein bee larvae, wild hen, garden-fresh shallot, plums of the deepest red, guavas with the strongest aroma and fish straight from the ponds in paddy fields. There would not be a single trip when our already overstuffed car was not rearranged to make space for more from the road.

And whenever the car broke down, we had no choice but to wait for hours for a friendly stranger to pass by. Mobile phones were still years away. These were the eighties; we seldom doubted the intention of strangers and even stopped when others gestured, asking for a lift.

War rumblings

In 1985, we moved to Imphal, 138 kilometres south of Kohima on the highway. The first friends we made were our neighbours, a Poumai Naga family from Oinam village. We communicated in English as we tried to find our way through the official language, Meiteilon, the tongue of the dominant valley-settled Meiteis. It was our proximity to this family that played a big role in changing my outlook to this road. Uncle Benjamin, the father of our friends, was the lawmaker who represented Oinam's Karong constituency.

I remember the tense summer of 1987. My friends' house was swarming with people; many seemed sick and in pain. There was talk of the Indian Army, and repeated mention of the words 'Assam Rifles'. This was when the fear of the Indian Army was driven in, sharp and deep. It was then that I was made aware of the military and its heavy presence in the region. Until then, the Indian Army for me was symbolised by Sunday outings to buy sweet and sticky jalebis at the Zakhama Military Station just outside Kohima.

The temporary check-posts seemed to have suddenly multiplied along the road and the men in uniform always seemed hostile. Maybe they were always patrolling, camouflaged, but I had never really noticed them before. Road travel had taken on a new meaning.

'Operation Bluebird' was launched on July 11, 1987 in retaliation for a raid on an Assam Rifles outpost by cadres of the National Socialist Council of Nagalim, or the NSCN,[1] near Oinam, the village of our friends. The undergrounds (as they are commonly referred to) made villagers transport stashes of arms and ammunitions that were grabbed in the raid. During the raid, most of the villagers were in their paddy fields; July is a busy month for farmers who try and make the most of the rains.

Recalling that day more than twenty-five years ago, P.L. Dowang, an elderly villager says he was in the field when he heard gunfire and assumed there was some training going on at the army camp. A little later he saw a cloud of dark smoke and realised it was more serious. He rushed back to the village only to find the underground boys carrying heavy loads of weapons, covered in black soot. The villagers were asked to assemble for a meeting and then made to carry the arms to the jungle camps of the NSCN. Dowang himself

---

[1] The NSCN was formed in 1980, opposing the signing of the Shillong Accord by the Naga National Council (NNC) with the Government of India. NNC, led by Angami Zapu Phizo, was the political mother of Naga nationalism, fighting for sovereignty. Armed conflict took a new dimension after the formation of the NSCN—which was further divided in 1998 into the NSCN-IM (Isak-Muivah) and NSCN-Khaplang, or NSCN-K. A ceasefire with NSCN-K is in place since 1997 with the Government of India. The NSCN-K abrogated their 2001 ceasefire with the Indian government on March 27, 2015, just a month before the truce was up for renewal.

was forced to carry two automatic rifles and a crate of bullets. The weapons were piled up like stacks of firewood.

Th. Ngulani, an elder from the Poumai Naga tribe that inhabits Oinam and the surrounding villages, jogs his memory. For three months they were uprooted from their homes and herded in the village ground, a tactic called 'grouping' of villages, often used by the Indian security forces in the 1950s and '60s to quell the activities of the Naga Army. The men would get to eat one meal in four or five days; luckier ones once in two days. Semi-starved, they were beaten and used like mules to drop off rations for soldiers of the Indian army in other villages.

On one occasion, the women and children were locked inside the Catholic Church for six days without a drop of water; they had to urinate and pass stool inside the church. Four of their village leaders were shot dead. Ninety-three of the good houses were selected and burnt to the ground. The villagers were then ordered to grow vegetables on those patches. The pigs and chickens being reared by the villagers were all eaten by the Indian army soldiers. Villagers had to abandon their rice fields for an entire year, which meant abandoning their only source of livelihood. Any upheaval means disturbing the social fabric of self-sustaining village life. For two years, their movements were restricted and they had to register at the army gate even to visit their fields. Oinam had more than 700 households and most had fled in the year that followed. Those left behind were mostly the elderly. For four or five years after the incident, army officers would land in their helicopters and at every such visit, women and children would be assembled, sweets would be handed out and photographs taken with the visiting officers.[2]

This is only Oinam village I speak of. Operation Bluebird was carried out in thirty contiguous Naga villages in Manipur state.

I am told that most of the men who were part of the group that

---

[2] A parallel strategy of aggressive psychological warfare and damage control, the Indian military undertakes community development (construction of local grounds, waiting sheds, supply of computer units, medical camps, etc.) accompanied by slogans such as 'Friends of the Hill People'.

was forced to carry weapons for the NSCN are now dead. The men were identified, singled out and brutally tortured by the Indian army for ostensibly aiding the undergrounds.

Many of the villagers from the old Oinam village have resettled in nearby towns and villages. The village school was destroyed during the army operation and homes that were burnt were never rebuilt. Villagers chose not to return to Oinam, a village of painful memories. There is a new Onaeme village just above the highway with the first settlers arriving in 2002. It now has a population of more than 1,400 displaced villagers from Oinam village.

KT Rose lives in this new settlement. She was twenty then. And twenty-eight years later she remembers 1987 like it was yesterday. She was one of the women taken repeatedly for interrogation, each time blindfolded. Her mother's biggest fear was the possibility of Rose being raped. She would act brave and comfort her mother while dying on the inside. On the last day of her interrogation she was told to reveal the hideout of a NSCN soldier. She had no idea whatsoever of his whereabouts. The soldiers told her they would rape her, burn her body and peel her skin off. To frighten her more, she was told there was nobody else in the room besides them. It was then that the headman of her village cleared his throat to indicate he was also present. She survived the episode, physically unharmed but psychologically scarred.

Naga history is rife with stories of sexual violence inflicted upon its womenfolk by soldiers of the Indian security forces. Four teenagers were raped at the altar of a church in Yankeli village in 1971; more than two dozen women were raped and dozens more molested in 1970 in Cheswezy village; twenty-four-year-old Angai was gang-raped in 1974, Luingamla of Ngainga village was shot dead when she resisted two Indian army officers on January 24, 1986.

A Tangkhul Naga girl named Rose (coincidentally the same age as KT Rose was during the Oinam incident) was gang-raped by soldiers of the Border Security Force in 1974. Rose committed suicide on March 4, 1974, two days after she was raped. These are translated excerpts from the letter she left for her boyfriend:

'Most beloved,

...I choose my own disgraceful death and lo! I will walk as an
outcast forever. My love when you remember me, turn your eyes to
the darkest horizon for I reside forever in the abyss of darkness. There,
you will find me treading all alone with a heavy sigh of regret in that
long darkness.

What remains of the sad tale I will narrate to you closely in another
lifetime, in another eternity...'

Back in present-day Oinam, Rose remembers two elderly women
dying and the army refusing to let their bodies be buried according
to tradition. She said the women carried the bodies and buried them
without the men.

Another woman gave birth to a baby on the village ground as
she wasn't allowed to go indoors even for delivery. The infant born
in intense distress is now a grown woman. I wonder what the story
of her birth means to her...the day when the village ground bore
mute witness to the writhing of her mother, surrounded by other
women desperately trying to maintain her dignity. The pain and
trauma of years of human rights violations by the armed forces has
been expressed in verse by many Naga women:

Our Story
The tears, the bitter tears
Of a people for amnesty
Professed, generous, on their return
That was no amnesty
But camp of concentration
Concentrating
On the strangulation of Naga spirit
By torture, rape and genocide
Of Naga man, woman, child, all
In whose veins flowed blood Naga.
Tears of a people forced
To witness the methodical
Desecration of their God's abode
By the pain, the blasphemy

Of their virgins done to death
Upon the altars of churches
Transformed
By India's soldiers to altars of lust.

—Easterine Iralu

As a child living in Imphal in the 1980s, I did not know that I was experiencing first-hand the effect of an armed conflict, this time between the Indian Army and the NSCN. But such violence would be repeated again and again and I would grow to understand it and yet, not quite understand it.

Travel on this road reveals that the highway is also the space where India exerts its ultimate sovereignty. Driving along, one inevitably crosses multitudes of army vehicles in long convoys. Sometime in the mid-2000s, I was in a car with some friends from New Delhi. As an army convoy drove past us, one of the passengers spontaneously pointed an imaginary gun at them and made gunshot sounds 'dishkyun, dishkyun.' The rest of us froze. She had no idea about the sense of fear that had suddenly gripped us with her playful gesture. Who in the rest of India, besides these states and Jammu and Kashmir, fears the army, after all?

Blockades and ballistics

The road, the lifeline in a region where rail and air transport is undeveloped, often becomes a bone of contention between two warring groups. Since it controls the supply of essential goods and military movement, it has been used as a means to hold the state to ransom. The longest ever economic blockade on this highway was for ninety-two days in 2011, during which the movement of supplies was cut off and prices of essential commodities skyrocketed.

My parents still live in Imphal, with its mindboggling presence of not only the army and paramilitary, but police and other state forces. It is infamous for 'false encounters' and extra-judicial killings. It was here that I first had a gun pointed to my head by Manipur police commandoes. It was sometime in the late 1990s.

My dog had fallen ill and I had to take him to the vet. Around 7 p.m., on our way back the soldiers stopped us for interrogation. I was with two other cousins in the car. We were taken to separate corners and asked questions. I figured that if any of our answers differed, we'd be potential undergrounds. The power abrogated by the police commandoes is unimaginable in a civilised society. We lived under the tyranny of state forces, which were supposedly meant to protect us.

I've also had a gun pointed at my head by NSCN soldiers. One of them jumped out in front of our car on the highway, brandishing a gun in broad daylight. This was barely two kilometres from a major Indian army check-post. The year was 2007. My sister and I were on the way to Ukhrul with two others. The soldiers got into our car and made us take another road in order to avoid the army camp. They were menacing. We travelled all day on that dilapidated road, stopping frequently for them to seek a mobile signal to speak to their 'boss'. We were the only travellers on that road. They sat in the back seat while my sister and I shared the passenger seat in front. All the while, my nails dug into her skin in absolute fear. Not knowing what they meant to do with us, not knowing whether they had any plans to press the trigger, made the journey hell. We were eventually released in Ukhrul after night fell. My sister and I stood in front of the vehicle trying to stop them from driving off with one of our cousins, but they sped away. He was released two days later, after much furore. It is a journey I would rather forget but, unfortunately, cannot ever erase.

Fear permeates the memories of too many civilians in this small but highly complex state. Renu Takhellambam is the President of the Extra Judicial Execution Victim Families Association (EEVFAM) and has been fighting for the rights of widows of those killed in fake encounters. In October 2012, a Public Interest Litigation (PIL) was filed by EEVFAM on behalf of 1,528 people they say were killed in Manipur in extra-judicial executions between 1979 and 2012. Takhellambam's husband was killed by Manipur police commandoes on April 6, 2007. She says she heard the gunshots that killed him;

it was in broad daylight in the middle of Imphal town. That day, they were celebrating the second anniversary of their life together as husband and wife. He had gone out to buy a camera film roll but never returned home.

Her own pain notwithstanding, Takhellambam now leads widows struggling to live a respectable life. She laments that there is stigma associated with those whose husbands have been killed, either by security forces or by undergrounds and that there is barely any support extended by society. She has no doubt that her young son will be taken care of by her in-laws if the need arises, but her own life has become a matter of concern. 'What about me? What is my place in society?' she asks, daring to voice her own needs.

Fasts as resistance

Given my location, it is not difficult to understand the problems of marginalised minority groups. Yet, I have asked myself again and again whether violence is the best way out.

As the years pass travelling along this road, I have also seen new characters and stories emerge. Through the debris of war and years of suffering, I have seen strong anti-war voices emerge. One of them is Irom Sharmila, whom we have come to know as a famous prisoner of conscience. Sharmila has not eaten a morsel of food voluntarily since November 2000 in protest against the Armed Forces Special Powers Act (AFSPA), a draconian law that is in effect in some Northeast Indian states and the state of Jammu and Kashmir. According to the Act,[3] troops have the right to shoot to kill suspected rebels without fear of possible prosecution and to arrest suspected militants without a warrant. My thoughts go back to Oinam in 1987. And onward to the repeated incidents of brutality by the armed forces that pushed Irom Sharmila to launch her non-violent protest.

Sharmila is forcibly fed through a nose tube and constantly monitored under judicial custody. Her home for the past decade

---

[3]http://www.mha.nic.in/sites/upload_files/mha/files/pdf/armed_forces_special_powers_act1958.pdf

and a half has been a special ward at the Jawaharlal Nehru Hospital in Imphal, close to her mother's home.

Sharmila's brother, Irom Singhajit, graciously gives us time to meet both his mother and himself. As in most traditional Meitei homes, there is a tulsi (holy basil) plant in the centre of the courtyard. Nearby stands a weaving loom with a sarong in progress, two kittens sleep by a spinning wheel and ducks swim gracefully in a nearby pond. On the face of it, this seems like an idyllic slow-paced life. Until Irom Sakhi Devi appears.

Sharmila's mother, Sakhi Devi, has vowed not to meet her daughter until her goal has been met. You can feel the burden she carries in her heart. As she weeps, her son chides her, saying that tears do not befit the mother of such a courageous woman. Sakhi Devi calmly says that she cannot help it and that any talk of her daughter saddens her. In 2011, Sakhi Devi had to undergo a cataract surgery and was admitted in the same hospital where Sharmila is lodged. Sharmila visited her mother with a pillow she had sewn herself, stuffed with dried leaves and flowers. The pillow is Sakhi Devi's prized possession. She rests her head on it at the end of each day. The task her daughter has set for herself seems stupendous, with her homeland caught in a seemingly endless cycle of violence.

Who is the enemy?

More than thirty armed groups operate in Manipur. Because it shares a porous border with Myanmar, guns are easy to procure and this makes it possible to form a rebel organisation overnight. Says Momo Mongmi, leader of the United Minorities Liberation Army (UMLA), 'Our organisation falls under the umbrella of the Kuki National Organization (KNO). There are fourteen to fifteen groups under the KNO. Three groups, the Pakan Reunification Army, Kuki National Army and us are in this vicinity.' We spend the night in Moreh, on the border with Myanmar and start the journey much before dawn to visit the UMLA, now stationed at Camp Hermon. UMLA was formed on October 17, 2007 to safeguard the rights of minority tribes. UMLA is an armed group with just fifty-two members. They believe by coming together and taking up arms, others will pay heed to their voice. Leaders of the UMLA say that after arming themselves, violence against minority groups in the area has also decreased.

En route to the camp of the UMLA, our journey is halted for half-an-hour at an army check-post. This check-post is secured with a padlock at 6:30 every evening and opens at 5:30 in the morning. We wake up a soldier who in turn passes on the message to another and then to another higher up who has control of the keys. We are allowed to pass after our baggage is checked. A student leader who was accompanying us tells us that residents here feel like they live in a zoo, their comings and goings always controlled. The soldier manning the gate acknowledges the nuisance. He says his job is far from enviable. For us, it is mere inconvenience. I wonder about those seriously ill, who have to be rushed to bigger towns for treatment. Would it be loss of precious time?

What is it like to travel the road now? It is not so much the fear of the army anymore. A little Hindi is enough to make a connection with soldiers of the Indian Army. But there is another fear: the ethnic. The Kukis are an ethnic group different from the Nagas and the fear of the 'other' refuses to go away. Because of recent ethnic clashes, whenever I cross a Kuki area, I am tense. I will try not to stop in Kangpokpi, the biggest Kuki town between Imphal and Kohima, or any Kuki area after dark, even to buy a bottle of water. It has to be a Naga village. How miserable is life when one neighbour fears the other, and the other the next. Wistfully I remember the days when we would be packed into that Ambassador car, always stopping at Kangpokpi because my mother had to buy dried mushrooms.

Identities are real but blurred. How does one relate to age-old neighbours, waking up one day to see them at war? The ethnic divide is thin and blurry, but at the same time firm. The individual has no space when communities are at loggerheads.

Manipur is a conglomeration of many ethnic groups; each has its phase of war with the other. The Naga-Kuki hostilities coalesced into violent clashes in the 1990s. Thousands were killed and hundreds of villages burnt. K. Matia, a Mao Naga, was forty and living in Maharashtra when the news of unending violence drew her homewards so she could help calm tensions between the two embattled communities. Her home was in Mao, which was then the main rest point for public buses travelling between Manipur and Nagaland. Matia and a few other women would board buses in Mao and travel until they reached Kuki areas so as to provide safe passage to Kukis travelling in Naga areas.

It is already dark when we reach the Mowzhu Prayer Center to meet Matia, so we decide to return the next day. When we see her home in the morning, there are no regrets about the time taken to make the second trip. For those of us who now live in big cities, the little prayer spot on a hill is like a nature resort. Flowers of all hues sway in the gentle breeze and a very healthy dog escorts us all the way up to the immaculate dwelling. People like Matia are best met in the day, the sun on her face to accentuate her gleeful and childlike laugh. Some people just exude joy.

She narrates a story of how she risked her own life to save the lives of a mother and daughter. One day while travelling on the bus to Imphal, in the thick of the clashes, Matia was so caught up in a conversation with fellow passengers that she did not notice the bus stop. When she realised that a non-Naga woman and her daughter had been dragged out of the bus and into the woods below, she tracked them down. It turned out that the captors were Nagas and she begged the boys to let them go. She was beaten and threatened and she even ran back to the road out of fear. But she managed to find her courage once again and went back into the woods to plead for their lives. She told the boys that this wasn't the right place for war and that their captives weren't the right people to wage war against. Matia eventually managed to get them both released. She continues to work to build trust between the two communities.

Life on the highway she says, has been tough because they have borne the brunt of army brutalities. 'As compared to those living in the interiors, we suffer a lot more. We are affected by all the problems that arise.' But she is quick to add that they have also been able stand for the cause of the Nagas. 'We know we have our rights and cannot compromise on this. After all, we are all ruled by blood.'

Are my fears a creation of my mind? Should I be ashamed to feel this way? And if I fear the Kukis, chances are, they fear us too. But would my people really harm Kukis were they to stop in our area? I know they would be safe. Before travelling to Kuki areas to shoot for the film based on this essay, I was in touch with Daniel Mate, the President of the Kuki Students Organization in Tengnoupal. We were complete strangers. I didn't know whether he would be doubtful of my intentions, me being a Naga and the subject of my film being political. But he was a brother to me during the trip and I trusted him. It made me think.

And then one night, our car breaks down in the Kuki village of Hengbung. I am frightened. My mind keeps telling me that this is a hostile area. A group of four boys approaches us. I immediately tense. One of them openly addresses my fears and says that no harm would come to us and that we could even rest in their village should we need to. Their offer to help seemed genuine. It made me think some more.

Territorial borders have no context with the lived and living experiences of the people. They are administrative tools, often tossing the local populace around between appropriating histories and perpetrating conflicts.

I was in Delhi in the summer of 2001 during one of the worst phases in Naga and the ethnic Meitei relations. Frenzied mobs took to the streets in response to the Indian government's decision to extend the ceasefire with the largest Naga armed outfit, the NSCN-IM, to outside of Nagaland state. Eighteen people were killed on June 18 when security forces opened fire to control the mob. Our home then was on the highway itself. The wall around my house was the only barrier between my family and the mob; men, women, children, holding torches and shouting impassioned slogans. I remember anxious phone calls to my parents by the hour as they stayed up, praying that the madness would end. Things have not returned to what they were in the aftermath of 2001.

So, here I am stuck in the lost land of my childhood, unable to move forward. I look to my left, there are a dozen groups like UMLA, I look to my right and there stands the monolith NSCN-IM, I look in front and see people pitted against people, I look behind and there is the law that has clenched us tightly in its fist. Where am I in between? I feel pulled in all directions, equally, violently, and I feel a desperate need for some sort of peace.

In wait

In all of this, it seems to be the women whose intervention becomes crucial when structure and civility collapses. It is women who wave the white flag in times of insanity. They are called to drown out the noise with their prayers. Women's groups have gained strength, but they are still viewed mainly as peacekeeping forces with very little representation in decision-making bodies.

Camp Hebron, headquarters of the largest armed Naga group, the NSCN-IM, is a little off the highway. I've had my share of uncomfortable history with them, so I am a little nervous when entering their imposing gateway. The Nagas have been fighting for their right to self-determination ever since the creation of the Indian state. The 1950s and '60s were especially tumultuous. My father remembers the times when they needed a password to walk the streets after dark because of indefinite curfew. Passwords were changed everyday. There has been a ceasefire between the NSCN-IM and the Government of India since August 1, 1997. Only time will tell if the 'Framework Agreement' between the two parties signed in early August 2015 can move towards resolving the seven-decade-long conflict.

Kanmichon Zingkhai, the commander of the women's wing of the NSCN-IM, has agreed to speak with us. The organisation has roughly 2,000 women cadres. She has given thirty-four years of her life to the organisation, half of it spent in extreme hardship as a guerrilla fighter. She narrates tales of war, about being tailed by Burmese soldiers, about their life on the move, and not a day spent in one place before the 1997 ceasefire. One would wonder about the kind of exhaustion the years must bring, but she still feels strongly about the path she has chosen and says she will continue to fight for what rightfully belongs to her people.

Zingkhai says that despite missing her family, the nation is more important. She says that at times the physical difference between men and women might be apparent and at such times one may feel weaker, but the one who carries the spirit of the nation feels no such difference. 'No nation is mature without the active participation of women; the Naga nation will also be incomplete without the participation of its women,' she says.

On this highway lie the graves of two boys who were killed on May 6, 2010 in Mao. The Manipur state government had banned NSCN-IM General Secretary Thuingaleng Muivah from entering the state to visit his native village. That day, Nagas had gathered in the state border town of Mao for a peaceful protest when state security forces opened fire. The two boys who died were not even part of the rally but had come to check on family members when they heard the firing. I cannot help wonder: would they still be alive had their lives not been linked to this road?

The story of these two boys takes me to August 30, 2014 when two other young men were shot dead by security forces of Manipur state during a protest in Ukhrul, where I belong. The wives of both were expecting their first child.

I remember the sadness and sense of desperation on the day of the killing that made me wake up in the middle of the night to write a poem.

Ambiguity
Were they willing,
whatever the consequence?
Them who died.
They say it was for us.
You, are you willing,
to stand in front?
Facing the bullet,
Consciously.

Your waiting companion,
Your crying child,
Your ailing mother,
who now spends her life,
the rest of it,
In naked grief.

We sing their eulogy,
And yes, we must!
For they have fallen,
Their splattered blood in our eyes,
In our hands.
For we are all to blame.
And we continue to blame,
Them, she, him, I.

Was this how it was to be?
The bullets in the flesh,
Did they hesitate?
Even for the slightest?
Or have they caused
just the impact desired.
Deep, broken, forceful, bloody, done.

I ask you, will you stand to take the bullet?
Do you want loud, real loud?
Do you want to hear cries,
If that is the only way to be heard?
Do you fear,
That yours is diminishing,
That yours is fading,
And that, we must hear cries,
We must see blood,
To be in the present.

And you, how do you feel?
To trample sans conscience,
To murder sans judgement.
To forget.
And to sleep.

And, O fool,
To let hatred fill.
We will go, like they have.
That is our only common future.

You, shouting from the rooftops,
You, dragging them in,
You, patriot!
You, coward,
You, traitor,
You, undaunted,
You, believer,
You, which one are you?
Which one am I?

He died.
And he too.
Lambs.
Sacrificed.
Martyrs.

My child sleeps,
I watch her.
This is my peace.

The journeys of my childhood were always more fun with my father at the wheel. On one occasion, he asked me whether I'd like to see a volcano. I was a teenager but still gullible enough to believe what he said and, needless to say, thrilled. When we passed an army camp near one of our favourite tea stalls he pointed to a signboard that said Jwalamukhi, which means volcano in Hindi. Imagine my disappointment! My daughter is still too young for me to try that trick.

I may have travelled this road a hundred times. And with every journey, a new complexity emerges. There are multiple layers of experience. Sometimes historical, sometimes contemporary. But, I can say for sure, it is always more difficult for women to find their space within this confounding maze.

Now married to an Angami Naga from Kohima village, I travel the stretch from my mother's to my husband's hometown several times a year. A good chunk of my life has revolved around this area and I can foresee a lot of my daughter's travels will be made along this length. Her father narrates anecdotes as he drives and I try not to pass on my fears. Fears, if at all, must be gathered through personal experiences and not inherited. I hope she will have a different story to tell.

About the Authors

Laxmi Murthy is consulting editor with *Himal Southasian*, the region's only political review magazine, published from Kathmandu. She also heads the Hri Institute for Southasian Research and Exchange, a research unit under the Himal banner. She is currently based in Bangalore and has been active in the autonomous women's movement in India for more than twenty-five years.

Mitu Varma is project director at Panos South Asia and has been leading the project on which this book is based. She is also director for Film Southasia, a biennial festival of documentaries for the region, and editorial advisor for *Himal Southasian*. She is based in New Delhi and is a founder member of the Community Radio Forum—India.

Zahid Hussain is an award-winning journalist and author. He is the former Pakistan correspondent for *The Times* of London and *The Wall Street Journal*. He has also covered Pakistan and Afghanistan for several other international publications, including *Newsweek*, Associated Press, *The Economist* and *India Today*. He is a regular columnist for *Dawn*.

Farzana Ali is the Peshawar bureau chief of Aaj News, a private television channel. She covers Khyber Pakhtunkhwa and the Tribal Areas. Her areas of interest include social issues and human rights, and as a journalist from a war zone, most of her work is related to conflict. She has produced four documentaries on different issues with national and international organisations, including 'Impact of Militarisation on the Dancing Girls of Swat' for Panos.

Muhammad Zafar is a reporter with the *Express Tribune,* an international newspaper in Quetta. He covers court proceedings, politics, crime, sports and health across Balochistan. He has also worked for the *Media Times, Daily Times* and *Daily Balochistan Express.*

Shazia Irram Gul has been working as a correspondent with Radio Pakistan, Peshawar since 2000. As head of the Peshawar University Media Research Centre, she helped set up and manage the first University Campus Radio in any university of Pakistan-Khyber Pakhtunkhwa. She has also worked with Deutsche Welle Urdu service. She has led teams covering the 2005 quake in the region and the 2010 floods in Swat for mainstream media.

Syed Ali Shah is the Balochistan Bureau Chief of *Dawn News* based in Quetta. He has been reporting on social issues, politics, growing religious radicalisation, sectarianism, the Baloch insurgency, tribal disputes and the menace of narcotics in the province for the past fifteen years. He has earlier worked with *Al Jazeera* and *The Balochistan Times* and contributed stories to CNN as well.

Shaista Yasmeen is currently working as a Project Coordinator at Uks Research Resource and Publication Centre in Pakistan. She combines the experiences gained from media and social development sectors to conduct trainings, produce radio shows, write articles and deliver lectures. She has earlier worked with Dawn TV, AVT Group of Channels, and Pakistan Broadcasting Corporation and contributes monthly articles to Sach Web TV. Her areas of interest include politics, current affairs, media, gender and human rights.

Deepak Thapa is the Director of Social Science Baha, Kathmandu. He has commented extensively on Nepal's contemporary political developments and writes a fortnightly column in *The Kathmandu Post*. He is also a widely published author on socio-political issues in Nepal.

Darshan Karki has been a journalist and editor at *The Kathmandu Post*. Before joining the newsroom, she worked as a researcher in various non-governmental organisations in Nepal.

Deepak Adhikari is a Kathmandu-based independent journalist. In a career spanning over a decade-and-a-half, he has covered many of the socio-political issues of Nepal including human rights, the environment, hydropower, tourism, and mountaineering. His work has appeared in the *New York Times*, *Time* magazine, *The Caravan*, *Himal Southasian*, *Al Jazeera*, and the *Nikkei Asian Review*, among others. He has also served as the Nepal correspondent for Agence France-Presse (AFP), the global news agency. Prior to joining AFP, he was with Nepal's largest media group, Kantipur Publications.

Sewa Bhattarai is currently a reporter at BBC Nepali Sewa, where she reports on the art beat in Nepali language. A bilingual journalist, she has previously worked with *Republica*, an English language daily in Nepal, and continues to write for several English-language publications. Her interests in reporting are art, culture, religion, gender, society and environment.

Siddiq Wahid is a historian of Central Eurasian and Tibetan political history and the Founding Vice Chancellor of Islamic University in Kashmir. Among his previous assignments, he has been Senior Fellow at New Delhi's prestigious Centre for Policy Research, Director of the UNESCO Institute of Kashmir Studies at the University of Kashmir and the Maharaja Gulab Singh Chair Professor at the University of Jammu. Wahid received his PhD from Harvard University and has lectured widely in the United States, Europe and South Asia. He has published in many anthologies and journals. He has also written widely as a public intellectual on the Kashmir dispute, for the resolution of which he is an activist.

Shazia Yousuf was born in downtown Srinagar, the summer capital of Indian-administered Kashmir. She grew up amidst armed conflict and decided to become a story-teller. After a Masters in Journalism, she joined a local newsmagazine, *Kashmir Life*, and also wrote stories of women in war zones for many international, national and local media outlets including *Guernica*, Inter Press Service, Women's Feature Service, and Anadolu Agency. She also teaches at the Islamic University of Science and Technology.

Zahid Rafiq is a journalist based in Srinagar. He has worked with *The Indian Express*, *Tehelka* and *The Hindu*. A Fulbright scholar, he studied journalism at the University of California, Berkeley, and has written for several international publications like the *New York Times*, *Christian Science Monitor*, *Foreign Policy* and *Vice News*.

Sanjay Barbora is a sociologist who teaches at the Tata Institute of Social Sciences, Guwahati Campus. He has worked with Panos South Asia in the past and is involved with several research initiatives on migration, agrarian change and the media.

Thingnam Anjulika Samom is an independent journalist based in Manipur. She has been associated with leading newspapers in Manipur such as *Matamgi Yakairol*, *Sangai Express* and *Hueiyen Lanpao*, besides writing for agencies and publications based outside such as the *North East*

Sun, Women's Feature Services (WFS), *Himal Southasian*, Infochange, Indiatogether, *Motherland*, *The Caravan* and Panos London Features. She has also made two short films on conflict widows in Manipur besides translating stories and poems from Manipuri to English.

Yirmiyan Arthur Yhome has had a long association with Panos South Asia. *This Road I Know* is her third documentary completed with the help of a Panos fellowship. She holds a Masters degree from the Mass Communication Research Centre, Jamia Millia Islamia. She is a Photo Editor with the Associated Press.

www.ingramcontent.com/pod-product-compliance
Lightning Source LLC
Chambersburg PA
CBHW051953270326
41929CB00015B/2645